Planning and Conducting Family Cluster

To
Jim and Pam and Linda and Robin
for all we shared together as LITs
at Greenlake

Planning and Conducting Family Cluster

Education for Family Wellness

Barbara Vance

SAGE PUBLICATIONS
The Publishers of Professional Social Science
Newbury Park London New Delhi

For information address:

SAGE Publications, Inc.
2111 West Hillcrest Drive
Newbury Park, California 91320

SAGE Publications Ltd.
28 Banner Street
London EC1Y 8QE
England

SAGE Publications India Pvt. Ltd.
M-32 Market
Greater Kailash I
New Delhi 110 048 India

Printed in the United States of America

Library of Congress Cataloging-in-Publication Data

Vance, Barbara.
Planning and conducting family cluster : education for family wellness / by Barbara Vance.
p. cm.
Bibliography: p.
Includes index.
ISBN 0-8039-3482-3. — ISBN 0-8039-3483-1 (pbk.)
1. Family life education. 2. Family—Religious life. I. Title.
II. Title: Title: Family cluster.
HQ10.V24 1989
646.7′8—dc20 89-30555
CIP

FIRST PRINTING 1989

Contents

Foreword

Barbara has taken the model of Family Cluster and shown ways to implement (operationalize) it in practice, not only within Family Cluster sessions but within other family enrichment experiences as well. To this end, it will be a helpful manual for practitioners.

Since I developed the Family Cluster model in 1970, it has been used all over the world with families from many cultures. Because of the process nature of work with family systems, as well as the nature of experiential education, the art of leading Family Clusters is a difficult one to "pin down" in writing. Barbara has succeeded in communicating this skill as well as in providing examples of leaders in practice. To this end, the manual builds on the first book written about Family Clusters, *Family Enrichment with Family Clusters* by M. Sawin (Valley Forge, PA: Judson, 1979).

Barbara has given many practical suggestions of books, songs, and games to use along with ways they might be integrated into sessions as teaching tools. Therefore, a tool does not become just an object to use but a learning experience that is integrated into the larger whole of learning objectives.

Barbara has not only written about practicing the art of leading or facilitating Family Clusters but she has also led them herself, and has trained students and others in leadership of Family Cluster. She has done this across cultures, in Israel and in the United States.

Amidst all of this productivity, Barbara has been living with the results of a massive stroke, which seems to have prodded her on to greater commitment on behalf of family wellness. We salute you, Barbara!

—Margaret M. Sawin
Manila, Philippines
December 1987

Preface

This book is something like an operator's manual for a car. It tells you how Family Cluster runs and how to keep it running. It is something you might want to keep close at hand, maybe in your glove compartment, so you can check up on how things are running in Family Cluster.

Unlike a car-owner's manual, this manual does not come with the already manufactured object that it was designed to explain how to keep in good operating condition. This is a manual for leaders-in-training (LITs) and already experienced and trained leaders of Family Cluster. Leaders are expected to put together the object that this manual is about—Family Cluster. As a matter of fact, this manual explains how to "build" a Family Cluster, what makes it work, and how to keep it going. The leader is the builder, operator, and mechanic for Family Cluster, all at the same time.

Once you learn how to "build" Family Cluster and operate it for a while, you will discover that not only do you have your own best way of doing things but that each Cluster is different from every other. Planning and conducting Family Cluster is not assembly-line work. It is building on uniqueness. Once you get the "hang of it," the Clusters you lead—although built on the same principles as any other (those principles described in this book)—will have a look all their own. Each will be "one of a kind," one with your particular stamp on it (along with that of your coleader in each case). That's the way it should be. This book is not about building Family Cluster clones. It is about building Clusters, each unique from every other.

This book is about a subject from which people in their "right minds" flee—the education of complete family groups, not just one family at a time but several at once. That is a daunting task when compared to the usual kind of education experience, which is designed for the individual. This book is about family life education at its best—education that includes the whole family. More specifically, it is about family life education with *several* families. Just as the motto for the Peace Corps suggests, being a leader of Family Cluster is likely to be the "toughest job you'll ever love."

A Family Cluster is a group of four or five families who meet periodically on a regular basis for an education experience together. They don't meet together for therapy. They meet together for education. The focus of *therapy* is major repair when something needs "fixing." It focuses on the individual family unit. *Education*, however, focuses on growth and "preventive maintenance." Because "fixing" is not part of the process (although I don't deny that it might happily occur incidentally), objectives in family life education focus on strengths that already exist in all families. It focuses on those strengths that the individual families composing the Cluster perceive to need improving. These strengths generally involve how the family members relate to each other. The objectives are specific, as are those in any other education process, but they are unique to each Family Cluster.

There is a great deal of discussion in the literature about differences among three forms of intervention with families: education, enrichment, and therapy. *Education* and *enrichment* often get used interchangeably. I simply have chosen not to include *enrichment* in the book title because I believe Family Cluster can be an effective means of *education* for the entire family unit. Of course, families are "enriched" by their education experience together.

This is a "how-to" book for leaders of Family Cluster. It is about a process I define as education for family groups. It is *not* a book about family therapy. However, Family Cluster can be an effective adjunct to therapy. In some cases, it might even be an effective alternative to family therapy.

The pages of this book are sprinkled with examples from my own work with real families. The people I talk about are real people. However, in order to protect the privacy of people with whom I've had the privilege of leading in Family Cluster, names and other identifying information have been changed. Sometimes the families I describe are composites of several families.

Perhaps you have noticed that I capitalize the initial letter in each of the words *Family Cluster*. I do that on purpose. To me, Family Cluster is a proper noun, the name of something. That means it deserves to have initial capitals just like any other proper noun.

Family Cluster is not something I dreamed up all by myself. Like Wordsworth's child who went forth and became a part of all she met, I too, am a combination of all that I have met. I don't know where I heard about Family Cluster, but I am very grateful to Margaret Sawin and Dorothy Becvar, who answered the endless questions I had about Family Cluster.

I'm also grateful for those who were my trainers as a Family Cluster leader: Richard Speck, the Reverend Claude Pullis, and Luel Hawley. I acknowledge the many ideas and support we leaders-in-training shared and gave each other as we worked together for a week of intensive training one summer—especially Jim Haas, Robin Coira, Pam Collins, and Linda Passmark, to whom I have dedicated the book. And, of course, we couldn't have had such a rich training experience without five wonderful families who were our "guinea pigs" during that week of intensive training, which included 12 separate sessions of Family Cluster. Not only did we learn volumes from one another, we learned to expand our circles of love.

In addition, I'm grateful for the encouragement from my colleagues at Brigham Young University in developing my leadership skills in Family Cluster, especially Wes Burr, former director of the Family Living Center, and Bob Stahmann, my department chairman.

I'm grateful to my editor and good friend, Terry Hendrix, at Sage Publications, for confidence in me and wise and helpful suggestions to improve the manuscript.

I'm grateful to colleagues in the United States and in Israel who have read the manuscript and made perceptive and wise suggestions, especially Ruth Liron and Ruth Katz in Israel.

Finally, I'm grateful to students (LITs) at Brigham Young University and to the families who made up our Family Clusters, for the many lessons they have taught me and the opportunity they have provided me to expand my skills and circle of love.

—Barbara Vance
Provo, Utah

PART I

Families and Family Cluster

The family is the basic unit of society. The focus in today's modern world, however, is the individual, not the family. Perhaps we take the family for granted.

Family means two or more people living in relationship to one another, 24 hours a day, day in and day out. I'm not going to define family more precisely because no one has yet agreed what a family is. Is a single person a family? Are a husband and a wife a family? Do roommates compose a family? Is a family only composed of parents and children? What about the extended kinship system so typical of the Middle East and other parts of the world?

The family is changing. All of what we call family today wasn't called that years ago. Our laws from ancient to modern times have been designed to support and protect the family (Hafen, 1983). The federal government cannot establish laws unless the impact on the family has been defined. And yet a look at the problems of today's society reveal considerable injury to the family. For example, one out of every two marriages ends in divorce, teenage pregnancy is rising at an alarming rate, there is a frightening increase in drug and alcohol abuse, and there is an increasing incidence of AIDS in the heterosexual population, to name just a few injuries to the modern family. Is the family too injured to recover? Of course not, but if families are going to grow and flourish, they need lots of support.

Most couples getting married have no idea what it will be like to bear and raise children. Someone once said that parenthood is the last profession open to amateurs. When everything nailed down seems to be coming loose, parents want to know whether to give up or to keep plugging along. They would like some evidence that all the hard work and stress are worth it.

Family Cluster is designed to support families by helping them to enjoy one another, to learn together, to serve and support one another. However, before jumping into the details of conducting/leading Family Cluster, a word from our sponsor—families.

The first chapter is an overview of Family Cluster. The second chapter focuses on the family as a system of interacting parts, people who reciprocally influence one another. The third chapter explores some of the key characteristics of healthy, strong families. The fourth chapter examines some of the research related to social support and Family Cluster and the possible effectiveness of Family Cluster as a family life education experience. These four chapters about the family and Family Cluster set the stage for Parts II and III, which examine in detail how to plan and implement Family Cluster.

Reference

Hafen, B. C. (1983, January). The constitutional status of marriage, kinship, and sexual privacy: Balancing the individual and social interests. *Michigan Law Review 81*(3) [Entire issue].

1. Family Cluster: An Overview

It's the greatest experience I've ever had with my family. —A father evaluating his experience in Family Cluster

I found out I'm really a member of my family. —A teenager evaluating his experience in Family Cluster (his new "family" is his aunt and uncle and their three younger daughters after the death of his own parents in an airplane accident)

I discovered some friends I like and who like me. —A 9-year-old girl evaluating her experience in Family Cluster

I'll never be the same. I didn't know our family could have so much fun together. —A mother evaluating her experience in Family Cluster

It is difficult to describe what can happen in Family Cluster. People change. Their feelings about one another change. They do things they normally never would do—and discover how much fun they have doing them. They discover themselves. They discover one another. They develop warm feelings for others that are impossible to describe. They laugh together. They cry together. Families grow stronger.

Pretend you have a zoom-lens camera. The first thing you do when you take a picture is to look through the viewfinder at your main subject (such as a landscape or unusual scene in nature). That first view of your subject is an overview. However, that scene consists of many details that might not be apparent in that first view. You use your zoom lens to zoom in on particular details of your subject, recognizing that the detail you look at through the zoom lens is only a part of the whole. Your zoom lens gives you a chance to examine your subject more closely—in detail. You are aware, however, that the details are not the whole. Again you take a look at the entire subject—a panorama view or overview. That view is different from the details brought into focus with your zoom lens. However important the details are, they are not the original subject but only a part of the subject. Those details help to make the subject what it is.

So, too, is Family Cluster a main scene composed of many details. The details are not Family Cluster, but they add important dimensions to the whole to make it the rich and beautiful scene it can be.

The purpose of this chapter is to give you an overview of Family Cluster, especially related to the two main processes involved in Family Cluster: planning and conducting a Family Cluster. *Planning* is that process that goes on behind the scenes in preparation for the actual implementation of Family Cluster. Often planning occurs many weeks before the first Cluster session begins. *Conducting* a session of Family Cluster is the actual practice, or doing, of Family Cluster.

This chapter will give you an overview of Family Cluster. The chapters that follow will be zoom-lens views of specific details important for the planning and conducting of effective Family Clusters. Keep in mind, however, that the details are only part of the whole, that Family Cluster is more than drawing, pasting, games, or songs.

What Is a Family Cluster?

Family Cluster is a term coined by Herbert Otto (1975). However, Margaret Sawin (1979), because of her pioneering work in the early 1970s in establishing and maintaining Clusters among Protestant congregations in North America, is considered the founder of Family Cluster. (Although Otto conducted a few Clusters in the early 1970s, his model and sponsorship were different from Sawin's.)

Sawin (1979, p. 27) defines Family Cluster as

> a group of four or five complete family units* which contract to meet together periodically over an extended period of time for shared edu-

cational experiences related to their living in relationship within their families. A Cluster provides mutual support, training in skills which facilitate the family living in relationship, and celebration of their life and beliefs together.
(*A family unit is made up of any persons who live in relationship with one another, i.e., a nuclear family, a one-parent family, a couple without children, one or more persons who live in one household, a single person who lives alone but has relationships with others.)

As used in this book, Family Cluster is defined as a form of support and education designed for four or five families who meet together consistently at the same time, usually once a week, for at least eight sessions. It is not necessary for the families to share the same religious faith nor, indeed, even to practice any sort of religious observance. However, it is helpful for all the families in a Cluster to share the same basic values and goals.

What is experiential education? Family Cluster is basically experiential education, which is based on the premise that one can learn best when one has experienced—or been involved with—a given learning event. Because each family system is unique (that is, it has its own history and set of rules and family boundaries that identify it as a unique social unit, different from any other in the society), what each family "learns" from a given learning event may be very different from every other family who "experiences" the same event. However, experiential learning provides learners an opportunity to become involved in a learning event (e.g., through the media of visual imagery, finger paints, crayons on paper, role-playing, puppetry, and picture books) and to discuss their experience of that event.

The discussion of a learning experience is called *processing* (see Chapter 13), an important factor in leading learners to individual insights relative to a given learning experience.

There are no guarantees that a learning experience will lead to insight. However, the experience is designed for maximum involvement of all participants. For example, if role-playing is the medium of involvement, *all* members of the Cluster participate in the experience as role-players.

Occasionally, a form of "telling" is used preceding a learning experience. For instance, during a learning event focusing on reflective listening in the family, the leader may describe two or three steps involved in reflective listening and give an example or two.

The Cluster members may then, through role-playing, practice the two or three steps. The role-playing is then followed by "processing," or structured discussion, to explore what Cluster members learned from the experience (that is, what "insights" they discovered).

In experiential education, the emphasis is *always* on involvement of the learner. There is very little emphasis on "telling" by the teacher. As a matter of fact, the person leading the Cluster is not designated as a "teacher" but as a *leader* or facilitator. The leader structures the learning experience, guides the involvement of Cluster members in the experience, and leads the discussion (processing) of the experience. Learners do not sit passively, taking notes, while the teacher lectures or "tells" (teaches?). Once the experience is under way, the most desirable role for the leader is that of observer/facilitator. The leader "gets out of the way" so the learners can learn.

Because "insights" in Family Cluster are often shared together as a family group, the education process is unique in that the education process focuses on ways to strengthen the entire family unit and not necessarily individuals within that unit. The family unit consists of a number of dyadic (two-person), triadic (three-person), and whole-family relationships. The focus of Family Cluster is strengthening those relationships. On the other hand, most education focuses on the individual, on his or her growth and progress. Relationship education is more complex, according to Mace (1981), and possibly more important in the long run. It is likely, however, that designing experiential education events is more complicated than typical classroom education because of the focus on relationships and the added challenge of providing experiences that will allow insight learning to take place in people who are in a variety of developmental stages. The classroom generally has learners who are one another's contemporaries (that is, who are in the same developmental stage). A family, on the other hand, such as one consisting of two teenagers and two school-aged children, could consist of individuals in at least three developmental stages, adulthood (parents), adolescence (teenagers), and the middle years (the school-aged children). Realistically, *each* person in the family is in a different developmental stage from every other family member, even though two people within the family may be the same age (such as parents, twins, or children in a stepfamily where each has biological parent not living in the home). Also, each family is in its own unique stage in the *family* life cycle. Family education, such as Family Cluster, is multigenerational (multidevelopmental) education.

Who Should Be in a Family Cluster?

Any kind of family is a likely candidate for Family Cluster. If the family is interested in sharing learning experiences and ideas with three or four other families, then that family is a prime candidate for Family Cluster.

Family Cluster involves everyone in the family. It is *not* passive learning. It can be messy at times—and an awful lot of fun. However, the family must be motivated enough to leave the comfort of the home and TV to get itself to a central place for each Cluster session. Generally, a family gets out of Cluster what it gives to Cluster. The family must have a desire to learn together and must trust the leaders enough to make a commitment to attend every Cluster session.

Family Cluster Is Not Family Therapy

Family Cluster is *not* therapy. Some families in Cluster, even when told in advance by leaders that Cluster is not designed to be a therapy experience, continue to expect Cluster to be a therapeutic experience. Therapy is designed to rehabilitate, to take what doesn't work and help the family make it work. Family Cluster, on the other hand, is designed to make "what works" work better. Every family has strengths. Every family has weaknesses. Sometimes the weaknesses are such that they threaten the very structure and identity of the family itself—thus the need for family therapy. However, most families have enough strong points that emphasis on those strong points can build the family, can make it a more satisfying, functional unit for its members.

This does not mean that Family Cluster should not include families who might be in therapy. It simply means that Cluster focuses on strengths while therapy focuses on weaknesses and their rehabilitation (on what needs "fixing").

It is likely that there are not enough family therapists to attend to the needs of all families who might benefit from family therapy. As a general rule, one therapist works closely with one family in therapy for a few weeks, months, or, occasionally, even years. It is possible that Family Cluster might shorten the length of time a family might spend in therapy. This is, as yet, an untested hypothesis. However, in a strong support group such as Family Cluster, families in therapy might see more vividly how they might change some dysfunctional family behavior, thus possibly reducing the amount of time required in therapy.

A word of *caution* is important at this point. Leaders of Family Cluster must focus on *strengths*, not weaknesses, in Family Cluster. Family Cluster leaders who also are family therapists may need to change the focus of their skills in order to lead a Cluster effectively. For example, a family therapist is trained to be a careful observer of family interaction, to make hypotheses about the functioning observed in a given family, and occasionally to confront the family with the observations and hypotheses. This can be very threatening to families not accustomed to confrontation. Confrontation requires trust and time—trust in one another to share honestly and to keep confidences (including those shared with the therapist), and time to work through the material brought up during the confrontation. The emphasis becomes "working through" something that the family generally doesn't want advertised. Family Cluster, on the other hand, concentrates on having fun—even absurd—experiences from which to draw insights. It requires a degree of risk (for instance, being silly or working with finger paints can be emotionally risky for some adults), but the risks do not require "letting it all spill out" (which often happens in family therapy in a given family when emotions become tender and perhaps even heated during confrontation). Laughter—even silliness and hilarity—are hallmarks of Family Cluster, but the emotional risks are seemingly not as great as those during family therapy.

Planning Family Clusters

Before a Family Cluster is held, sponsoring organizations must be found, families must be enlisted for the Cluster, a time and a place must be reserved for Cluster, Cluster sessions must be planned, and myriad other details related to "planning" must be addressed before the first Cluster session is held.

Who Sponsors a Family Cluster?

Anyone can start a Family Cluster. However, if an organization sponsors the Cluster, it is more likely that a Cluster can be held and will be effective because of supportive interest from the sponsor.

It is important that a Family Cluster have some type of institutional sponsorship such as a college or university, a business or industry, a religious congregation, or a governmental unit. Experience with Family Clusters (M. M. Sawin, personal communication, 1988) has shown that starting Family Clusters without institutional support tends to lead to a short life for Clusters and even dependency. Dependency occurs when families attend Cluster primarily because of loyalty to the leaders or to other families. An unexpected and sad result can be overdependency on leaders and other families. Family Cluster, to the contrary, should support families in developing self-reliance, not dependence.

Number of Sessions Required for Family Cluster

It is a good idea to plan at least eight sessions for the first group of Cluster sessions, although twelve to fifteen would be better to allow the time needed for change to take place. This provides enough time for Cluster members to get well acquainted and to bond with one another, to have enough sessions that they feel they have "learned" something, to establish rules and policies for those participating in the Cluster, and to prepare for terminating the Cluster. If a Family Cluster wishes to continue meeting beyond the initial eight sessions, the members should recontract to meet together for at least eight additional sessions. Though the Cluster members decide how they want to spend their time together, it takes at least eight Cluster sessions to deal with any learning topic to any degree of completion and Cluster member satisfaction.

Where Do Cluster Families Come from?

If there is an organization sponsoring the Family Cluster, usually the organization will advertise among its members for participating families in a Cluster. For example, if a business such as an insurance agency tells its employees that a Family Cluster will begin at a particular location on a particular date and time and will be held each week for eight weeks, briefly describing what a Family Cluster is all about, families can sign up on a first-come, first-served basis. If a Cluster for families with preschoolers and younger children, school-aged and adolescent children, children with disabilities, stepfamilies, and so forth are planned, those requirements should be stated in the initial advertising by the sponsoring organization.

The cost of the Cluster also should be indicated in any advertising about the Cluster unless the sponsoring organization plans to pay for the Cluster.

Length of Each Cluster Session

A Cluster session where families have a short meal together (usually sandwiches, possibly also including light refreshments that were prepared for everyone in Cluster by one of the families) might be scheduled for two hours once each week. If a meal is not served, but refreshments are served at the end, each Cluster session should last one and one-half hours at the same time and place once each week.

One of the challenges in scheduling Cluster sessions is finding a time when each family can attend at the same time as other families. Sometimes a late Saturday morning or early Saturday afternoon session is most convenient for all the members of a Cluster (Saturday sessions are not recommended for observant Jews or Seventh-Day Adventists because Saturday is the Sabbath).

Often children have paper routes or music, dancing, or sports lessons in the hours preceding the evening meal and after school. Often it is difficult for families to get together on weekdays or even early evenings on weeknights. Considering a sandwich meal together on a weeknight might be a good idea and a wonderful break for the person who usually prepares the meal (sandwiches are generally easy to prepare in advance). "Breaking bread together" can be a very effective way for families to drop barriers and become well acquainted with each other. There should not be emphasis on what is eaten. This may create a form of competition, which can destroy the purpose of the Cluster. A half hour should be set aside for the meal—no more—soon after everyone arrives at the beginning of the session. Then Cluster members, after a quick meal cleanup, should be ready to go on with other Cluster activities.

Staffing a Family Cluster

Every Cluster requires two leaders. This is necessary because managing a Cluster can be too overwhelming for one person. The planning and preparation for each Cluster session are time-consuming. In addition, while one leader is conducting a learning experience, the other leader can be an observer and assist the one conducting to recognize when it is time to change the activity of the Cluster or to assist Cluster members in activities to maintain motivation and satisfaction in the learning processes. Leaders gain a great deal by supporting each other and planning together. There is an old adage that applies to leading a Cluster: two heads are better than one. In addition, it is easier to maintain an even energy flow during a Cluster session when two leaders are involved.

Making Home Visits

I would recommend that each family who will be in the Cluster receive a visit from the Cluster leaders before the first Cluster session. This gives the family an opportunity to get acquainted with the leaders and the leaders an opportunity to get acquainted with the members of the family in their own living space. It is also an opportunity for family members to commit themselves to attending Cluster.

Equipment and Materials for Family Cluster

Equipment. The equipment needs of a Family Cluster are simple and basic. Generally, it is a good idea to have carpet on the floor where the Cluster meets so Cluster members can sit on the floor at will (it is helpful to little children to have adults at their level; many young children, when living in a world of adults, see nothing but knees!). There should be enough wall space so that instructions and words to songs on newsprint or computer paper or butcher paper can be attached with masking tape. Artwork, personal portraits, and other "masterpieces" made by Cluster members should also be attached to the walls with masking tape. Low chairs and tables, cushions, and occasionally audio-recording equipment and video playback equipment can be helpful for Family Cluster, but are not absolutely necessary for low-budget Clusters. Picture books and wooden blocks (colored and refinished or not) are helpful, especially if the Cluster has young children (i.e., children under the age of 6 or 7).

Supplies. The simpler the supplies are, the better. Newsprint is easy to get and often costs nothing because it can be obtained where newspapers or books are printed. I have conducted a Family Cluster using only newsprint on which to print instructions, songs, and the like. Sometimes, for variety, some Clusters will want to purchase a roll of butcher paper for the printing of instructions and so on. Computer paper is often discarded, and it can be used for the same purposes. Masking tape is an absolute necessity. Black marker pens can be used for printing instructions, songs, and the like, and colored marker pens in a variety of colors can be used by Cluster members in a variety of Cluster activities. Crayons are nice to have, as are pencils (sharpened), paste (school paste), old magazines, yarn, string, and a whole host of "beautiful junque." Sometimes if Cluster families scour their homes they can find supplies that might become part of the supplies for Cluster. Plastic food cartons can be saved and used to store Cluster supplies such as markers, crayons, pencils, and paste.

Objectives for Family Cluster Sessions

Each Cluster session revolves around some topic related to family growth and strength, such as communication and self-esteem. Specific topics are not enough, however. Objectives (that is, expected learner outcomes) must be planned related to the subject matter of each Cluster session. Insight objectives are the prime focus of Cluster activities (see Chapter 7).

The Cluster Session Agenda Plan

Each Cluster session generally consists of the following six types of learning experiences: gathering (meal, when included), Cluster meeting, game, theme activity, closure, and refreshments. These activities generally focus on family strengths that need improving as revealed by performance on the Family Strengths Inventory completed by each family in the Cluster (see Chapter 7).

Gathering. Not all families arrive at the Cluster session at the same time. It is a good idea to have an activity for Cluster members to engage in that will capture their interest immediately and assist them in making the transition from what they were doing before Cluster (probably rushing) to the Cluster itself. It is an event that allows immediate individual involvement, is most likely interesting to all Cluster members, does not require a great deal of thinking and planning on the part of the individual, and is something that can be done at one's own pace. It is an opportunity for the Cluster to gather together as one unit again after a week of being apart from one another. It is unstructured enough to allow Cluster members to greet one another and to get "psyched up" for their time together. When Cluster members get well acquainted with each other, they often save up things they want to share with other Cluster members outside their families. Often teenagers will greet each other with "high fives" or such comments as "What a cool outfit. Is that new?" or "Sorry your [football] team lost at state." When the Cluster is new, the gathering can focus on get-acquainted activities.

Meal. Sometimes a simple sandwich meal follows the gathering phase. Each family brings its own food. Refreshments can be served following this meal or at the end of the Cluster session, or families can bring their own dessert as desired. This provides a time for families to visit with other families—and with one another in the family—in a very relaxed atmosphere. When a meal is included in each Cluster session, an occasional potluck adds additional interest, stimulation, and reinforcement, especially when Cluster members are well acquainted with each other.

Cluster meeting. The Cluster meeting generally follows the gathering phase (or the meal, if a meal is included). It usually provides ritualized activities that mark the Cluster as a unit. As Cluster members become acquainted with each other, it might be a good idea to discuss briefly what has happened in the lives of Cluster members since the last Cluster. For example, one father had lost his job just before the Family Cluster began. During the fourth Cluster session, he announced excitedly that he had found a new and exciting job in another city, to begin a couple of months after the last Cluster session. Members of the Cluster had the opportunity to pat him on the back and to express their feelings of pleasure at his good fortune. One high school sophomore, a girl, won an essay contest and announced it excitedly to the Cluster at the Cluster meeting. This gave the Cluster members an opportunity to affirm this member in ways that neither they nor the young recipient will soon forget.

Another ritual that Clusters I conduct enjoy is that of Warm Fuzzies. I generally hand out a couple of Warm Fuzzies to each family in the Cluster and suggest that they hand the Fuzzies to anyone in the Cluster they would like.

The Cluster meeting also allows Cluster members an opportunity to talk about what they discovered during the past week about learning events from the previous Cluster session or sessions. It also is a good time to discuss "homework" that might have been assigned at the previous Cluster session.

If leaders are wise, they will include singing as part of each Cluster meeting. Generally, Cluster members enjoy singing, especially if the leaders enjoy it and are not afraid to sing with or without instruments (like guitars, ukes, banjos, harmonicas, and autoharps). No one is born with a monotone voice. All of us can benefit from singing. Sometimes words can be written to melodies with which people are already well acquainted. (Sometimes Cluster members will volunteer to do this.) Perhaps someone in the Cluster will compose a song they wish to share with the Cluster. Singing is contagious. Often young children, particularly, will be heard at home during the week singing songs they learned at Cluster, especially if the songs are short and have catchy words or melodies. (See Chapter 9 on music in Family Cluster.)

Game. Following the Cluster meeting, Cluster members are usually ready for a change of pace. So a game usually changes the pace, allows the Cluster members to be a bit silly, and helps them experience something related to the learning objectives for the session. Games can be tremendous equalizers in that adults can be just as silly as their children and can get on the same level with their children. Games should be of such a nature that everyone in the Cluster can participate, including the younger ones. They should involve and be enjoyed by everyone in the Cluster.

Theme activity. Following the game, the major learning experience related to the insight objective for the Cluster session is implemented. The theme activity generally is planned to take up at least half of the Cluster session time. Now is the time for Cluster members to engage in such activities as puppets, guided imagery, role-playing, clay sculpturing, coloring with crayons or colored markers, and so on. Following the theme activity, Cluster leaders *process* the event (see Chapter 13 on "processing" in Family Cluster), although processing can and should occur during the Cluster meeting and following the game.

Closure. It is important to stick to a time schedule in Family Cluster. If it has been agreed that Cluster will last an hour and a half, then that contract should be kept by the leaders. Closure is the way to bring the events of the session to a close, perhaps through a song or chant or some other ritualized means of bringing the Cluster to a close. A ritual often enjoyed during Cluster is a favorite song or finger play during closure. If there are any homework assignments related to the theme activity and learning objectives, they should be made during Closure.

Closure is a good time to acknowledge what has taken place during the Cluster session and those who have participated, to reinforce what people learned (as discussed during the "processing" of the theme activity) by briefly summarizing what has been learned and ways the learning might be included in daily activities, and to acknowledge the family (or families) who brought the refreshments for the session.

Refreshments. With the possible exception of the first Cluster session, refreshments, if desired by the Cluster families, should be assigned, each Cluster session, to families who are members of the Cluster. If a meal is served, the refreshments should be served at the end of the meal. As a general rule, refreshments should be very simple and low in calories.

Cluster Leaders Working as a Team

Cluster leaders, although they may have a general idea of what themes or learning objectives they wish to pursue during each of the Cluster sessions, need to plan the details of the next Cluster session immediately following the current session while ideas and insights gained from Cluster observations are still fresh.

Cluster leaders have the opportunity to contribute their strengths in the planning of Cluster sessions. One leader will observe in the Cluster group what the other leader might miss. Together, the leaders can compile their ideas about how the next session should be planned. They can be as creative as they wish to be, drawing from their experience and sharing feelings and ideas openly and honestly. Wise leaders will not take personally what the other team member says or does, but will confront issues as honestly as possible when they occur.

It is important to plan Cluster sessions to fit the members of the Cluster. Who does the talking in the Cluster? Who is getting left out? Who seems to be the most needy and demanding? What can be done to match Cluster plans with team member observations? What seems to be working?

Conducting a Cluster Session

Before the Cluster Session Begins

It is a mistake to arrive at the place where the Cluster session is to be held just minutes before the session begins. I'm always surprised at the things I miss in preparation, although I have always prided myself on being a good detail person. In addition, I need time to get set up leisurely before a Cluster. I get confused when people start arriving while I'm in the midst of preparations. My confusion is contagious among Cluster members.

I often talk with Cluster leaders in training about knowing the "geography" of the session. It is important to have in mind the layout of the session from beginning to end. Unexpected things can and will happen. However, it is better to be overprepared than underprepared. If I know exactly where I am going to conduct each learning activity, how I am going to bridge the transition from one activity to another, and if I have all my supplies and equipment ready to go and in order before the Cluster begins, I can relax a few moments before the first family arrives and be prepared to meet that family enthusiastically.

Summary and Conclusions

This chapter has provided an overview of a family support and experiential education program called Family Cluster, focusing primarily on the two major processes of planning and conducting a Family Cluster.

The chapters in Parts II and III will zoom in on the details of the two processes, *planning* and *conducting* Family Cluster. Keep in mind, however, that the focus of this book is Family Cluster. Family Cluster is not gathering activities, theme activities, games, or music. Such activities are tools in a larger process of learning. Remember the larger view when you focus on the details.

Before the details of planning and conducting Family Cluster are discussed, three chapters follow that discuss critical issues related to Family Cluster. Chapter 2 discusses the family system. Because Family Cluster is made up of family groups, it is important for the leader to understand how the members of the family affect one another's behavior. This reciprocal interaction is the focus of the idea of system, the family system. Because Family Cluster focuses on strengths, not weaknesses, of families, Chapter 3 discusses eight characteristics of strong families as revealed by research relative to family strength. Finally, Family Cluster has been the focus of research. Does Family Cluster experience lead to stronger families? Chapter 4 might answer that question.

References

Mace, D. (1981, October). The long, long trail from information-giving to behavioral change. *Family Relations, 30*(4), 599–606.

Otto, H. A. (1975). *The use of family strength concepts and methods in family life education*. Beverly Hills, CA: Holistic Press.

Sawin, M. M. (1988). Personal communication with the author.

Sawin, M. M. (1979). *Family enrichment with Family Clusters*. Valley Forge, PA: Judson.

2. The Family as a System

It was the final Cluster session. All Family Cluster members had agreed in their contract to attend all Cluster sessions, unless an emergency arose. In the event of an emergency, they would notify one of the leaders.

No one had called either of the leaders before this last Cluster session began. Cluster plans for that final session included *each* Cluster member. This was the last time the Cluster would meet together as a group. *Each* person would be the focus of a special good-bye. Termination of something so special as Cluster can be painful. The leaders had planned well to ease the pain of ending Cluster. Some relationships would end, bringing the inevitable pain that comes with loss of pleasant relationships. Some relationships would continue outside of Cluster as families kept in contact to support one another through a variety of life events.

Everybody arrived *except* the parents in one of the four families. In place of the parents came the maternal grandmother of the four children, who ranged in age from 7 to 16—three girls and one boy. There had been no warning and, therefore, no preparation to include a new member of the group.

Two rules in the Cluster contract had been broken. First, the parents did not notify one of the leaders that they would not be in attendance. Second, they did not request permission for someone new to enter the group. The rule was that if someone wanted to bring a friend or relative, one of the leaders would be notified and asked permission to bring the guest.

During that last Cluster session, almost all the other Cluster members made special efforts to include the grandmother in Cluster activities and to help her feel right at home. One father explained the routine of Cluster. A mother invited the grandmother and the four children to join their family during the potluck meal. The grandmother willingly and enthusiastically joined all the Cluster activities. She told the leaders afterward what a wonderful time she had had and how grateful she was that her daughter's family could be a part of that Cluster.

But something seemed very out of place about that Cluster session. The children in the family seemed to spend an inordinate amount of time focusing on "Grandma." The focus seemed to shift from experiencing termination to including a new member of Cluster. As a matter of fact, the entire Family Cluster system had changed.

A Family Cluster is made up of far more than the individuals who reside in the families of which that Cluster is composed. In other words, the whole is greater than the sum of its parts. In the same way, a family is far more than its individuals, as important as they are; a family is greater than the sum of its parts. A family is a *system* of individuals. Because Cluster becomes a larger system composed of four or five other systems, family systems, it is important for Cluster leaders to recognize the characteristics of a family system in order to make effective plans for that larger, or Cluster, system and to interact effectively with the members of that larger system.

This chapter describes the major characteristics of a family system, characteristics that cannot be ignored if effective Cluster planning and implementation are to take place. But first, here are some thoughts about the concept of *system*.

In recent decades the family has become more and more the focus of research. Methods of studying individuals just don't work when studying families. Families are *groups* of people, not just groups made up of individuals. The workings of a family cannot be explained by the workings of any of its individuals. The family must be studied as a unit, as a whole. This complicates matters. A major assumption of the system idea is that what individual family members do interacts with and influences what every other family member does. The workings of the family are explained by this reciprocal interaction process, just as my putting my hand behind my back can only be done by taking the fingers and thumb and wrist and arm along, too. Putting my hand behind my back can be explained only by taking into account the reciprocal interaction of fingers, thumb, wrist, and arm. Studying the workings of these individual elements involved in putting my hand behind my back does not explain what happens when I put my hand behind my back.

The functioning of "family" can be likened to that of a symphony orchestra. I play the violin, one of the stringed instruments in a symphony orchestra, which also includes violas, cellos, and contra-basses (or double basses). Even though I have been trained as a soloist, when I play with a symphony orchestra I subdue that solo tendency in order to cooperate with other instrumentalists in producing beautiful music, written, most often, by composers specifically for symphony orchestras. If I insisted on playing solos, no matter how beautiful, the purpose of the symphony orchestra would not be met, and I would soon be out of a job.

In a symphony orchestra there are many different ways to play a composition. It is the job of the conductor not only to interpret what the composer has written but to inform the players, or instrumentalists, how he or she has interpreted the composition and what signals will be used to notify us when there are changes in dynamics, rhythm, melody, and so on. Though the musical score is in front of each one of us, it is the conductor's job to lead us so we can produce a piece of music that will reflect a unified whole, not one that is a cacophony of many solos.

There are many kinds of families and many ways to interpret effective or "healthy" family living. Usually the parents interpret how the family "should" function. One or both parents, sometimes with interchangeable assistance from and negotiation with some or all of the children, "conduct" the family in making its own unique "music" together.

Sometimes individual family members, for one reason or another, don't want to participate in the business of making "music" with the family. Individuals play "solos" (that is, disengage themselves from the family, or attempt to make their own rules) and disrupt the "music" played by the family. The family may become dysfunctional or unhealthy because it isn't making "beautiful music" together. It is what happens in the family as a whole when it does not make "beautiful music" that provides work for family professionals, such as family therapists and family life educators.

Effective or functional family living occurs when not only the family is growing but when each member of the family is growing (and thus changing) and progressing. Growth and progression within the family result from the interactions of the members of the family. No one grows in a vacuum. Each member of the family influences every other member of the family. Thus the family can be seen as a system of interacting parts, each part influencing every other part. When the parts are well oiled and kept in good repair, the family becomes effective or "healthy." When the parts are not lubricated or well maintained, the potential of the family and of its individual members may not be realized without intervention.

A *system* is any unit made up of interacting parts or elements, which endures over a period of time, is goal oriented, and has both structural and functional parts.

The *family system* is a social system (that is, it is made up of people) whose elements are the individual members of the family who interact in patterned relationships to achieve family goals. These patterned relationships can allow growth and progress of individual members or can stifle growth and progress, depending upon the nature of the patterns. Every member of the family influences the growth of every other member of the family. In other words, interaction of family members affects growth and development of individual members.

Characteristics of a Family System

There are several elements that characterize each family system. The Kenyon family will exemplify these characteristics as they are described (see Figure 2.1 for the Kenyon family genogram).

Chad Kenyon (age 40) met his wife, Mary (age 37), at a fraternity party in college. He was a senior and she was a sophomore. Mary was 20 and Chad 23 when they were married. Today they are the parents of four children, 16-year-old Ted, 13-year-old Linda, 10-year-old Monica, and 7-year-old Tami. Since they were married, the Kenyons have lived in the same town where they both grew up and went to college. Chad went to work for a soft-drink manufacturer soon after graduation and has worked his way up in the organization from a truck driver who delivered soft drinks to supermarkets and other customers in the valley to the manager of

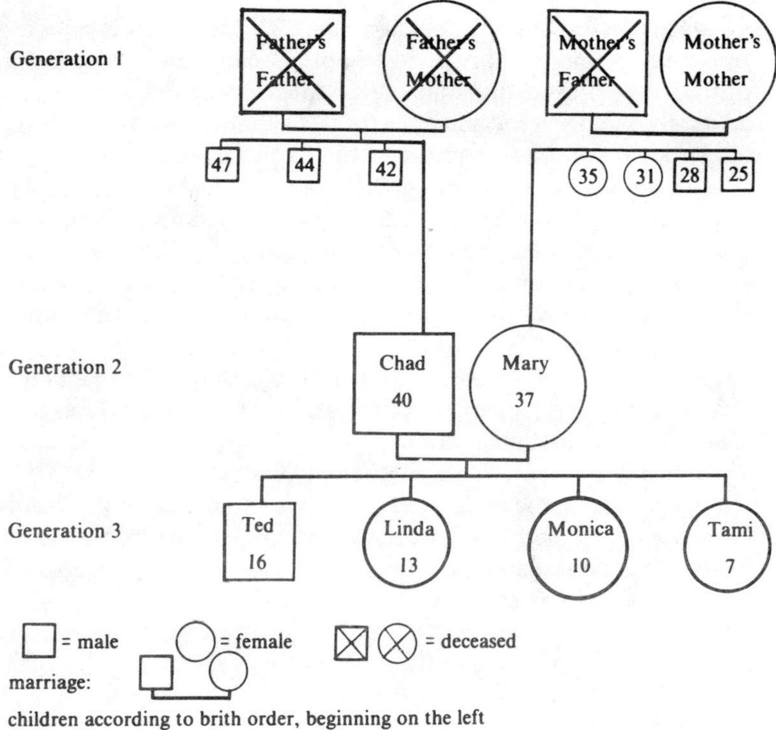

Figure 2.1. Three-Generation Genogram of the Kenyon Family

distribution in the company. He is responsible for several truck delivery routes and their drivers. He is a sports enthusiast who enjoys autumn football games at the local university, winter basketball games at the university, playing an occasional round of basketball with Ted at the basketball hoop Ted and Chad built in the back yard, and fishing the nearby streams in the spring and summer with Ted, his older brothers, and some of his friends at work. Mary finished her sophomore year in college, but never returned. She has been a full-time homemaker and mother since she and Chad were married 17 years ago.

The Kenyon family lives in a modest one-story four-bedroom home. Ted and Monica have their own bedrooms in the basement. Linda and Tami share a bedroom on the main floor, where their parents' bedroom is also located. A small kitchen (with a small laundry just off the kitchen), dining room, and living room constitute the remainder of the main floor of the Kenyon home. There is a small lawn in the front yard and a larger lawn in the fenced backyard with a couple of hardwood trees and a ring of well-kept flowers around the lawn and up against the house. A sandpile, swing set, the basketball hoop, and a hard-top surface for playing dot the back yard. The family dog, an Irish setter named "Cutter," lives in his dog house and dog run at one edge of the backyard.

Three months earlier, the Kenyon family had joined a Family Cluster sponsored by their Protestant congregation. The family goes to church every Sunday, mainly at the behest of Mary, who is a member of the congregation. Chad doesn't like organized religion, but joins the family when they go to church and supports Mary in her church activities during the week.

Chad is the fourth child in a family of four sons. One of his older brothers was recently divorced. Both of Chad's parents are dead. Mary is the oldest of five children, with two younger sisters and two younger brothers.

The characteristics of the family system described in this chapter are adaptations from those discussed in Galvin and Brommel (1986).

(1) Goal orientation: The family system has two basic goals, productivity and stability. As suggested earlier, any human system is goal-oriented. The goals of a family constitute the purpose of the family, its reason for being together. Although the goals are generally unconscious and, therefore, implicit, they nevertheless infuse the family with its purpose for being and influence the behavior of all family members. The goals of the family system are productivity and stability.

Productivity has nothing to do with the production of goods to be sold and distributed to society. It is not part of the economic system that runs society. However, it is an important reason why society can exist at all. Productivity refers to those values and rules, usually absorbed from the parental families of origin, around which the new family unit is organized, that uniquely identify the family as a unit. Those things that are considered valuable by the family and around which family rules of behavior operate constitute the productivity of the family.

Productivity marks the family as a unique social unit. Even

though the family members subscribe to the same values as its subculture, those values are interpreted behaviorally in unique ways that identify the family for who and what it is.

Hard work is one of the goals of the Kenyon family. Chad goes to work at 7:30 every morning and puts in a long and busy day at work, returning home by 6:30 in the evening, when Mary usually serves dinner. Mary, too, has a busy day, waking when Chad does, preparing breakfast for Chad and the children, then doing domestic chores. Usually in the afternoon she participates in community volunteer activities or church-sponsored activities and occasionally has lunch with a friend, one of her sisters, or her widowed mother.

Honesty is important to the Kenyons. The children have been taught to use only what belongs to them and to tell the truth and avoid cheating in school. Responsibility is important, as well. The children are expected to clean their own rooms and to participate on a rotating basis with household chores. They are expected to do their homework each evening, asking for assistance from other family members as they need it. Physical aggression is a no-no, although children are encouraged to express their strong feelings verbally and to choose appropriate ways to act on their feelings.

Family togetherness is important. The family goes to church together, after which they go to their maternal grandmother's home for Sunday dinner. They take family vacations together once a year. They often go bowling, on family picnics, visit relatives or friends, and even fishing and to sports events as a family.

These are just a few examples of family values important to the Kenyons.

Stability, or maintenance (Hoopes & Harper, 1987), is a goal that relates to the maintenance of good relationships in the family. It relates primarily to how the members of the family feel about each other and what they do to maintain those relationships. It is the "glue" that keeps the family together. It focuses primarily on the feelings family members have about each other. It focuses on emotional issues, rather than on those value issues that maintain the productivity of the family.

Family members may feel overclose to one another or wish they were more separate from one another. The ideal is a healthy sense of cohesion, where family members are bonded to one another but feel a sense of individual uniqueness that is valued by other family members. They don't have to be clones of one another in order to be valued, important people in the family system.

Chad and Mary feel it is important to be close, not only to one another but to their children. Chad likes sharing his enjoyment of sports actively with his son Ted. He enjoys his daughters and has always enjoyed being with them when he is home. He encourages them to share the events of the day with him and to share their thoughts and feelings. Mary, too, spends a lot of time with her children. She has been the main one to encourage them in their schoolwork, to go to parent-teacher conferences, to work as a homeroom mother with the PTA, and to encourage the children in their church activities. Both Mary and Chad encourage their children to engage in activities together so that they will become one another's friends. Mary feels that the family attending church together is an important way to help family members cement bonds with each other and with others in the congregation.

To help maintain their relationship with each other, Chad and Mary always reserve Friday night as their "date night." The children know that, after dinner that night, the parents will go to a movie, for a walk, or do some other activity they enjoy away from the home, just the two of them. When the children were younger, Mary's mother would be the family "baby-sitter" on date nights. Now the children take care of themselves when Mom and Dad have their dates.

(2) Interdependence and reciprocity: The behavior of each family member is related to and dependent upon that of every other. When changes occur in individual family members, they also occur in the family. Every member of the family influences the behavior of every other member. This is the concept of *reciprocity*, which is the hallmark of any human system—that the members of the group, in their interactions with one another, mutually influence one another. The only way one cannot *not* influence another member of that group is to get out of the group. And even leaving the group sends a message of some kind to the larger group, influencing each of the members in some way.

This characteristic also refers to the inevitable changes that occur within the group as a whole. One person changes and the whole group changes. This can be a process of growth, sometimes necessarily painful but always dynamic. Groups do not stay together very long if they do not change. This dynamic changing of a human system is called *morphogenesis*. It is something like the idea that, just when you get used to things the way they are, they change. We can never go back to the "good old days" (which probably weren't as good as we often think they were). At the same time, it seems to be a natural thing among humans—and certainly in physiological systems—to keep things the same, to maintain the *status quo*. This is called *homeostasis* in physiology and *morphostasis* in human systems.

Family systems change as they move through the stages of the family life cycle. What each family member does influences every other member. What each member does is dependent on what other members do. Thus family members experience *interdependence*.

Mary and Chad had their first child a year after they were married. That first year alone they had a chance to grow even closer as marriage partners, and to get acquainted with those "tremendous trifles" that helped to make each what he or she is and that occasionally bothered the other.

When little Ted came along, life for Mary and Chad changed forever. No longer were they an exclusive duet. Now they were a trio. Chad was surprised how much he enjoyed his little son. Mary, after postpartum depression, loved being a mother to an infant. Occasionally she was jealous of the attention that Chad seemed to focus on Ted. Chad, as well, felt somewhat jealous of Mary's being able to spend all day every day with their son.

And then almost three years later Linda came along. Chad fell in love with his little girl. He wasn't sure how to hold her, how to treat her, but he got used to her. He even helped Mary change diapers now and again. Once he even bathed his little daughter while Mary took care of an emergency with Ted. Ted wanted a dog, not a sister. At the very least, he wanted a brother. But, instead, he got a sister. Mary and Chad had to watch Ted carefully during those first few months after Linda's arrival because he was so rough with his little sister. But Ted seemed to enjoy holding his little sister. He often invited people into the house to see her, bragging to them that Linda was his little sister. Soon afterward Chad and Mary bought a dog, mainly because Ted wanted one so much.

Then came Monica and, finally, Tami. Chad and Mary do not plan to have more children. As each child has entered the family, he or she has brought major changes not only into the lives of the individual family members but also into the family system itself.

As family members grow and change, they become more and more *interdependent* on one another. That is, the functioning of one person is dependent on the functioning of the others in the system. For example, the household functions more effectively when someone prepares the meals, someone does the food shopping, someone sets the table, and someone cleans up after a meal and puts the food away. If both of the parents are the breadwinners in the family, everyone needs to pitch in to do the household tasks that make the household—and family—function smoothly. Older brothers and sisters can assist younger siblings with their homework. Family members communicate with one another and are dependent on the sharing of messages with one another, for moving from activity to activity, and for dealing with emotions. Almost everything that is done in the home is dependent on what someone in the family does. This can create a healthy family interdependence.

(3) Wholeness: The individual members of the family are important, but once they become interrelated, the relationships as a whole complex take on a life of their own. This is another way of saying that the whole is greater than the sum of its parts. Once the members of the family get in the habit of interacting in certain ways with one another, those interactive habits almost take on a life of their own. They become the "right" way to do things because they have always been done that way. Seldom do families stop to examine their ways of doing things. Examination of what is going on can be painful and, at the very least, might require change, which most people don't like to do.

There is a law of physics called inertia that suggests that, once an object is moving, it tends to stay moving. Once it is stopped, it tends to stay motionless. There is great energy involved in interaction with one another in a family and, therefore, change. Families engage in these patterns because they are accustomed to them, possibly because they feel a degree of predictability and control with the patterns. The energy expended in the enactment of these patterns is greater than the sum of the energy coming from the individuals. This is one of the reasons it is difficult for some families to face the possibility of change. The change seems overwhelming and too difficult to even attempt.

In a system, $1 + 1 = 3$. That is, the whole is greater than the sum of its parts. A dyad, which consists of two persons, consists of the two persons *plus* their relationship, the third element in the dyad. In a relationship, the individuals are not independent of one another. That is, they mutually interact with one another. They, as individuals, plus their relationship, make the whole.

The Kenyons have adapted to a routine of interaction so predictable and habitual that they are not even aware of the pattern. The times everyone has to be to work and school differ in the morning, but everyone gets up at approximately the same time. After breakfast together, the members of the family go their separate ways. When the children, especially the girls, come home from school, they excitedly tell their mother about the events of the day. They compete with each other to tell Dad about their day when he arrives home from work in the evening. The way Dad teases his girls and his son is predictable, but no one has ever thought of changing it—or that it might need changing. The bedtime routine is always the same. Changing any of these routines would create great strain in the family. Their ways of interacting are so habitual they are not even aware of the powerful energy that is expended in those routines and how that energy might be molding the family system. The family system acts as a whole with patterns that have become unconscious and habitual.

(4) Patterns/self-regulation: Family members develop regular, redundant patterns of interaction that make life manageable and predictable. Every human system needs some set of standards by which it defines itself and that help it to maintain itself. The routines of a family generally grow out of the standards the family has set for itself. These standards grow out of the values that the family thinks are important, generally those values that have come from the parental families of origin and have been blended and implemented in a unique way within the new family.

As members of a system interact with one another, they establish redundant patterns that provide a degree of predictability and manageability within the system. Rules of behavior are established within the system to maintain integrity related to the standards and values of the family.

Family *values* consist of a system of ideas, attitudes, and beliefs about the worth of ideas, entities, or concepts and provide general guides to behavior. Values in the middle-class American home generally revolve around the worth of work, productivity, the individual, education, consumption, use of time, efficiency, orderliness, practicality, use of reason, cleanliness, freedom, equality, and democracy. Rules are generated around these values.

Rules are family regulations for family conduct or behavior. They reflect the values of the family and determine the behaviors that influence relationships and patterns of family interaction.

Such rules can be *explicit,* that is, clearly defined, specific, and within the awareness of each member of the family. When rules are explicit, choices become feasible and family members can participate consciously in forming rules that will facilitate individual growth.

Many, if not most, family rules are *implicit* in nature. That is, they are not directly expressed and generally are outside the awareness of family members. Implicit rules can provide for growth and development in the family or can be rigid and exploitative of family members.

For example, every family has implicit rules about who can talk to whom and what one may speak about. In a growth-oriented, functional family system, the implicit rule would be that one may talk to the person about whom a reaction is experienced or with whom one wishes to discuss thoughts and feelings. In a rigid, dysfunctional family system, such an implicit rule might be that if the child wants the father to know something about the child, then the child must tell the mother, who, in turn, will tell the father (in other words, the mother acts as a go-between; the child is not allowed to go directly to the father).

An implicit rule in a growth-oriented family about how and when a family member wishes to go outside the family to relate to others or to be alone would be to go in and out of the family when the need is recognized. Such "leaving" behavior is not perceived as a hidden message that the person is rejecting the family. In a rigid, dysfunctional family, the person who prefers to be alone or to be with others is suspected of not caring about family members or of being angry.

An implicit rule about expressing feelings and ideas in a growth-oriented family is that one may comment upon what one feels and thinks at any time. One makes such comments upon considering the context and the feeling level of others to whom one wishes to speak. One's perceptions are not judged by others as having ulterior motives. Responses of others to the ideas and feelings are heard as additional information, not as put-downs of the receiver. In a rigid, dysfunctional family, one does not express feelings, particularly if they are strongly felt. One does not say what one really feels and thinks, *or* all feelings and ideas must be expressed and are perceived as family property, not as owned by the person expressing them.

Occasionally the family needs to recalibrate its rules if, like temperature in the home, the behavior of family members appears too far off course. In order to do this, the family needs information to recalibrate its rules. Information comes in two forms: positive feedback and negative feedback. *Negative feedback* is information that will help the family to maintain its standards while minimizing change. Negative feedback is a way of maintaining homeostasis or morphostasis. Change may not be necessary.

Information that the rules need changing, that the family might need to change, is called *positive feedback* because it results in change or morphogenesis.

Families have their own rules for recognizing and doing something about negative and positive feedback. In general, change is difficult and resisted.

When Chad was promoted from a truck driver delivering soft drinks to clients of the company to the distribution manager, his time schedule at work changed as well. No longer did he have to be up at 5:00 in the morning and on the job by 7:00. When his time schedule for work changed, so did the time the family had breakfast and got up in the morning. As a matter of fact, the entire routine of the day changed for the family. Mary would get up to make Chad's breakfast and would eat breakfast with him before he went to work and before the children got up to get ready for school. Now that everyone gets up at about the same time, rules for using the bathrooms (one upstairs and one downstairs), and rules for eating breakfast and doing tasks before breakfast and school have changed. (Linda and Monica practice the piano for a half hour each before they leave for school each morning.)

The rules now seem second nature to the family, but when they were first changed as a result of Chad's job change, there was great upheaval in the family. The children constantly complained. Mary missed her breakfasts alone with her husband. The kids weren't sure they liked having Dad around for breakfast. But all that has changed now that the family has adjusted to its new rules. Change was difficult—even painful—but the family is back on a predictable, manageable schedule now.

However, Mary wants to go back to college and get her degree. That means she will have to leave in the morning before the children do to attend her classes. Adjustments in the morning routine will have to be made again—the rules will need to be changed. And Mary's relationships to each person in her family will change as a result of her new experience as a returning college student.

(5) Mutual influence/punctuation: In a family system, once an act occurs, it is both a response to a stimulus (an effect) and also a stimulus for another act (a cause), thus making it difficult, if not impossible, to determine which is cause and which is effect. Someone might ask, "Where did __________ begin?" in a given family. The idea of system looks at responses as circular, being both causes and effects. Therefore, people just go in circles when they attempt to figure out what started what. Everything is *both* a cause and an effect, a response to a stimulus and a stimulus itself.

Major family problems often end up in a circular argument about where to attach blame. In the concept of system, there is no such thing as blame. Each event is examined on its own merits, without making an attempt to determine its cause. Children often get caught in tangles of blaming one another for something. Each child perceives the "cause" differently. Parents collude in this process by asking their children who caused what—that is, they attempt to find the blame for the event. It most likely would be more functional and effective simply to begin with the event, an effect, and go from there to solve the problem, rather than to discover a cause and to attach blame.

Mary has wanted Chad to join her church ever since they started courting each other, but Chad would not join because he doesn't believe in organized religion. Mary, in her heart of hearts, admits that Chad lives a "religious" life perhaps more effectively than anyone in her congregation. Chad supports her in her church activities and probably gives more quiet service to members of the congregation than anyone else. Occasionally Mary and Chad get caught in an "if only . . ." verbal battle. That is, Mary will say, "Chad, if only you would join the church, __________ would work out fine." Chad usually will make some such reply as, "Mary, that doesn't have anything to do with it. Even if I joined the church, that wouldn't make any difference with __________." Possibly what they both need to do is talk about what Mary *wants* and go from there instead of attempting to find the cause of an effect. This problem of placing blame has not yet become a major problem for Mary and Chad (and, therefore, the remainder of the family), but it could escalate because both are attempting to place blame (cause) instead of to deal with the wanted event itself.

Both Mary and Chad discipline their children by first attempting to find the source of the blame for undesired behavior. This leads to dead-ends, but they continue to seek the blame. If they dealt with the undesired behavior without seeking the cause, they would likely be more successful in their efforts to teach their children desirable behavior patterns.

(6) Adaptation: Change or adaptation in the face of developmental or other stress is a predictable part of a family system. The family is capable of adaptation. That is, the family is capable of change. As a matter of fact, the family must change in order to survive. However, the family will attempt to stay the same (morphostasis) until forced by circumstances, by life events such as transitions, to make a change, to adapt to a new set of rules and ways of interacting with one another (morphogenesis). In other words, the family system is dynamic. It will experience morphostasis for a while, then morphogenesis as change becomes important and necessary. For example, the arrival of the first child is the kind of developmental stress or life event that requires change or adaptation within the family unit. When the first child enters school for the first time (including preschool), the breadwinner(s) lose employment, or the grandparents come for a visit, changes or adaptations must be made in the family system to adjust to the new challenge to the family as a unit.

The Kenyon family goes to Mary's mother's home for dinner every Sunday after church. Recently Mary's mother broke her leg and was in the hospital for a week. She hobbled around with a cast for several weeks. For a couple of Sundays, Grandmother could not prepare the usual Sunday meal for her daughter's family. Mary, of course, was very concerned about her mother's health, as was Chad. Mary fussed about how her mother was going to take care of herself at home alone (she is a widow). She wanted her mother to come stay at her home. Ted would enjoy sleeping in a sleeping bag in the living room for a while. Grandmother refused. She wanted to stay in her own home, although she expressed appreciation for the offer from Mary and the family. Grandmother fussed about missing the dinner for the family on the two Sundays she was unable to prepare the meal. Even now she hobbles around on crutches as she prepares the meal for Mary and Chad and the family each Sunday. The children were very concerned about their grandmother's accident. Nevertheless, although they did not say anything about it to their parents, the change in their Sunday routine bothered them. Everyone was grateful to get back to "things as usual" when Grandmother insisted on fixing dinner while hobbling around on her crutches. The family adapted to this necessary adjustment in their Sunday routine for a while. The family probably could have adapted to a more serious health problem. But life is a series of such adaptations to life events, which often are very stressful and require change in accepted patterns of family life.

(7) *Openness: A predictable process in a family system is interchange with other people, ideas, and social systems in order to sustain the family unit*. There is no such thing as closed human systems. That is, human systems, including the family, must interact with elements outside the system in order to survive, they must interact with the larger ecosystem of which the family is a part. No person or family is an island. That openness means that the family becomes vulnerable to change. No longer can the family operate as an independent unit in society. It depends on farmers and distributors for its food, clothing, and household items—for virtually everything family members need in a material sense. In addition, the members of the family come in contact with others in the society who can change individual goals or behavior, such as an outstanding teacher or a drug-using friend. Television has become a powerful source of influence within the average family. People, ideas, and other value systems affect the family almost outside the awareness of the family members. Even in earlier times when families produced their own food, clothing, and shelter, they became interacting parts of their larger ecosystem. They couldn't get food unless they prepared and cared for their crops and their livestock, nor could they get their clothing or shelter unless they cooperated with the larger ecosystem of which they were a part.

Chad and Mary were shocked one evening when they viewed a videotape Ted had brought home to view. The profanity and sexually explicit scenes were beyond anything they had allowed their children to see before. The movie was something that "all the kids liked." Chad and Mary wondered how they could do a better job of monitoring what Ted viewed on TV. They had not allowed Ted to go to "R-" and "X"-rated movies. Now they were viewing such a film in their own home. They were very concerned about the impact of such a film on such an impressionable mind as Ted's. They realized they wouldn't be able to stop Ted from viewing videotapes of which they didn't approve. They faced up to the possibility that they no longer had as much control over Ted's behavior as they had had in the past. They seriously wondered if they had been as effective in teaching Ted about making choices as they had hoped. They realized they wouldn't always be around to put the brakes on or to give the go-ahead for every major decision Ted had ahead of him. At the same time, they realized the powerful influence that other people and the media can have on their son.

(8) Equifinality: In family systems, there is generally more than one effective way to accomplish a goal. Equifinality means that there is more than one way to achieve a goal. For example, two families may believe in the concept of responsibility; both families will teach responsibility in different ways—and yet the children learn responsibility in *both* families.

When a man and a woman marry and start having children, each has his or her own ideas about how children should be raised even though both may share the same basic goals. Parenting, partially, is a blending of those two sets of ideas about how to raise children. The values of the parents may be the same, but their ideas about how to achieve those values may be entirely different.

Both Chad and Mary agree that children should learn how to work. Therefore, they assign household tasks to the children as soon as the children are capable of doing the tasks. Mary carefully monitors the children when they do their tasks. She makes sure that the children make their beds, take out the garbage, clean their rooms, set the table, clean up the dishes after meals, mow the lawn, and so on. Her children say she is very strict about getting tasks done around the house (which may have something to do with the influence of birth order on Mary; for a thought-provoking theory of birth order and its effects, see Hoopes and Harper, 1987). Chad, on the other hand, although he agrees that the children should have household tasks to do and should get them done, is more "laid back" about the accomplishment of those tasks. Mary has never felt that Chad was strict enough with the kids. She feels they can "get away with murder" around their father. This has always bothered Mary. Occasionally she and Chad argue about this. Mary now sees that Chad will never change. He refuses to be strict. He thinks that "understanding talk" will motivate the kids to do their tasks as much as "nagging" from their mother. Tasks usually get done in spite of the differing ways of motivating the children in the Kenyon family. It is likely that these and other ways are effective in getting the children to do their tasks, to "learn how to work." There is no one "right" way to motivate the children—there are several ways, each as effective as the other.

(9) Hierarchical relationships: Every family contains interpersonal and person/psychobiological subsystems that must be considered to understand the whole. Every dyadic (two-person) relationship in the family has its own set of rules and forms a family subsystem. The functioning of the family can only be understood within the context of this complex of functioning subsystem relationships. As the family increases in size, the complexity of these interpersonal relationships (and, therefore, subsystems) increases geometrically.

As the number of members of the family increases, the system becomes more complex and more complicated. The following is the formula for determining the number of dyadic relationships in any given family or human system (Miller & Janosik, 1980):

$$x = \frac{y^2 - y}{2}$$

where x = the number of relationships (dyads) and y = the number of persons in a family. For example, the number of relationships in a family with both parents and one child (three people) would be as follows:

$$x = \frac{3^2 - 3}{2} = \frac{9 - 3}{2} = \frac{6}{2} = 3$$

Notice the tremendous increase in relationships in the following family consisting of two parents and four children (six people):

$$x = \frac{6^2 - 6}{2} = \frac{36 - 6}{2} = \frac{30}{2} = 15$$

In other words, even though the second family is only double the size of the first one, the number of two-person relationships jumped to five times as many in the second family compared with the first.

The family system is made up of this complex of hierarchical relationships. That is, the family cannot be understood unless the subsystems that make up that unit are understood. Every dyadic or triadic (three-person) relationship in the family has its own set of rules, its own boundaries, its own unique characteristics.

These subsystems can become problematic in a family, especially triangles. A *triangle* occurs when the first child arrives in the family. In social systems, triangles are the most difficult to maintain and keep functional. That is, it is easy for two people (a dyad) within the triangle to form an alliance against the third member. For instance, the mother and newly arrived baby can be viewed from the father's perspective as forming an alliance against him. After all, the mother carried the baby around in her womb for nine months and probably has far more vested in the infant than the father because of her necessary physical closeness to the child. Many women spend their entire first pregnancy planning for their first child. Sometimes the father gets left out of this planning (or at least partially left out). The father can become something like an extra thumb in this first family triangle.

A triangle becomes problematic when this alliance process is consistently formed the same way within the same triangle and within other triangles in the family.

Mary and Chad were excited about their first child's birth. They spent hours planning what they were going to name their baby, where he would sleep, what he would wear, and what he might need as an infant to learn and be happy. Chad was in the delivery room when Ted was born. As a matter of fact, he has was in the delivery room when each of his four children was born. Mary occasionally feels pangs of jealousy when she sees Chad and Ted playing basketball outdoors or going off on fishing trips together. Ted is the catcher on his high school baseball team. Chad and Ted practiced for many hours so Ted could be the catcher. They have been "pals" ever since Ted was born. Chad, on the other hand, "spoils" his "little girls." Mary and Chad have talked endlessly about how to relate to their children. But they have noticed that there are dyads between the children as well. Ted teased his little sisters unmercifully while they were in their early childhood years. Just recently he and Linda have become good friends and often talk about what is happening in school and with their friends. Tami hasn't formed any noticeable bond with anyone in the family. She is the family "baby" and "Princess" (her father's favorite name for her). These assigned labels or *roles* can become expected sets of behaviors, which are difficult to get out of because they are not negotiable.

A *role* is a set of culturally defined behaviors expected of a person in a given social position. It defines what a person in a given situation should do. (It is *not* the actual performance of the expected behaviors.)

Each person in a family occupies several *social positions*. To each position are attached several roles. For example, a person in the *mother position* in the family might be expected to play the roles of housekeeper, child caretaker, child socializer, child teacher, child counselor, and so forth. The person in the *father position* in the family might be expected to play the roles of provider, child playmaker, child teacher, child taskmaster, and so forth. The person in the *wife position*, on the other hand, might be expected to play the roles of companion to her husband, sexual partner to her husband, playmaker with her husband, and so on. The person in the *husband position* might be expected to play the roles of companion to his wife, sexual partner to his wife, playmaker with his wife, and so on.

Such roles are *explicit* or formal roles because they are generally accepted as the roles of mothers and fathers and husbands and wives in society.

Another type of role is played by all family members primarily to meet the emotional needs of family members and maintain equilibrium in the family. This is the *implicit* or informal role. Some of these roles stimulate growth, while others hinder growth in family members. Such implicit roles include mediator, family jester, encourager, harmonizer, initiator, compromiser, follower, blocker, dominator, attention-seeker, martyr, pal, tease, and scapegoat.

Sometimes family members have labels attached to them that are hard to get rid of and that tend to become self-fulfilling prophecies because family members so labeled tend to engage in those clusters of behavior that characterize each label. Such labels include the "responsible" one, the "popular" one, the "socially ambitious" one, the "studious" one (or "egghead"), the "family isolate," the "irresponsible" one, the "sickly" one, the "spoiled" one. Such labels usually come in pairs. That is, if someone is labeled the "irresponsible" one, someone else in the family will be labeled the "responsible" one; if someone is labeled the "sickly" one, someone else will be labeled the "healthy" one; and so on. Such labels tend to be generalized by the child and affect his or her self-esteem.

A family system contains at least three levels of hierarchical relationships: the family system as a whole, the subsystems (dyads and triangles) that make up that family system, and the individual or personal psychobiological systems in the family. In order to understand the whole, the subsystems at each of the other two levels must be understood.

(10) Information processing: Every family system has its own patterns of processing information and transmitting messages. The way the family passes information from one person to another is *information processing* (communication). Sometimes these patterns are functional (that is, they allow for growth of individual members) or dysfunctional (that is, they retard growth of individual members). Before information processing can be understood, the concept of power in the family system needs to be understood.

Power is the actual or potential ability of one individual to control or influence another person's behavior. The person (or persons) in a family who makes the decisions is generally considered the person with power in the family. In authoritarian families all members of the family share the belief that one person has the right to control the behavior of the others in the family. In democratic or authoritative families all members of the family participate in the decision-making process to the degree they are able, and one person, generally a parent, presides and makes final decisions if the family is unable to come to a consensus on the issue.

Power in any given family is ascribed to those family members who control the rewards and punishments of others, who are perceived as having the greatest physical and/or mental ability, who are perceived as having some special knowledge or skill or expertise, who are believed to have the ability to punish noncompliant individuals, and/or who are most persuasive in explaining the necessity for some change. It is important in a family that levels of authority between parents and child be explicit, specific, and clear.

Unequal (dominant-submissive) power structure. The unequal (dominant-submissive) power structure is illustrated in Figure 2.2. This unequal power structure functions on the assumption that all people are not equal (that is, not of equal worth) and that some people, because of such factors as age, size, experience, wealth, social status, and degree of education, should exercise power and dominion (dominance or control) over others. Such power and dominion can take the form of benevolence or malevolence. If some people are dominant, this suggests others must be weak and submissive to such power.

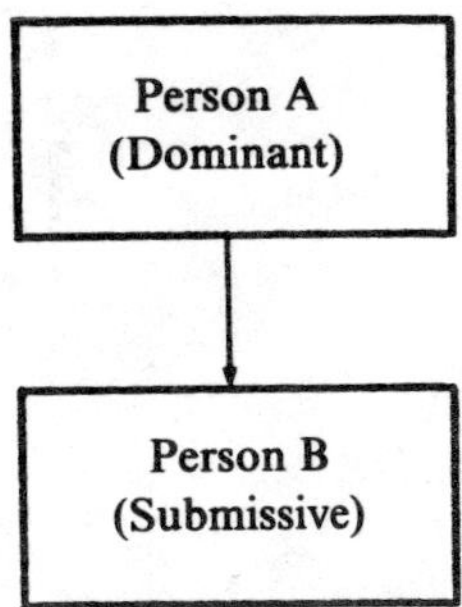

Figure 2.2. Unequal (Dominant-Submissive) Power Structure

This type of relationship between the powerful and the weak, the dominant and the submissive, assumes that some people are better than others. If some people are better than others, it follows that the "better" ones have the right and responsibility to set the goals for the "inferior" ones. This suggests that the "inferior" (or submissive) ones are not capable of setting their own goals. It then follows that the person who sets the goals of another must also take responsibility for the achievement of those goals because he or she, not the submissive person, is the one who makes the commitment to such goals. The role of the "inferior" or submissive person in such a relationship is to accept without question the goals set by the dominant person and to carry out any directives related to the goals. Thus neither the dominant nor the submissive person changes, grows, or progresses because both are locked into a rigid power structure.

Feelings in such a dominant-submissive structure are considered unimportant. In fact, it is common in such relationships to deny feelings (whether positive or negative) because they are considered to be signs of weakness. Both dominant and submissive persons are taught to deny, repress, or suppress their feelings.

Position A (dominant) in Figure 2.2. is thought by many people to be more desirable than Position B (submissive). Thus we can see people in families with an unequal power structure trying to put other people down by whatever means they can in order to become the dominant (and thus "better") persons.

The consequences of an unequal power structure in a family

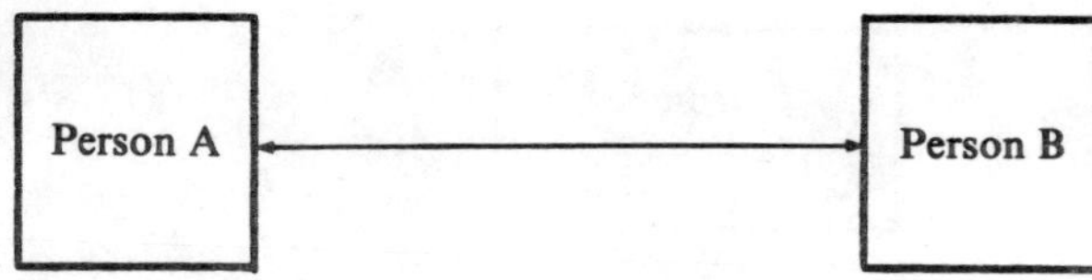

Figure 2.3. Equal (Parallel) Power Structure

vary according to the degree of dominance and submission within the family. Typical consequences of this kind of structure include feelings of anger and frustration, quarrels, competition, ambition for social status, self-gratification and selfishness, withdrawal from society, greed, and even violence. Relationships based on such an unequal power structure can be seen between management and labor, between teacher and student, between different religious sects, between parents and children, and between siblings within the family.

Equal (parallel) power structure. Equal power does not suggest there are no differences in size, age, experience, wealth, or knowledge. However, these differences fade in the face of the fact that *all* people are of equal worth. The child may be younger, weaker, and less educated than his father, but both the child and his father are of equal *worth*. Equal power suggests there is no hierarchy among people in a family, no authoritarianism, not even "benevolent" rule from parents or older siblings. *All are equal in opportunity, rights, and social status although not necessarily equal in talent, education, age, size, experience, or wealth.* Such an equal power structure is illustrated in Figure 2.3.

An equal (parallel) relationship is based on the assumption that those involved in the relationship are of equal worth. One may be older, more experienced or skilled, richer, better educated (may even be more intelligent, as measured by an intelligence test); may be higher in social status or prestige; may hold a more visible and coveted social or professional or political position; or may be physically stronger than the other. Regardless of these differences, the individuals in the relationship are viewed as equal in worth.

Such equals set their own goals to the degree they are able. A young child, for example, is less capable than an adult of setting his or her goals because physical and mental development are not yet complete. Thus the child cannot take the responsibility for all of his or her actions. Each person in an equal relationship assists the other to achieve his or her goals through encouragement, praise, and physical and/or psychological assistance. Each person from the age of about 8 is responsible for the choices he or she makes, takes the consequences of his or her actions, and evaluates achievement of his or her own goals.

Communication patterns. Communication is the processing of information (or energy) between a sender and receiver. Communication serves to bind the subsystems of the family together into a cohesive whole and to maintain the entire family system.

Communication is the most important part of the structure of the family system in facilitating the achievement of the family goals. It is critical that the family provide a nurturing environment where the individual can develop feelings of self-worth and a sense of trust in and caring for other individuals. This is accomplished best through clear and functional communication patterns within the family system. Satir (1972, p. 31) describes the importance of communication:

> I see communication as a huge umbrella that covers and affects all that goes on between human beings. Once a human being has arrived on this earth, *communication is the largest single factor determining what kinds of relationships he makes with others and what happens to him in the world about him.*

Functional communication refers to clear transmission and reception of both content and feeling in any verbal or nonverbal message. When you listen to others, you are listening to abstracts called verbal symbols. These verbal symbols can be called "messages." These messages are of two types: content and intent (or feeling). The message is considered *content* when it consists mainly of an idea or series of ideas about things, people, places, and/or events. The message is considered *intent* (that is, feeling) when it consists primarily of words related to emotion or affect and/or nonverbal signals revealing strong emotional involvement of the sender. All of us send both content and intent messages. Functional communication in the family allows for maximum growth and development of the individual members of the family.

Although the purpose of this chapter is to describe the family as a system, it is important at this point to provide some "how to's" related to functional, or healthy, communication among family members. These communication skills are related primarily to feelings because so many people have trouble communicating their feelings or "hearing" the feelings of others. These skills include paraphrasing (or reflecting) feelings and direct expression of feelings (sometimes called "I" messages).

Paraphrasing (reflecting) feelings. Family communication that is functional—that is, focused on the growth of the individuals involved and thus focused on equal power structure—tends to concern itself a great deal with the feelings of family members. One effective way to do this is to listen carefully to what the other person is saying (and feeling) and then to reflect back to the person, in your own words, what you perceived the other person to be saying. The prefix *para* means "a going beyond; like or resembling." In other words, when you listen to the comments of another person, you try to imagine what it is the person is really trying to say. Paraphrasing feelings is an appropriate way to respond to another person's comment if you perceive it to be basically an "intent" message (that is, a message about feeling, emotion, or affect) and you are almost certain you understand what feeling is being expressed. You paraphrase feelings by doing the following:

—put in *your own words* the feeling message you perceived
—using *affect, feeling, or emotion words* to describe the perceived feeling and
—using a *voice inflection indicating a statement*; then
—*pause* for the other to respond.

For example, suppose at the dinner table Barney excitedly told his family: "Today I hit a home run and knocked in two other guys ahead of me! We won 10 to 9!" His father replied: "Boy, I'll bet you felt terrific." Here the father's comment is related directly to the child's feeling. It is his paraphrase (or reflection) in his own words of the feelings behind the boy's comment, a reflection of the "intent" of the comment. It accepts the feeling without agreeing with it, judging it, or criticizing it. It sends a nonverbal message to the child that it is OK to have such feelings. If the father is incorrect in his perception, the boy can easily correct it because he has not been put on the defensive by his father's remark.

Many adults, when responding to the comments of others, tend to do one of several things. Sometimes they *agree* or *disagree* with what the other person said. Sometimes they *evaluate* what the person said, thus tending to moralize, give advice, command, or compare the other person with someone else. Sometimes they use the other person's comment as a *springboard* to discuss a related topic. Sometimes they respond in a way that is *irrelevant* to what the other person said. Sometimes they simply *ignore* what the other person said. All of these ways of responding essentially tell the other person that the adult doesn't care. Furthermore, such comments often are perceived as punishers, effectively eliminating in the future the type of response the other person has made—but not the feeling. If the parent, for example, has established an equal (parallel) relationship with the child, the parent will feel no necessity to do other than respond to (and thus recognize and accept) the feelings of the child.

One typical parent response to a comment such as Barney's at the dinner table is this: "That's nice. Pass the potatoes." This response *ignores* the child's feelings by barely acknowledging his comment before going on to something irrelevant to his feelings.

This is another typical parent response: "I'm proud of you, son." This is expressing the *father's feelings about the boy's performance* rather than paraphrasing the boy's feelings. The boy may perceive he is valued by his father only when he accomplishes something important. A third typical parent response: "It isn't polite to brag about things you have done well." This is an *evaluation* of the boy's comment and a put-down to his self-esteem.

Another typical parent comment: "Maybe you'll hit two home runs in the next game." This, again, is a *put-down* because it suggests the father won't be satisfied until his son does an even better job of playing baseball.

It is not necessary to paraphrase a person's feelings every time that person makes a comment. When the other person seems obviously aroused, in either a positive or a negative direction, you could focus your response to the other's comment on the feeling behind that comment. This helps the other person to put a label on his or her real feeling—something children are often unable to do without adult assistance—and also helps to reduce the magnitude of the other person's feeling and helps that person find appropriate ways to deal with it. When a person is highly aroused, it is difficult for him or her to be rational. When you paraphrase the other person's feeling, it helps to "reduce the steam" so the other person can control his or her own behavior. The person knows he or she has been listened to and so doesn't have to hurry through what he or she wants to say or try to say something that will please you.

Adults as well as children have comparatively small feeling vocabularies. Perhaps this is because we are afraid of feelings and, therefore, deny them. When we deny feelings, we can't develop a large feeling vocabulary. A child who has a large feeling vocabulary because his or her feelings are accepted (that is, his or her feelings are often paraphrased) also is likely to develop several behavior alternatives related to a feeling and make wiser choices of behavior than the child whose feelings are consistently denied.

Paraphrasing the other person's feelings tends to do the following for that person (including a child):

(1) It reduces the magnitude of a negative feeling;
(2) it creates a warm, trusting, caring relationship between you and the other person;
(3) the other person becomes less afraid of his or her negative feelings;
(4) it opens the way for the other to deal appropriately with his or her feelings because it pinpoints the feeling instead of denying it;
(5) the other person tends to recognize the feeling instead of denying it;
(6) the other person tends to paraphrase the feelings of others because of the model set for him or her; and
(7) the other person is more likely to take responsibility for his or her own behavior rather than depending on others to tell him or her what to do.

Directly expressing feelings. It is not only important that you learn to recognize and accept the other person's feelings (by paraphrasing feelings), it is also important that you learn to recognize and accept your own feelings. It is impossible to act constructively with regard to your own feelings unless you are aware of and can label your own feelings at any given moment in time. This is what some people call "being in touch with yourself." It isn't always necessary to tell people what you are feeling, but *you* should always know, particularly if the feelings are very strong, in either a positive or a negative direction. When these strong feelings threaten the development of an effective relationship with another family member or with a friend, it may be appropriate to communicate such feelings to the other person.

When you share your feelings with others directly, you engage in the process of *self-disclosure*. That is, you allow people to know the real you because you reveal your feelings as well as your thoughts.

There are appropriate and inappropriate ways of communicating strong feelings to others. It is always inappropriate to thrust the responsibility for your feelings upon another person or group. No one can make you feel anything. For instance, saying to another, "You make me feel stupid," ignores the fact that your feelings are created by your own unique perceptions and interpretations of what someone else does and says. The other person cannot create those perceptions and interpretations; you do. Your interpretation of another person's behavior may create such strong feelings inside that it is helpful to share with the other person what you are feeling to help you find a way to change the feeling. This is done by

(1) *describing the behavior in the other* that you perceive is creating your negative feeling (don't blame; just describe):

"When you leave your clothes lying all over the furniture in your room . . . "

(2) stating *your feeling* about the consequence the behavior produces for you:

" . . . I get upset . . . "

(3) and stating *the consequence*:

". . . because the clothes get terribly wrinkled and the room looks messy" (Dinkmeyer & McKay, 1976).

For example, suppose a child is watching TV with his feet propped up on a new upholstered chair. Mother notices this and probably feels like saying:

"You know better than to put your feet on that chair."

However, this is an *indirect* expression of feeling. It is ambiguous and projects the responsibility for the mother's feeling to the child.

Now notice the change when the mother expresses her feeling directly:

> "Your feet are on the chair . . ." (she describes the *behavior*)
> " . . . and I feel anxious . . ." (she describes her *feeling*)
> " . . . because the chair will get dirty" (she describes the *consequence* of the child's behavior).

In this case, when the mother describes the feeling (anxious) as her own, it generally is much easier for the child to receive (or accept) the feeling. The emphasis is on the mother's own feeling and on here-and-now behavior of the child, behavior that can be changed. It is not likely the child will become defensive. It leaves the choice up to him whether to change his behavior or not. Because he doesn't have to defend himself, he is more likely to change his behavior than if his mother had accused him of causing her feeling.

Now notice what happens if the mother were to use the pronoun *you* instead of *I* when expressing her feeling: "You're making me feel anxious right now . . ." This is attaching the responsibility for her feeling onto the child. That's a big load to carry, and it is unfair to the child. By using the pronoun *I* when expressing her feeling directly, she takes the responsibility for her own feeling (this process is sometimes called sending an "I message.") In other words, she "owns" her own feelings; she takes responsibility for her own feelings.

When you directly express your feelings to others, you are taking the risk of (that is, becoming vulnerable to):

- —your feelings not being understood and accepted by the other person;
- —having your feelings denied;
- —having your feelings ridiculed, judged, or laughed at;
- —being manipulated because the other person might use his or her knowledge of your feelings to force you to do things you do not wish to do; and
- —feeling guilty if you feel having feelings and expressing them are undesirable characteristics.

Patience is important when you express feelings directly. Others may not know how to be as open and honest with their feelings as you are. It is difficult not to be hurt when your openness is not accepted and understood. If you are open and direct, you will serve as a role model for those who are learning how to express their feelings directly.

It is important to use wisdom in directly expressing feelings. There are times when it is *not* wise to express feelings directly. Sometimes

(a) the risks are too high (e.g., someone in authority over you cannot accept your openness and may be threatened by it, thus possibly making decisions that may put obstacles in the way of your growth);
(b) the need for action is too pressing (e.g., your child is breaking a rule and running out into a busy street);
(c) the person is in no condition to accept your feelings (e.g., your spouse is too upset to really hear what you say; your child is too young to understand);
(d) you will be in physical danger for expressing your feelings directly.

When you express your feelings directly, be sure to avoid the following *traps*:

(a) labeling the other person or his or her behavior (e.g., using such terms as *nice, brilliant, stupid, rude*);
(b) evaluating the other person's behavior (e.g., "You deliberately cut me off");
(c) ascribing motives or intentions to the other person (e.g., "You always want to be boss"; "You always insist on being the center of attention"; "You're just trying to show her up");
(d) engaging in name-calling (e.g., "You're being stubborn").

There are several ways you can identify your feelings when you express them directly. One is the conventional way of simply *labeling* them (e.g., angry, embarrassed, happy, worried). Sometimes it is hard to find a suitable label for a feeling. In that case you might try using *simile* or *metaphor* (e.g., "I feel as lazy as a summer day"; "I'm as keyed up as a lion stalking prey"). If you can't find a label or a simile or metaphor to express what you are feeling, you might try *action* words (e.g., "I'm so happy I could leap the tallest building"; "I'm feeling so frustrated I could kick in a steel wall").

It is easy to get the idea that direct expression of feeling should only deal with conflicts in relationships or should occur only when negative feelings are being felt. Don't be afraid to express your positive feelings about someone or something. This reinforces positive feelings in others. Also be sure to let people know how much you appreciate it when they try to change their behavior to improve their relationships with you. It makes you feel better when you can "accentuate the positive" whenever possible.

When you communicate your feelings honestly and openly with others, you serve as a role model for appropriate expression of feelings, you help clarify the relationship between you and the other person, and you help establish a trusting, open relationship with the other person. Communicating your honest feelings to the other person is a way of showing love and concern. It shows that you trust that person enough to take the risk of being open and honest. *This does not mean license to share* all *your feelings with others. It is appropriate to share only those feelings that are directly associated with the effectiveness of the relationship.*

Information processing (communication) is the means by which the members of the family system interrelate. The information processed in the family contains the messages about how people wish to relate to each other. How this information is processed determines whether the family is a functional (growth-oriented) or dysfunctional (growth-retarding) system.

Mary and Chad have shared their feelings, whether "good" or "bad," ever since they met each other. They talk about everything and have attempted to teach their children to do the same thing. Their greatest difficulty in communication is confronting the natural and normal conflicts that occasionally come up. For instance, Chad so thoroughly enjoyed his daily route delivering soft drinks to company clients that he felt he had been "put out to pasture" when he was promoted to distribution manager. Now he doesn't have the daily contacts he once had with the clients. He misses those contacts. He has never told Mary how he feels about his job. However, Mary suspects that something is wrong. Unfortunately, she thinks Chad's occasional "bad days" are her fault, and yet she doesn't know what to do about them. She is stuck in the trap of "reading his mind." In the meantime, Chad feels something must change at his job or he won't be able to continue being an effective distribution manager. He wants to talk about his problem with Mary but he doesn't know how. He'd really like to go back to his old job. But he is afraid that Mary will encourage him to keep working his way up because the family needs the money.

Conclusions

This chapter has described 10 characteristics of a family system, including goal orientation, interdependence and reciprocity, wholeness, patterns/self-regulation, mutual influence/punctuation, adaptation, openness, equifinality, hierarchical relationships, and information processing (communication). Examples from the six-member Kenyon family have illustrated these characteristics.

Every human group, if it remains intact over a period of time, develops each of these system characteristics. Ignoring or denying these important elements in the system can create tension and even disruption of the relationship between those who serve the family system and the family itself. An understanding of these characteristics can lead to effective service to and interaction with family units.

Family Cluster, like the family, is a system that eventually takes on similar characteristics of the family system as it grows and progresses. Thus the Family Cluster becomes a larger system, or *suprasystem*, that contains four or more other systems, the families it comprises. The particular Family Cluster will become unique, just like each family of which it is composed, as it takes on these system characteristics. Thus each Family Cluster is unique in relation to every other Family Cluster that has ever existed, now exists, or will exist.

When Family Cluster plans are being made, consideration of the characteristics of the systems of which the Cluster is composed should form the basis of effective planning. Leaders should carefully observe the families as they interact in the home and at Cluster to discover how each family exhibits each of these 10 characteristics. Leaders also should consider carefully how the Cluster itself exhibits these characteristics.

This chapter began with the description of an event that changed the Family Cluster system during its terminating, or closing, session—the unannounced visit of a maternal grandmother instead of the parents in one of the Cluster families. This was the Kenyon grandmother. As later explained to the Cluster leaders,

Chad had been suddenly called out of town by his company. He wanted Mary to go with him. It would give her a brief vacation. It would give them both some extra "date time" that week. They both felt bad about missing the closing Cluster session. They wanted the children, at least, to experience that last session. So they asked Grandma to be the parent substitute, to which she readily agreed.

Chad and Mary's reasons for missing that last Cluster session were laudable. They had no idea the effect Grandma would have on the entire Family Cluster system, as benign as it may seem. The leaders had failed to explain the reason why they were reluctant to give permission for guests to come to Cluster when the Cluster contract was developed during the second session of Cluster. As a result, they were disappointed in the outcome of their careful and painstaking planning for the last (terminating) Cluster session.

Cluster plans can be more effective when characteristics of the families that make up the Family Cluster, and of the Family Cluster itself, are carefully considered when making those plans.

These system characteristics are "hidden." That is, family and Cluster members are unaware of them. However, effective Family Clusters can occur only if leaders are aware of how these characteristics are uniquely exemplified by the families that compose the Cluster.

References

Dinkmeyer, D., & McKay, G. D. (1976). *Systematic training for effective parenting: Parent's handbook*. Circle Pines, MN: American Guidance Service.

Galvin, K. M., & Brommel, B. J. (1986). *Family communication: Cohesion and change* (2nd ed.). Glenview, IL: Scott, Foresman.

Hoopes, M. M., & Harper, J. M. (1987). *Birth order roles and sibling patterns in individual and family therapy*. Rockville, MD: Aspen.

Miller, J. R., & Janosik, E. H. (1980). *Family-focused care*. New York: McGraw-Hill.

Satir, V. (1972). *Peoplemaking*. Palo Alto, CA: Science and Behavior Books.

3. Characteristics of a Strong Family

For many years the medical model was used in treating individuals with psychological problems. That is, they were considered ill. Therapy was designed to "cure" them of the illness that had made them sick.

Do families get sick psychologically? It depends on your philosophy of family intervention. A doctor cannot, however, tell a family to take some pills, drink lots of liquids, go to bed, and everything will be all right. This just does not work for families. And it probably doesn't work for individuals with psychological problems either.

The focus of family intervention, whether therapy, education, or enrichment, is on how well the family is functioning. To be specific, it focuses on the strengths of families.

Just as an automobile needs maintenance now and again (an oil change, a lube job, even a tune-up), so do families. This is what education and enrichment are all about. Therapy does major repair work on families.

Just as the auto mechanic needs to know what the car does when it functions well, so do leaders of Family Cluster need to know what families do when they function well. Only then can a diagnosis be made concerning whether the family needs maintenance (the focus of Family Cluster) or repair (the focus of family therapy).

This chapter focuses on the characteristics that research indicates make strong families. It is assumed that most families have at least some degree of each of these characteristics. Most families, just like smoothly running automobiles, would probably benefit from some preventive maintenance now and then. Preventive maintenance makes strong families stronger. It makes what works work better. That is what Family Cluster is all about.

The following characteristics of strong families are derived from the work of David Olson and his colleagues (1980) at the University of Minnesota and from a study of 3,000 families by Nick Stinnett and John DeFrain (1985).

Strong families are not without problems, without troubles. They have their share of problems and troubles just like anyone else. Stinnett and DeFrain (1985, p. 8) suggest that strong families "can best be defined as places where we enter for comfort, development, and regeneration and places from which we go forth renewed and charged with power for positive living." The characteristics of strong families described in this chapter define this source of "comfort, development, and regeneration" as revealed by the research of Olson and his colleagues (1980) and Stinnett and DeFrain (1985).

Probably the most frequently used assessment of family strength is FACES III (the Family Adaptability and Cohesion Evaluation Scales; Olson, Portner, & Lavee, 1985), a short family assessment instrument completed by individual family members and developed at the University of Minnesota. It is based on the Circumplex Model of family strength (Olson et al., 1980), which is a two-dimensional model focusing on what are purported to be the two major strengths of families: adaptability and cohesion.

(1) The strong family is a cohesive family. According to Olson and his colleagues, cohesion is the major affective strength of the family. Cohesion refers to the emotional bonding that takes place between and among family members.

Cohesion has two extremes: disengagement and enmeshment. On a five-point scale, the strong family would tend toward the center of the scale, which would be true cohesion. That is, each family member is emotionally bonded to every other family member, but there is a healthy sense of separateness, of individuality, of being "one's own person" among the members of a cohesive family.

Some families tend toward *enmeshment*, one extreme of the cohesion continuum. That is, family members seem emotionally engulfed in other family members, so much so that their separateness, their individuality, is swallowed up in their blending with others in the family. Such families tend toward the enmeshment extreme of the cohesion dimension.

On the other hand, some families tend to be emotionally *disengaged* from one another, the other extreme of the cohesion continuum. In a sense, they use the home basically as a motel and filling station. They protect their individuality, their separateness, from others, by avoiding emotional bonds with other family members. They feel threatened by emotional bonds.

(2) The strong family is adaptable. Adaptability is the second dimension in the Circumplex Model. This dimension of family strength refers to the rules in the family, how they change, and who makes them. Like the dimension of cohesion, adaptability has two extremes: rigidity and chaos.

At one extreme is the *rigid* family, where rules are strictly adhered to, punishment for breaking a rule may be severe, rules are usually made and enforced by one or both of the parents, and there is little opportunity to negotiate change in the rules.

At the other extreme of the adaptability continuum is the *chaotic* family, which tends to operate without many, if any, ground rules. Family members in a chaotic family system tend to operate by their own individual sets of rules and values and go their individual, separate ways. There is no need to negotiate changes because rules can change according to the individual's desires. Punishments are few, if any, because there are no rules to break.

The ideal on the adaptability continuum, similar to the cohesion dimension, is somewhere in the middle of the continuum, where rules are followed by family members, are explicit and open to negotiation when needed (i.e., they change), and are determined by consensus of family members. A family that is *adaptable* tends toward the center of the continuum.

Olson and his colleagues remind us that families are dynamic. They change, grow, and meet challenges during each of the stages of the family life cycle, which might move the family toward either extreme on the cohesion or adaptability dimension. Strong families, in spite of crises and unexpected challenges, tend toward the center of each continuum. If both dimensions, adaptability and cohesion, were placed like cross hairs on a target, and a circle drawn around the center just like a target, the strong family would tend toward the bull's eye. The farther away from the bull's eye the family is located, the less strength that family has and the greater their need for preventive maintenance and perhaps even therapy.

(3) The strong family has an invulnerable sense of commitment. This and the remaining five characteristics are derived from research

with over 3,000 families—primarily families in the United States but including some families in foreign countries—that was headed by Stinnett and DeFrain (1985).

Commitment relates primarily to the dedication of family members to the promotion of each other's welfare and happiness, to the unity of the family. The family comes first in the lives of a committed family.

Possibly the greatest human fear is that of being abandoned, psychologically as well as physically. Commitment is the glue that keeps the family together, that makes it possible for individuals in the family to know there is always a place where they are loved unconditionally, where they are trusted, where they are safe and secure, where they are valued for what they are and not for who they are. In spite of troubles, of bad times, commitment to one another is steady and unwavering, something that can be counted on no matter what and no matter how long. Commitment is a long-term sort of thing.

Central to commitment in the family is sexual fidelity between husband and wife. An extramarital affair by either, or both, in spite of "swinging door" sex common in our society, may be the greatest enemy to a family's existence. It strikes at the very heart of family. It sends messages that people are not valued, that they are expendable. Although an extramarital affair in a marriage does not always end a marriage, nor does it mean the end of the family, it is extraordinarily rare for strong families to remain so following an extramarital affair of one of the marriage partners.

Most families live in the fast lane, with outside pressures threatening the very existence of the family. Often both parents are employed outside the home. Even when both parents are not employed outside the home, children, as well as their parents, are pulled in a hundred different directions, with volunteer community service, PTA, music lessons, sports events, and church service making their various demands on the time of family members. Wise families determine what their goals are and consciously plan how to spend their time to achieve their goals. They take periodic inventories of their progress toward goals and change priorities, including goals, if necessary. The commitment to each other in a strong family, the centrality of the family, makes it possible for strong families to let go of some things they would like to do in favor of those things that would best help them achieve their goals.

For example, one family that values commitment (which requires time together) might limit to one evening a week time when Mom and Dad can attend meetings related to their outside employment or service in the community, while each of the children is limited to one evening activity per week. Incidentally, the parents do not bring work home from the office and each spends only 40 hours each week on the job. The family spends one night together *each* week. Mom and Dad have at least a four-hour date with each other *each* week. Parents have occasional dates—one-on-one—with each of their children, such as lunch together or a visit to Dad's office. Family togetherness is a top priority in this family. They build their commitment to each other by building into their schedules time together and limiting those activities that pull them away from one another. They don't live on what is left over from the week to be together. They willingly sacrifice some preferences to have time together.

In a committed family, individuals are 100% there for each other. When they are together, they are not wishing they were someplace else or distracted by thoughts of something else. They have the delightful capacity to be individually 100% in the moment.

Committed families have a rich repertoire of traditions, those events that give a family a sense of continuity, of who and where they are in history. *Traditions* are the "we always do . . ." of a family. For instance, "On Thanksgiving, we always have a turkey with all the trimmings. At our table is always both sets of grandparents and Uncle X and Aunt Y and Cousins A, B, and C," *or* "We always celebrate each person's birthday by putting a special gift on the kitchen table when they come to breakfast on the morning of their birthday," *or* "On Sundays we always have a roast, vegetables, and potatoes and gravy for dinner after church," *or* "At the end of the Sabbath [Saturday] we always celebrate *havdalah* with the lighted braided candle and the cup of wine and the ritual chant," and on and on. These traditions help cement the family together, to define for them who they are, to commit themselves to one another, to feel obligated to one another by golden bonds of loving devotion.

(4) The strong family frequently expresses appreciation to family members. Strong families express their appreciation to one another frequently and in a variety of ways. Virginia Satir (1972) likens a person's self-esteem to a bucket that can be filled and emptied. Sometimes others dip into that bucket and take out some of the

self-esteem by negative comments or criticisms. In strong families, the emphasis is on filling each person's bucket of self-esteem by frequent comments and actions about how each person is appreciated, by affirmative words and actions that tend to result in fuller self-esteem buckets, not emptier ones. Family members focus on the pluses, not on the minuses. Everyone has faults as well as good qualities, but a strong family focuses on the good qualities. They mine for the gold and find it in one another. Expressing appreciation is contagious. In a family atmosphere where appreciation is frequently expressed, everyone gets in on the act eventually. Even negative things can be recast in positive ways (e.g., instead of saying to a child practicing the violin such a negative comment as, "Ouch! Those were pretty sour notes when you played that scale," you could recast it into something positive, such as "You held the violin very well while you played that scale; now try the scale again while I watch and listen."). Recasting also helps family members look for the positive instead of the negative.

Appreciation doesn't have to be verbalized all the time. Strong families find lots of creative ways to express appreciation. For example, in one family notes are frequently pinned on the pillow or stuck to the refrigerator, bathroom, bedroom mirror, or inside a cupboard, or tucked inside a briefcase or lunch box saying such short, appreciative statements as, "I'm glad I married you!" "I love you," "I'm glad you're in our family," "To the world's greatest mom (dad)," or "Thanks for the help just when I needed it."

People blossom with reminders that they are appreciated. Two days before I wrote this chapter, one of the student receptionists in our department office drew a large basketball on a sheet of typing paper. Above the ball was penned these words: "On-the-Ball Award to Dr. Vance" (I had turned in my textbook order as soon as I got the notice the order was due). Below the ball, Rosalie had written these words: "Thanks for being so prompt with your textbook order. You sure make my job a lot easier. /s/ Rosalie." I had been having one of those rare, terrible, horrible, no-good, very bad days. Everything changed when I read that note in my box at the end of that long day. My self-esteem bucket was quickly filled. I felt like jumping up and down. So I went to a basketball game and did just that—and our team won!

Receiving messages of appreciation is almost as important as giving them. Instead of responding to the compliment, "You're the greatest dad (mom) I know," with "I'm the *only* dad you have, so you don't have much to compare," try saying a simple, "Thanks for telling me." Responding to an appreciative message negatively is a form of denial, not only of the message but of the person giving it. An acknowledgment of the message, with a short but honest expression of feeling, can do so much to fill the self-esteem bucket of the giver.

Members of strong families are gracious receivers as well as givers of appreciation messages. In the words of Stinnett and DeFrain (1985, p. 55), "Being appreciated is like good music. We can listen to it over and over again."

(5) The strong family has effective communication patterns. Communication probably is the umbrella under which all of the family strengths are clustered. People who live together are communicating all the time. That is, they are sending to one another and receiving either verbal or nonverbal messages. The only way family members can avoid communicating with each other is to get out of the family, out of one another's presence. Even *that* communicates something!

Strong families tend to spend lots of time conversing with one another. Although most of what they talk about may be trivial, their conversations reflect caring for one another and occasional dips into serious and even solemn matters. But they enjoy conversing with one another no matter what the subject. In addition, conversations are spontaneous and flow easily among family members. They are indicative of caring relationships in the family.

Strong families have conflicts and disagreements like everyone else. However, their communication patterns are marked by openness and honesty and a willingness to deal with problems when they come up. Problems and conflicts are not brushed under the carpet to gather more dust and debris. When a conflict arises, it is dealt with the moment it occurs.

Strong families have two basic communication skills that tend to deepen relationships and increase caring for family members. That is, they actively *listen* to one another, and they inform one another of their *feelings*.

Strong families tend to check out the accuracy of the messages they hear from one another. They don't assume they know what the other is trying to say. They attend carefully to what the other says, attend to facial expression, gestures, and voice tone, and clarify the information they don't understand. Therefore, they don't manipulate one another. If they want something, they say so explicitly. They do not expect others to read their minds.

When conflicts occur, which they always do even in the best of human relationships, strong feelings are generated frequently. Members of strong families directly express their strong feelings, label them for what they are, accept them as their own, and explore verbally with other family members possible ways to deal with the feelings without hurting others. Directness and kindness often go hand in hand. Brutal honesty is replaced by owning one's own feelings, labeling them, and exploring ways to deal with them. Members of families with effective communication skills avoid unacceptable communication behaviors such as criticism, evaluation, and acting superior to others, as well as bullying, outwitting, blaming, dominating, or controlling. They don't manipulate others by silence or playing on dependency or guilt. They say what they mean and mean what they say.

Strong families are real people in a real world. They have their disagreements. Their mistakes can be monumental at times. They get tired and overstressed. However, they don't hoard grievances. They deal with one problem at a time. They don't lack problems, but they have the communication patterns that reflect respect and caring for one another.

(6) The strong family spends lots of time together. In his book *The Broken Heart: The Medical Consequences of Loneliness,* James Lynch (1977, p. 3) suggests that

> human relationships *do* matter. . . . The fact is that social isolation, the lack of human companionship, death or absence of parents in early childhood, sudden loss of love, and chronic human loneliness are significant contributors to premature death. . . . Almost every cause of death is significantly influenced by human companionship.

Strong families seem to have an intuitive understanding of the possible consequences of loneliness. Although it is possible to be lonely in a crowd, strong families spend lots of time together. It is difficult to be lonely when often surrounded by those who love you the most and are the most committed to you. Strong families intuitively realize this.

Family togetherness can be one-on-one, with Mom out shopping with a daughter while Dad is off to a hockey game with a son. However, strong families report that they spend lots of time together—as a whole family, including times gathered around the dinner table in the evening, visiting the grandparents as a family, celebrating a holiday together, spending at least one night a week together, and taking family vacations.

Often when children leave the home, they remember most fondly those things the family did together. At the time the events occurred, they had no idea they were building such memory bank accounts. When I get together with my brothers and sisters, often we reminisce fondly about our times together as a family when we were children, even if it included backbreaking work like weeding potatoes as volunteers on the church welfare farm. Those times together brought laughter, tears, shared experiences we'll never forget, experiences that cement us together as a family even though we've gone our separate ways to build our lives in new families, new families that are extensions of the old.

The nurturing of relationships takes time. Strong families nurture relationships by spending time together. Nurtured relationships can weather loneliness, which is something everyone experiences at least once in a while—it is a human condition. Even chronic loneliness (such as that experienced by so many in their golden years) is survivable with memories of close family relationships, of lots of family togetherness, in the memory bank account.

Family togetherness also helps create a sense of family identity. It seems to clearly mark the boundaries of the family. Members of strong families can say with pride, "That's *my* family because . . ."

(7) Spiritual wellness is typical in a strong family. It is not necessary for a family to have a formal affiliation with religion to be spiritually well. A strong family has a sense of strength, purpose, and direction in life that appears to be based on a sense of a power greater than its members are, a greater good or power, that guides their lives. This belief in a greater good has a powerful influence in the lives of members of strong families.

The important thing about spiritual wellness is not the type of conviction (such as Christian, Jewish, Buddhist) but the sense of a shared conviction within the family. This conviction leads to direction in life, to a sense of shared meaning and purpose, even to a sense of peace.

Spiritual wellness has deep roots in a shared connection to all humanity and a sense of overriding meaning in life that transcends the moment, a sense of some type of divine Presence that is guiding the universe.

Strong families have their troubles just like everyone does. In spite of death of loved ones, chronic illness, or loss of employment, however, life goes on with a sense of purpose and connection in strong families, often marked by quiet moments of meditation and even prayer. This means an abiding faith in fellow mortals, a faith that gives the assurance that, even when people *do* dumb things, they *are* still worthwhile, needed, and wanted.

Strong families put into practice their spiritual principles. They meditate or pray, they engage in religious rituals with enthusiasm, they celebrate their religious heritage (if attached to formal religious groups), they rejoice in communion with those who share their religious or moral convictions, they volunteer for work to make their communities better places to live. They practice what they preach—in their families, in their communities.

The hallmarks of a spiritually well family are a sense of "hope, love, family, an elevation of spirit, a reverence for life, and a sense of the sacred" (Stinnett & DeFrain, 1985, p. 119).

(8) A strong family has the ability to cope effectively with crises and stress. They see crises and stress as opportunities for growth. A crisis is something sudden and overwhelming that changes the direction in life of the family, such as the birth of a baby, the loss of employment of the family breadwinner, the wedding of a member of the family, the death of a member of the family. Although we generally think of crisis as something negative, it can be an opportunity in a strong family. The sudden upheaval in the family caused by any given crisis can tear a family apart—or it can cement the family in unique ways.

For three years of my professional life, I conducted research with families of pediatric burn patients in the burn unit of a major regional medical center. I was struck by the frequency of family dissolution in the families of the children who were patients in the unit. Parents, particularly, often had such an overwhelming sense of guilt that they abdicated their involvement with other members of the family *or* they simply abandoned the child, psychologically if not physically (we called this the "Broken-Toy Syndrome"). Blame and overwhelming feelings of grief (including anger and depression) and, often, divorce took their awful toll among the families of the patients. Crisis in many of these families seemed to pull them apart, not strengthen them.

Stinnett and DeFrain (1985) discovered six strategies that strong families use when crisis strikes. Forgive my reference to a personal crisis. Margaret Sawin, in her foreword to this book, has already alluded to my experience with a massive brain hemorrhage. I'll use that experience to exemplify the six strategies strong families use when coping with crisis, as described by Stinnett and DeFrain.

(1) A strong family has the ability to see something positive in the crisis and to focus on that positive element. I was on sabbatical leave in Israel when I had a stroke—a massive brain hemorrhage. I was almost 10,000 miles from my home in the United States. You can imagine what such news would do to four brothers and sisters, their families, and my elderly parents. Brain surgery saved my life—but not without some anxious days for my family as my life hung in the balance and news of my progress was transmitted overseas. My family had come together on the telephone (a brother and a sister live in neighboring states with their families) to give permission for the surgery and to talk about their feelings during my crisis. Family permission for my surgery was telephoned to my chief surgeon in Israel (I had three surgeons working on me during a 10-hour surgical marathon). My life was spared. My entire family fasted and prayed for me (these are some of the religious rituals we share when crisis occurs). When word reached my family that I would live, they were convinced my life had been spared for a purpose—a purpose beyond me and even beyond them. To this day they firmly believe in this higher purpose for my life.

(2) Members of a strong family unite to face the challenges of a crisis. My brothers and sisters have heavy responsibilities in their own families (I have 28 nieces and nephews). Because I have no husband nor children, they all wanted to fly to my side as soon as possible to be with me through my crisis and let me know that family was with me. That would have been impossible at the time, as well as foolish. I have no memory of the first two weeks following my stroke. However, Israeli friends as well as friends in our little congregation in Jerusalem frequently visited me and provided whatever companionship I needed in Israel. (They became my surrogate family.) I needed to return to my home in the United States, however, to continue my recovery. I couldn't do that alone. My sister and brother-in-law, in a neighboring state, took time out

from very busy schedules at work and in the home and took money desperately needed for a new car from their quickly dwindling bank account to fly to Israel and accompany me home. I have only meager information about the many long-distance telephone calls among my siblings until a way could be worked out to bring me home. We are not a wealthy family. My parents were too elderly to travel such a long distance or to provide the assistance I needed on that long flight home. I'm convinced that all six of them (two sisters, two brothers, both parents) would have flown to Israel to give me aid had it been wise or feasible. When I returned home, they visited me frequently, made arrangements for me to visit them for extended periods, and in general spoiled me. I loved every minute of it. But, more important, my crisis had united our family in a way it hadn't been united in years. The potential was there. It just needed a crisis to bring it out in the open. My crisis was their crisis. Already it has made an indelible mark on the family—one we will always cherish and appreciate.

(3) During a crisis a strong family seeks out valuable support from others. Often during a crisis the members of the family can't do all that is needed. Others are needed to fill the gaps. I have already alluded to the fact that Israeli friends and members of my religious congregation in Jerusalem became my larger family. They visited me daily. I never lacked visitors. They brought me tapes to listen to on a personal tape stereo (they brought that, too).

One friend, a physical therapist, taught me how to sit up in my hospital bed, how to get out of the bed, and how to walk about the hospital. (One of my "inconveniences" as a result of the stroke was the destruction of my sense of balance, causing me to stagger when I walked and grope for balance toward any person or solid object nearby; I needed to learn all over again how to navigate in a world of gravity.) One visitor always gave me a foot rub when he came to visit me in the hospital.

One of my fellow patients, an elderly woman preparing for surgery for a brain tumor, fed me my meals when she saw them always going back to the kitchen untouched. (She didn't know that another one of the "inconveniences" resulting from my stroke was destruction of the appetite center in the brain, making it almost impossible for me to eat and keep anything down.)

When I returned to the United States, the women in my church congregation prepared my meals for two months until I was able to prepare my own. A 14-year-old neighbor took me for short walks each day for several months. Another neighbor did my food shopping for three months. Another took me to my physical therapy sessions three times a week for five weeks. My family could not have done all of this for me. So my friends in Israel and in the United States filled in where my family could not.

(4) In time of crisis a strong family draws on spiritual resources. Just as they draw on their physical and emotional resources during crisis, strong families draw on their spiritual resources as well, which provide perspective, hope, and comfort during and after the crisis. During my own crisis, my family and I drew on our spiritual resources frequently. Without enumerating all the ways we did so, suffice it to say my life will never be the same. I have a perspective I may never have reached any other way. The memories of the hope and comfort I received will always nourish my life, especially because I could share in this spiritual resource with my family.

(5) During time of crisis, a strong family uses their communication skills to solve problems and allow open expression of feelings. The younger of my two sisters, the mother of eight children, was the sibling who coordinated everything within my family during my crisis. Finally she openly expressed her feelings of frustration at not being able to be with me and do what she felt I needed from at least one member of the family while I was in Israel. Her oldest child was soon to leave on a church mission to a foreign country. She was torn between her empathy for my seemingly desperate situation in Israel and the needs of her son. It was then that my other sister and her husband recognized more clearly what needed to be done and thus made changes in their own lives so that what needed to be done could happen. Communication skills are important during times of crisis—to solve problems and allow strong feelings to deflate by their open expression.

(6) During time of crisis a strong family is flexible and adaptable. Just as trees along the coast of the ocean tend to bend, instead of break, in the face of strong storms, so do strong families bend instead of break in time of crisis. This ability to bend, or be flexible, this ability to adapt to the storms of life, is a characteristic strategy of strong families when they face the seemingly overwhelming odds of a crisis. This is something like the idea that "when the going gets tough, the tough get going." I don't know how my sister coordinated everything so well with everyone else in the family dur-

ing my crisis. But I know she did. She didn't break. She bent in the direction of the storm. I don't know how my sister and brother-in-law could afford the time or the money to come to my aid in Israel. But they did. And they now have their new car. And life went on for all of us. We bent with the storm, but did not break. We have become a stronger family because of the crisis. That adaptable, flexible strength will serve as an important resource in our family emotional bank account in the future when we are called upon to meet future crises (and they *do* and *will* come—even strong families have their share of crises).

However, crisis is not generally an everyday thing for most of us. Yet we live with pressures—with stress—every day of our lives. Strong families take stress in their stride. Instead of looking at all that needs to be done, and feeling overwhelmed by it, they take life one day at a time and do one thing at a time. They have a broad perspective on their goals and do only those things that will help them achieve their goals.

And, last but not least, strong families have the capacity to laugh, mainly at themselves. They can wear their halos just a little bit cockeyed and see the humor in the crazy things that happen in their lives. This helps them to bend, to see things in perspective, to avoid being overwhelmed by stress, to enjoy life in spite of its stresses and strains.

These are eight characteristics of strong families. These, as undoubtedly you have noticed, are not mutually exclusive characteristics. They overlap. Each is an important part of the fabric of the other one. For example, families wouldn't enjoy spending time together unless they had effective communication skills and were committed to one another.

Some families have all of these characteristics in generous portions. Some have most. Some have just a few. All families have at least a little bit of each. Most families could benefit from education and enrichment experiences, such as Family Cluster—some preventive maintenance to tune up some or all of these characteristics.

These characteristics of strong families are so important that I have developed a short and easy-to-complete Family Strengths Inventory (FSI) to measure each of these strengths in the family. The individual members of our Cluster families complete the FSI before Cluster begins. Each family's profile on the FSI is then computed and discussed with the family. Each Cluster family selects from the inventory those items on which they would like the Cluster to focus its education experiences. The curriculum of the Cluster is based on these family strengths as selected by the families in the Cluster. How to do this is explained in later chapters.

This chapter is not about perfect families. It is about strong families, our friends and neighbors next door, maybe ourselves. These probably are not the only important characteristics of strong families. For example, Curran (1983) describes 15 traits of "healthy" families. However, the 8 characteristics described in this chapter seem to include all 15 of Curran's traits.

In the meantime, research continues to search out those qualities most characteristic of strong families.

References

Curran, C. (1983). *Traits of a healthy family*. Minneapolis, MN: Winston.

Lynch, J. J. (1977). *The broken heart: The medical consequences of loneliness*. New York: Basic Books.

Olson, D. H., Portner, J., & Lavee, Y. (1985). FACES III [Family assessment instrument]. St. Paul: University of Minnesota, Family Social Science.

Olson, D. H., Russell, C. S., & Sprenkle, D. H. (1980). Circumplex model of marital and family systems II: Empirical studies and clinical intervention. In *Family intervention, assessment, and theory* (Vol. 1). Greenwich, CT: JAI.

Satir, V. (1972). *Peoplemaking*. Palo Alto, CA: Science and Behavior Books.

Stinnett, N., & DeFrain, J. (1985). *Secrets of strong families*. New York: Berkley.

4. Family Cluster as the Focus of Research

The idea of Family Cluster captures the interest of all kinds of people interested in family education and family enrichment. Those who have experienced Family Cluster can speak glowingly of the great experience they and their families have enjoyed in Cluster. Family Cluster apparently is so new, however, that the unbiased eye of science has had little opportunity to examine it under the microscope of description and experimentation.

Research Focusing on Family Cluster

It is reported that about two dozen studies have been done focusing on Family Cluster. However, most of these studies have been done by those studying for the ministry (M. M. Sawin, personal communication, April 1988). This research has not been published in professional journals that can be accessed by the typical university or college library. Therefore, the research reported here focuses on what has been published in professional journals accessed by computer literature search. Only three such studies were found.

Does Family Cluster Reduce Isolation Among Urbanites?

Pringle (1974) describes six Family Cluster groups drawn from the congregation in a Dallas Protestant church. The six Family

Clusters were organized as a result of the previous experience in Cluster of a committee from the congregation delegated to study the possibility of Cluster in the congregation. Because urban living tends to separate and isolate people, Pringle's research described how people in six Cluster groups from the congregation achieved friendships with and social support from others outside the immediate family. Members of the congregation, whether married or single, were invited to join Family Cluster. An organizational meeting was held in the church for all those who had signed up for Cluster, and six groups were organized from among this volunteer group. Each Family Cluster group met once a week, usually for a potluck supper. It is not clear who the leaders of the separate Clusters were, or even if each group had leaders. It isn't clear how long each Cluster met each week, nor where each met, nor what the curriculum was for each Cluster.

At the end of two months, all six Cluster groups met in an all-Cluster meeting. Participants discussed what they were learning in Cluster. There seemed to be a consensus that all Clusters shared the following values: (a) getting to know others in depth and with greater honesty and intimacy; (b) becoming aware of the reservoirs of goodwill in people different from oneself; (c) providing contact with children for those who do not have children in the home; (d) providing opportunities for children to form relationships with other adults and children outside the home; and (e) finding out how people in other families fulfill their roles. These values seemed to grow out of a variety of activities, including potluck meals, sensitivity sessions, camping trips, kite flying, ice skating, bicycling, trips to the theater, cookie making, singing, and even building a sandbox.

After the Cluster groups had been going for four months, half of the Cluster members responded to a questionnaire, which apparently consisted of a checklist that indicated how Cluster might have made Cluster members' lives better or worse. Most indicated they had gained "interesting companions," and over half indicated that Cluster had been a "positive experience." About half of the respondents indicated there had been conflicts in their Clusters. In half of these cases the conflicts were perceived as unresolved, perhaps suggesting that the Cluster leaders should have skills in conflict resolution.

The Pringle study indicated that one-third (two) of the six Cluster groups fell apart during the first three months. Reasons given for the breakups included inadequate organizational leadership, key members moving out of town and, therefore, out of Cluster, disagreements over expectations for Cluster, and personality clashes. There is allusion to the possibility that new Cluster members were recruited from earlier congregation volunteers. Therefore, it is not clear whether or not all six Clusters continued in Cluster for the duration. The length of time each Cluster group met is not clear, although half the subjects filled out questionnaires at the end of four months. If the Clusters met weekly, this would be 14–16 Cluster sessions before the conclusion of the study. Four of the original six Clusters reportedly were still in session nine months after they began.

The Pringle (1974) study is a descriptive study. Would those who found companionship outside their nuclear families have done so anyway? Would those who got close to and were hurt by others have had such experience had they not experienced Cluster? What are the long-term effects of such hurting, if any? Studies like Pringle's raise more questions than they answer. That is one of the advantages of research. Subsequent researchers can stand on the shoulders of those who went before.

Knowledge of and Participation in Family Cluster

Bowen (1985) reports on interviews with 664 married couples in the air force randomly selected from 24 bases around the world. Interviews included questions on overall marital satisfaction, degree of marital communication, and satisfaction with marital sexuality and companionship. Couples were also asked their feelings about raising children in the air force; the nature of parent-child relationships; linkages with parents, neighbors, friends, and work associates; and their knowledge of and participation in various family enrichment and support programs.

Only 12% of the husbands and 15% of air force wives had heard about Family Cluster. Couples with weak community ties were less likely to have heard about this program than those with strong community ties. Only 3% of the couples had actually participated in a Family Cluster. All of the wives in that 3% found Cluster helpful, while only 35% of their husbands did. Of the parent education, couple communication, couple enrichment, and family enrichment programs mentioned and described in the interview, air force couples were least enthusiastic about Family Cluster.

If Family Cluster were offered, 30% of the husbands and 43% of the wives indicated they were at least likely to attend. The authors suggested that one possibility for such low interest may have been the lack of knowledge about Family Cluster among the couples.

Leadership Training for Leaders of Family Cluster

Dyer and Dyer (1986) describe leadership training for four marriage and family enrichment programs, including Family Cluster. Although this is not research focusing on Family Cluster, Dyer and Dyer ask questions about leadership training that should be carefully considered by those of us who are trainers of leaders in Family Cluster.

Although Dyer and Dyer obtained their information about the training of leaders from Family Clustering, Inc., an organization that no longer exists, the questions they ask about training are important. They focused primarily on three basic questions as they interviewed leaders of and read about leadership training in four different marriage and family enrichment programs:

(1) Who should be trained for leadership? This is the question regarding the selection of those who will be trained to be leaders of Family Cluster. Should only professional people be trained to be Family Cluster leaders? Can nonprofessional people become effective Family Cluster leaders? Because Family Cluster has been developed with the idea of lay leaders (nonprofessionals) leading Clusters, this is an issue that deserves careful consideration and research.

(2) What should the training consist of? This is the issue of the content of training. What should that content be? What processes should be involved in the training?

(3) How should competence be determined? Most professions have certification requirements designed to provide at least minimal competence in the profession. What does a competent Family Cluster leader do? How can this be measured? Who should certify the competence of Family Cluster leaders?

Dyer and Dyer suggest that perhaps the field of marriage and family enrichment is at the point where the various programs should get away from training that focuses on the specific program and, instead, focus efforts on training for "process," especially related to experiential learning. They also suggest that training should include intergenerational dynamics. These issues need to be addressed by Cluster trainers, and additional research into leadership training in Family Cluster is needed.

Does Family Cluster Strengthen Families in Trouble?

Family Cluster focuses on strength, not weakness. However, I am pursuing the hypothesis with several colleagues in the United States and Israel that Family Cluster strengthens families awaiting family therapy and shortens the therapy process. This requires an experimental approach to research.

Family Cluster as Social Support

Frequently throughout the pages of this book, I refer to the idea that Family Cluster is a form of social support; that is, in the many forms of interaction available in Family Cluster, the individuals who participate will find support from other families outside their own family boundaries who can help them cope with the daily stresses that face us all. Family Cluster becomes a kind of "buffer" that can cushion one's reaction to stress or crisis.

But what is *social support*? Most of us have an intuitive idea what it means. However, intuition does not necessarily make good research. In the past, social support had other names such as "community integration," "social participation," and "attachment" (Barrera & Ainlay, 1983).

The dictionary defines *support* as an act or process that assists, helps, or holds up something else. Support, therefore, is not "doing for" the other person, but assisting or holding up while the other person does the work. This is an important idea in social relationships, especially those that exist within the family unit.

Social support always involves a recipient, a provider (sometimes called a donor), and some sort of exchange, ranging from the provision of goods and services to the provision of caring listening (Schumaker & Brownell, 1984). The desired end result is the enhancement in some specific way of the recipient, primarily a feeling that he or she is cared for and loved (Cobb, 1976).

Lin (1986, p. 7) defines *social support* as follows: "Social support denotes forces or factors that sustain human beings. Accordingly, social support can be defined as forces or factors in the social environment that facilitate the survival of human beings." She then gives a research or "synthetic" definition of social support: "The synthetic definition of social support is *the perceived or actual instrumental and/or expressive provisions supplied by the community, social networks, and confiding partners*" (p. 18).

Barrera and Ainlay (1983) suggest that four categories should be included when defining and doing research with social support:

(1) *Material aid and behavioral assistance*: Providing tangible materials in the form of money and other physical objects; sharing of tasks through physical labor;
(2) *Intimate interaction*: Behaviors such as listening, expressing esteem, caring, and understanding;
(3) *Guidance and feedback*: Offering advice, information, or instruction; providing individuals with feedback about their behavior, thoughts, or feelings.
(4) *Positive social interaction*: Engaging in social interactions for fun and relaxation.

Cobb (1976), in his frequently cited article on social support, examines convincing evidence that social support is overwhelmingly effective in helping people cope with such events as hospitalization, life transitions, illness recovery, stress and crises, bereavement, aging and retirement, loss of employment, and the threat of death. Hammer, Gutwirth, and Phillips (1982) found that parents need social support, that the nature of social support for parents focuses primarily on kin (family), and that parents in the lower class are more likely to have few social support networks and have a greater tendency to depression. Sosa, Kennell, Klaus, Robertson, and Urrutia (1980) found that a mother in labor and delivery having someone (a nonprofessional) with her during labor and delivery lowers birth complications and improves the bonding between the mother and her infant.

Possibly closer to the possibilities of Family Cluster as a social support system is Roskin's (1982) study of 45 adults who had recently experienced two or more stressful life changes such as death of a family member or close friend, illness in the family, or personal illness or injury. These adults had received no professional help to assist them through their specific crises. Half of the group attended six seminars led by a social worker. The seminars were designed to help members ventilate their feelings and to provide support for one another. Those in the second, or control, group attended the seminars following the experimental group. In measures of five different health dimensions, including mental health, taken following the seminar attendance of the experimental group, there were significant differences between the groups in favor of those in the experimental group.

Social support may suggest weakness. Certainly this is not what I mean when I suggest that Family Cluster is a means of social support for Cluster members. Caplan (1974, p. 7), in his frequently cited work related to social support, says this about social support and weakness:

> The idea that a person receives support or is in need of support usually carries the connotation that he is weak. From this point of view our term is unfortunate, because what we have in mind is not the propping up of someone who is in danger of falling down, but rather the augmenting of a person's strengths to facilitate his mastery of his environment.

Later Caplan (1974, p. 9) goes on to say about the family group:

> The essential elements in a . . . family group, from the point of view of its acting as a support system, are attitudes of sensitivity and respect for the needs of all its members and an effective communication system. It is significant that in most cases where individuals have not been protected from illness, and have therefore become accessible to study in our clinics and hospitals, their families have shortcomings in both these aspects.

Caplan comes as close as anyone to describing social support as it might be experienced in Family Cluster.

Social support involves some sort of interaction between people, primarily to mitigate stressful events (Schumaker & Brownell, 1984). However, social support research to date has not done a very effective job identifying what is being studied, except in very general terms. Confusion exists, for instance, about who the recipient is, who the provider is, what was exchanged, how the exchange took place, how the recipient perceived the "support," and the short- and long-term effects of the "support."

Gottlieb (1983) suggests additional questions that need to be addressed in social support research: (1) Is access to a single source of support enough to attenuate stress or are multiple sources needed? (2) Is contact with the primary group, the family, more helpful than other, less-primary, forms of support? (3) What is the nature of social ties? How do these help or hinder a person working through stress? (4) What is the best way to measure social support? Self-report (the most common)? "Phenomenological" changes? Observed changes? (5) How long must someone be exposed to the social support in order for it to work? (6) How does the process of social support work?

These are issues that need to be dealt with in research on Family Cluster as a means of social support. It seems fairly obvious that the members of an entire Family Cluster are the "providers" of the support. The individual members of the Cluster, and perhaps entire family groups, are the "recipients." Thus Family Cluster is seen as a reciprocal support system where the recipients also become the providers. There is no generally accepted format for Family Cluster social support (this book is an attempt to provide one)—that is, a structured format providing for specific exchange. And what does that exchange consist of to provide social support? Is it the same as experiential learning experiences, which are the focus of Cluster? What about all those unstructured, incidental exchanges that occur between and among the members of Cluster? And how are the effects of these interactions measured? When I suggest that Family Cluster is an effective means of social support, I am speaking from an intuitive base, not from a broad research base.

Conclusions

There are some distinct challenges to those doing research with Family Cluster that may spur the creativity of the investigator or overwhelm it. Not the least of these challenges is the fact that Family Cluster involves people interacting with other people. What works in researching individual differences doesn't seem to work when researching people interacting with other people. New methodologies explaining patterns of interaction must be developed and tested. What is the nature of this interaction and how does it work? How does it work as social support? Is it effective in strengthening families and helping them become social support systems for one another? The challenges of research with people in interaction with one another is compounded by the fact that each Family Cluster that is the focus of research is entirely different from any other Cluster. Therefore, it is not possible to compare studies—even if methodologically similar, because of differences in populations. Someone's meat may be someone else's poison.

Researchers who study Family Cluster must remain outside the Cluster in order to remain unbiased and avoid "tainting" the groups they study. Talking "about" Family Cluster (which the investigator must do) and being a part of it are two very different things. Anything I say about Family Cluster, if I am studying its processes and effects, will be colored by my own experience in the process. I can make my expectations come true in a Cluster, in spite of the fact I think I am unbiased. This is called a "self-fulfilling prophecy"—unacceptable in scientific research.

Describing Family Cluster is different from studying its effects. When I describe something, I observe something and report what I observe, something like what a newspaper reporter should do. I do nothing to influence the outcome. I simply describe what I observe.

Experimental research, on the other hand, is an attempt to make some changes occur. It answers the question, "What causes X?" Descriptive research merely describes X. In experimental research there are at least two experimental groups—a treatment group (the group that receives the treatment) and the control group (the group that does not receive the treatment). Both should be randomly selected from a larger population and thus be representative of that population. The members of the experimental group should be assigned randomly (i.e., by chance), as should the members of the control group. Thus the experimental and control groups are considered essentially the same before the experiment begins. The experimental group receives some kind of treatment (such as Family Cluster) whereas the control group does not. At the end of treatment *both* groups are measured in exactly the same way. If the experimental group differs in any significant way from the control group, then there is evidence to support the statement that the treatment "caused" that difference.

It is likely that most research focusing on Family Cluster, at least in the beginning, would relate to the *description* of the elements of Family Cluster and the overall process, *not* to *cause and effect*.

It is too soon to draw any conclusions about the effectiveness (cause and effect) of Family Cluster. Such research requires the experimental approach. To my knowledge, such research is not available concerning Family Cluster. It has yet to be done.

However, there is evidence from those who have participated in Family Cluster that Family Cluster is appealing (one of the hallmarks of Cluster). The strongest proponents of Family Cluster are those who have actually experienced it as members or leaders. Such word-of-mouth advertising reveals excitement about participation in what is perceived as a very important process in their lives. However, questions about the changes that Cluster might make in the lives of those who participate in it will remain until a considerable body of experimental research can be conducted with Family Cluster.

References

Barrera, M., Jr., & Ainlay, S. L. (1983). The structure of social support: A conceptual and empirical analysis. *Journal of Community Psychology, 11*, 133–143.

Bowen, G. L. (1985, October). Families in blue: Insights from air force families. *Social Casework: The Journal of Contemporary Social Work*, 459–465.

Caplan, G. (1974). *Support systems and community mental health*. New York: Behavioral Publications.

Cobb, S. (1976, September-October). Social support as a moderator of life stress. *Psychosomatic Medicine, 38*(5), 300–314.

Dyer, P. M., & Dyer, G. H. (1986). Leadership training for marriage and family enrichment. *Journal of Psychotherapy and the Family*, 97–100.

Gottlieb, B. H. (1983). Early theoretical formulations. In *Social support strategies: Guidelines for mental health practice*. Beverly Hills, CA: Sage.

Hammer, M., Gutwirth, L., & Phillips, S. L.(1982). Parenthood and social networks: A preliminary view. *Social Science and Medicine, 16*, 2091–2100.

Lin, N. (1986). Conceptualizing social support. In N. Lin, A. Dean, & W. M.Ensel (Eds.). *Social support, life events, and depression*. New York: Academic Press.

Pringle, B. M. (1974, April). Family clusters as a means of reducing isolation among urbanites. *The Family Coordinator*, 175–179.

Roskin, M. (1982). Coping with life changes: A preventive social work approach. *American Journal of Community Psychology, 10*, 331–340.

Sawin, M. M. (1988, April). Personal communication with the author.

Schumaker, S. A., & Brownell, A. (1984). Toward a theory of social support: Closing conceptual gaps. *Journal of Social Issues, 40*(4), 11–36.

Sosa, R., Kennell, J., Klaus, M., Robertson, S., & Urrutia, J. (1980). The effect of a supportive companion on perinatal problems, length of labor, and mother infant interaction. *New England Journal of Medicine, 303*, 597–600.

PART II

Planning a Family Cluster

The architect lives in a world of fantasy. That is, he or she imagines what a given building will look like. Then he or she draws the plans and specifications for that building down to the smallest nail, nut, and bolt. These architectural plans become the guide for the builder, the contractor. No architectural plans, no building.

The Family Cluster leader is the architect of Family Cluster. Working in teams of two, Family Cluster leaders imagine what families in the Cluster will be like, what their needs are, what they might do in Family Cluster. They *plan*, just like an architect, the specifications for Cluster, the educational experiences for families. They leave nothing to chance. A Cluster leader's plans and specifications are called session agenda plans.

The chapters in this part detail how to plan goals and objectives of Cluster, how to plan each Cluster session agenda, and how to select activities, games, books, stories, and music for Cluster.

5. Leaders of Family Cluster

Probably because Family Cluster is primarily a family education/enrichment process—a group experience in learning—the person who directs the activities of a Family Cluster is called a leader rather than a teacher. Teaching undoubtedly is taking place. However, the primary role of the leader is to set the stage for learning—for insight—to take place.

A leader is "one who goes before," a person who leads the way, a person focused on people, one who has vision and foresight, a person who is willing to do what he or she expects others to do. A leader is an example, a model, rather than a "teller." A leader essentially says to those he or she leads, "Do as I do," rather than, "Do as I say."

Two Leaders Required for Each Family Cluster

The world probably wouldn't collapse if only one person took on the task of leading a Family Cluster, although the leader might! That leader and Cluster would probably pay a high price for such folly.

As the old adage goes, "Two heads are better than one." While one person is leading an experience in Cluster, the other is nearby to provide emotional support, to provide materials, to keep an eye on the clock if things begin to drag, and especially to observe. At the close of a Cluster session, the two coleaders can discuss what they have observed during the session including such things as who is getting left out, what the needs of individuals appear to be, how well activities for the session seemed to go, what changes in planning need to be made, and what the goals and objectives of the next session should be.

Even though it is possible to use ready-made Cluster session agenda plans (there are some in this book), any already prepared session agenda plan must be cut to fit the wearer, the particular Cluster, just as cloth is cut to fit the person who will wear the outfit. Cluster is made up of individual persons and families, and Cluster plans, to be most effective, need to be suited to the individuals in the Cluster. In addition, Clusters are held in a variety of physical surroundings, including homes, schools, churches, and community buildings. The "geography" of a session plan must be adapted to fit the uniqueness of the Cluster physical surroundings. Two leaders making such plans are likely to produce more efficient, effective, and appealing plans than just one leader.

Characteristics of Cluster Leaders

There are a variety of characteristics that mark the effective Cluster leader. I'm not aware of any scientific study of the most critical characteristics of effective Cluster leaders. However, I would like to suggest the following as a result of my own experience leading Clusters and training Cluster leaders. Perhaps you can rate yourself from 1 to 10 on each characteristic, with 1 too little, and 10 the ideal. If you rate yourself 5 (about average) or below on any given characteristic, it probably would be a good idea for you to find ways to improve in that characteristic. I propose that an effective Cluster leader would have a rating of 5 or above on *each* of the following 15 characteristics:

(1) He or she is flexible and adaptable. Flexibility and adaptability suggest that a leader can "roll with the punches." Learn to expect the unexpected. Perhaps something dear to your heart is not working in Cluster. An effective leader is flexible enough to recognize what is not working, to let it go, and to change to something that is more likely to work. Human beings don't always function according to expectations. There needs to be a degree of "hang-looseness" in an effective Cluster leader so that plans can be

changed at the last minute and possible disappointments at every turn avoided.

I'm not suggesting that one must compromise principle. But rules, which are our guidelines or regulations in life, are derived from our values. Sometimes our rules, not the values, need to change to fit changing circumstances, just as bedtime needs to change to fit the growth needs of people of different ages in the family. Ask any set of parents how their rules have changed as the home has adapted to the changing growth needs of children. Perhaps the rule "everything in order, everything in its place" must shift to accommodate growth needs of young children who may take a long time to learn that rule. Some never learn it. But children are more important than rules. Cleanliness and order are important values but the rules related to these values probably need to change with the growth needs and learning abilities of children in the home.

When you find yourself grumbling about a rule being broken, ask yourself what value the rule is related to. Could you survive without that rule in your life? How much difference will it make in your life if it is broken now and again?

If your life is very uncomfortable unless you are surrounded by lots of rigid rules, perhaps you need to choose another way to serve than to become a Cluster leader.

(2) He or she enjoys people of different ages in the same group. Almost by definition a family is made up of members of different ages. Each of us has grown up in a family. A Family Cluster is made up of four or five families. The age range can be broad (at this writing I am leading a Cluster with four families—a total of 30 members, including 22 children ranging in age from 3 to 19). Cluster can be noisy, messy, seemingly chaotic. An effective leader enjoys such diversity—indeed, thrives on it. There are endless possibilities to observe individual personalities in a kaleidoscope of manifestation. This very diversity becomes a major focus of interest and observation. Each person in the Cluster becomes a kind of "book" to be read, not always from cover to cover, but certainly known through a series of "short stories."

(3) He or she is healthy. It is up to the leader of the Family Cluster to model the desired energy level of each Cluster session. It is difficult to maintain this energy level when the leader has had little to eat, no exercise, and little sleep. It is *very important* that the

leader maintain adequate blood sugar levels through wise eating habits and be able to maintain energy and enthusiasm through adequate exercise, primarily cardiovascular exercise. A wise leader needs to treat his or her body well or that leader will not treat the Cluster well. It's just as simple as that.

Leading a Cluster is not backbreaking work, but it can be very stressful. If you have poor eating habits (including missing meals because you are too busy), if you get little or no cardiovascular exercise (that is, walking, riding an exercycle, doing aerobic dance, or some other aerobic exercise regularly), if you don't get enough sleep at night—leading Cluster may be too stressful for you. You need enthusiasm and energy to plan, prepare for, and conduct Cluster. Don't cheat Cluster and yourself by cheating the health of your body. Well-conditioned Cluster leaders are usually satisfied leaders.

(4) He or she is assertive. Cluster is not a place for shrinking violets. Planning an effective session is not enough. Those plans must be put into effect with wise preparation, enthusiasm, and modeling of desired behavior. The members of a Cluster usually take their cues from the leaders regarding what to do, how to do it, and how much energy to devote to it. Effective leaders don't hang back. They see what needs to be done and do it when needed.

When you have an idea, do you share it with others? Do you get excited by other people's ideas? When you get an idea, do you act on it? When you don't like something, are you able to say so without offending others? If you think you have something to add to a suggestion to make it a better one, do you say so? Are you willing to work with the ideas of a coleader and to try things out before deciding they're no good? Affirmative answers to these questions auger well for healthy assertiveness as a Cluster leader.

(5) He or she is creative. This characteristic is difficult to define, yet important. It has something to do with seeing things in new or novel ways. For instance, one of the delightful characteristics of an effective Cluster is what I call its often "off-the-wall" functioning. That is, there seems to be a new twist to everything and nothing is taken too seriously. Who could have imagined that a small group of floppy animal hand puppets could have created so much learning and so much fun as they did in one Cluster session I attended? We were having an experience related to self-esteem. Each family

had been handed a card with a situation typed on it. Each family was asked to create and practice their role-playing situation with the puppets and then perform it for the entire Cluster. A long table had been turned on its side and each family crouched behind the table and presented their skit to the rest of us. With each skit, all of us dissolved in laughter, including each family "on stage." For instance, clever leaders had written on the cards instructions similar to these:

> Your great uncle, whom you had never met, arrived today from Mars. He will be staying with your family for two days. You are seated in the living room, after a delicious meal, discussing your plans for your great uncle during his stay. What will you do with your great uncle during his two-day visit? Create and act out the conversation in the living room, using the hand puppets.

Creativity in a leader means generating novel ways to experience the objectives for each Cluster session.

The best way I have discovered for me to generate creative, effective, appealing Cluster experiences is to brainstorm ideas with a coleader. We brainstorm ideas for a while. We don't discuss or evaluate them. We just get them out in the open. In other words, we get them down before we make them good. After we've tossed ideas around for a while, we pick the ones that seem most promising and "do-able." Then we plan how and in what order to implement them. If every plan must be perfect before it comes out of your head, you'll probably be happier doing something other than Cluster leadership.

(6) He or she is an effective problem-solver. To an effective Cluster leader, problems are challenges, opportunities for creative juices and new energy to come to the fore. For instance, the very family you planned a special Cluster experience for may not be in today's Cluster because one of the children has the whooping cough. What do you do? Cancel Cluster? Give up the idea entirely? No. You go ahead with the plan but find a way to extend it to next week's Cluster, when it is likely the family will be back. But what if Family X can't come to Cluster next week either? Well, you'll face that issue if it comes up. In the meantime, you modify your plan to fit today's Cluster grouping. Then you enter Cluster with the same energy and enthusiasm you always do.

Cluster can be a problem-solver's dream or nightmare, any way you choose to look at it. Murphy's Law may work overtime for the average Cluster (you know, the law that says, "If anything can go wrong, it will"). Some people think Murphy's Law says, "If anything can go wrong, don't try it." However, an effective leader is an effective problem-solver, facing each problem as another challenge to be met. I'm convinced that life was never meant to be comfortable, and problems make lots of people uncomfortable. But problems can be terrific ways to help us grow, if we let them.

(7) He or she has high self-esteem. The effective Cluster leader feels enough self-worth that he or she is not dependent on others for praise and commendation to keep jacking up a flagging self-esteem or ego. But this is an un-self-conscious kind of thing. The Cluster leader is able to separate him- or herself from the Cluster and recognize that what occurs in Cluster does not reflect on the self. He or she is able to forget self in the process of Cluster, to enjoy Cluster, to be in the "now."

I have been in Cluster where leaders or leaders-in-training (LITs) seemed so unsure of themselves that they constantly drew attention to themselves. This is drawing energy away from its necessary focus on educational experiences for the Cluster families.

Feeding the egos of Cluster leaders is not the purpose of Cluster. An effective Cluster leader doesn't need or want such care and feeding. The leader with high self-esteem is fed by the enrichment taking place in the lives of Cluster members. The life of an effective Cluster leader who feels comfortable with his or her own self is enriched by the very act of being a leader.

(8) He or she has a good sense of humor and knows how to have fun. An effective Cluster leader wears his or her halo just a little cockeyed. The comic is always just around the corner, just under the surface. It is neither necessary nor desirable to be a comedian in order to be an effective Cluster leader. However, the effective leader can smile, laugh, have fun—often. Such laughter and fun are contagious and uplifting for the human spirit. The humorous in all aspects of life is appreciated and often shared with others.

(9) He or she appreciates the imperfect. A person who can appreciate the imperfect is likely to appreciate Cluster, a group of always imperfect individuals. Such a person is likely to recognize small gains toward goals—in self as well as in others. It is easier for someone who appreciates the imperfect to share warmth, support, and encouragement—to affirm others—because we're all imperfect.

A perfectionist tends to be too hard on self, too hard on others. Unfortunately, the perfectionist is *never* satisfied, because goals constantly shift forward and are never achieved. The rigidity of the perfectionist can create a very stressful environment—for self and for others.

One who appreciates the imperfect can enjoy the now. It is important that Cluster members learn to enjoy the now because that's the only time there is. Perfectionists tend to live in the future. Remember, today is the tomorrow you dreamed about yesterday.

(10) He or she is sensitive to group dynamics. This is a difficult one to pin down that nevertheless is important. An effective leader essentially listens with the "third ear," that inner ear that tells him or her when the time has come to begin an experience—or end it, when the energy level of Cluster is low and needs an injection of adrenalin, when something occurs that needs to be talked about right now, when some Cluster members are not "up to par" for any number of reasons, when an observation needs to be verbalized during Cluster. A leader brings his or her whole self into the Cluster, not just a body. One's whole being is focused on and attuned to what is happening, in each family, to each individual, in Cluster as a whole. It is a kind of sixth sense that gives a clue at the last minute when to try something else instead of what you had planned or when to continue with your plan. All of your sensory antennae are up and working. They vibrate when Cluster is going. Their messages are decoded at once and acted upon as needed.

(11) He or she is willing to work hard in less-than-ideal circumstances. Perhaps the room where Cluster meets is not as close as it should be to running water or the bathroom. Maybe it is cramped when all members of the Cluster are present. Maybe Cluster members can't be as messy—or as active—as would be ideal for Cluster plans when they are implemented. Nevertheless, the effective Cluster leader works with what is available, without complaint, and continues to make Cluster work in spite of less-than-ideal circumstances.

Maybe a snowstorm or a rainstorm has kept some Cluster members away from a Cluster session. Maybe there has been a death or other crisis in one of the Cluster families. These are circumstances no one can control. However, the effective Cluster leader will acknowledge these crises without breaking stride. Just as the "show must go on," so must Cluster go on, if the decision has been made to hold Cluster in spite of a given crisis. Cluster members are trusted to be capable of weathering the bumps and bruises along the way when any group comes together. The Cluster leader creatively problem-solves and allows the crisis to take its place among important learning experiences in Cluster.

(12) He or she enjoys working with others. An effective Cluster leader has had enough experience working with others to know whether he or she enjoys it. There is nothing bad about not liking to work with others. But if you prefer working alone and being in control of everything, Cluster leadership is not for you. Cluster leaders depend on one another, trust one another, plan together, evaluate together, and frequently need to bounce ideas off one another.

(13) He or she is willing to compromise preference, but not principle. Preference is related to things I like and don't like. Maybe I like scrambled eggs but not fried eggs. Maybe I prefer quiet over noise. Maybe I like classical music, but not rock 'n' roll. Sometimes I'm willing to compromise preference by eating fried eggs if that's the only thing available, getting involved in a noisy party when I would much prefer being alone if being at that party is important to someone important to me, or even listening to rock 'n' roll if it is important to a friend that I hear something that is special to him or her. But I needn't compromise the value of health and, therefore, the principles of good nutrition, if I eat a fried egg instead of a scrambled egg. I don't have to compromise the principle of the importance of quiet calm in my life to listen to some noisy rock 'n' roll that someone important to me wants me to hear.

Sometimes, when a Cluster is establishing its ground rules—its contract for working together—one or more of the teenagers might want to bring their portable stereos and play rock 'n' roll during Cluster. I'm willing for this to happen at a specified time—and for a very short period of time—but I am not willing to listen to rock 'n' roll for the entire Cluster session, session after session. Calm is too important in my life to have it broken over and over by what seems to me to be ear-splitting noise. I'm willing to discuss this with Cluster. However, I let the Cluster know what I am willing to do. This is a matter of principle for me, not preference. If the Cluster, by consensus, agrees to have rock 'n' roll blaring from "boom boxes" each Cluster session, I would help them find another Cluster leader. If I am not clear on the differences between my principles and preferences, I can't help Cluster members, through my own modeling, differentiate the difference between the two.

(14) He or she can express feelings directly and effectively. Strong feelings can be our enemies or our friends. Identifying my strong feelings in words helps me to control them. Otherwise, I repress them, deny them, and thus let them control me. If someone is missing from Cluster who hasn't notified me in advance, I might find myself making comments or acting in a way that shows I am disturbed by that person's absence because I was not notified and I miss the presence of that person (yes, every person *does* make a difference in Cluster). It clears the air and helps to avoid expectations that someone will read my mind if I directly express my feeling by saying something like, "I notice that ________(the missing person) is not here. I miss him/her. I wonder if ________is all right. ________signed a contract, as you all did, promising to let me know if he/she could not be in attendance at any session. I have not heard from ________. I am concerned. I wonder if a contract has been broken or if there is an emergency." This would give Cluster members an opportunity to share information about _____ and their own feelings. This would be setting a model for Cluster members when they have strong feelings about something in Cluster.

Strong feelings, when not articulated, tend to be denied and repressed. However, like a forest fire that is almost out, they are likely to burst into flame someplace else. Verbalizing feelings helps to reduce the strength of the feelings. It also avoids the trap many fall into of attempting to read another person's mind.

There is a difference between feeling and the behavior that goes with it. When feelings are expressed directly (that is, the person acknowledges what the feeling is and what he or she perceives to be the cause of the feeling), the person is much more likely to choose whether or not and how to adequately express a response to the feeling.

(15) He or she can listen reflectively. One of the most valuable tools of an effective Family Cluster leader is the ability to reflect what another person has said or done.

Reflective listening is not a passive "hearing" experience. It is verbalizing to the other, in your own words, what you have just heard. For example, 9-year-old Sam came into Cluster one afternoon and told me excitedly, "Boy, did we ever scare those slime dogs!" (A group of school-aged boys, in their gang, had discovered a dark, slippery substance on the sidewalks and on rocks nearby that they decided was caused by "slime dogs"—their own creation!) I didn't know what Sam was talking about. However, I could tell he was pretty excited about something, so I reflected his feelings: "Your voice tells me you're pretty excited about something. Why don't you tell me about scaring the slime dogs." When you reflect what someone else tells you, especially when strong feelings seem to be attached, it's a good idea to put in your own words (that is, reflect) what you think the other person is feeling. Then pause for the other person to respond. Sometimes people are so shocked by a reflective response, especially one related to feelings, that they are stunned into silence. Children, generally, will get right into such an invitation to share more.

Reflective listening is an effective way to say "I care" without making a big deal out of it. It does not indicate agreement or disagreement, nor does it preach or moralize. It simply acknowledges in your own words what you think the person said.

These are 15 important characteristics possessed by effective Family Cluster leaders I have known. Perhaps you can think of others. If you rated yourself 10 on each, you would have a total score of 150. However, the overall score is not important. What *is* important is whether or not you have enough of *each* characteristic to become an effective Family Cluster leader, a leader who enjoys planning and conducting Family Cluster.

6. Preparing for a Family Cluster

This chapter focuses on some of those important details you need to attend to when preparing for a Family Cluster. Questions about who will sponsor the Family Cluster, where the Family Cluster will be held, how the participants will be selected, compensation for leaders, and so on need to be answered, and preparations need to be made for the beginning of Family Cluster.

Who Will Sponsor the Family Cluster?

The first Clusters organized and led by Margaret Sawin were sponsored by Protestant congregations. As a matter of fact, religious congregations are probably the most frequent sponsors of Family Cluster to date. Religious congregations are made up of families. They have a stewardship to meet the spiritual needs of the members of their congregations. The family is the bedrock of any congregation.

Religious congregations usually have resources to provide for Clusters, including space in which the Cluster can meet and compensation for Cluster leaders. They may even have materials and supplies needed for Cluster as well as electronic equipment such as overhead projectors, screens, VCRs, tape recorders, and so forth. Sometimes their libraries contain books appropriate for Family Clusters. In addition, most current leadership in Family Cluster comes out of religious congregations, including Jewish, Middle Eastern, and Far Eastern groups.

A largely untapped source of sponsorship is *business and industry*. Today many businesses and industrial complexes have included sports and exercise facilities for their employees. They recognize that rising health care costs, especially insurance, can be reduced by reinforcing and supporting healthy life-styles among their employees. However, employees live in families. Absence from work is costly to business and industry. People often are absent from work because of needs of others in the family. Often those needs relate to psychological problems of other family members. Those problems probably can often be traced back to relationship problems in family living. It is likely that absenteeism could be cut considerably if businesses and industries would sponsor for their employees' Family Clusters. Because Family Cluster focuses on what works, on the strengths of the family, it helps to cement family bonds and probably would help to eliminate much stress faced by millions of employees. If business and industrial leaders could be persuaded that sponsoring Family Clusters would cut employee absenteeism, they probably could be persuaded to sponsor Family Clusters. Space and even funds for materials, supplies, and equipment could be provided by businesses and industries. Their funding of Family Cluster, if it could be shown to reduce absenteeism, could easily pay for itself many times over. Profits are the bottom line for businesses and industries in any capitalist country. Happy employees commit their talents and creative energies to the provision of such profits. Happy employees come from happy, strong families.

Educational institutions, such as public schools, colleges, and universities, can be sponsors of Family Cluster, especially when Family Cluster is offered as a part of the curriculum of one of the academic departments, such as family studies, child psychology, or child development. Family Clusters can provide internship opportunities for students in high school, college, or the university who are studying family life education or one of its variations.

Compensation for Family Cluster leaders is important. The sponsoring organization probably is in a better position to provide such compensation than the families in a Cluster. The compensation needs to be agreed upon in writing between the sponsoring organization and the leaders of the Clusters.

Sponsoring organizations may have lists of potential Family Cluster families. In addition, they may provide the publicity for Family Clusters as well.

Public schools depend on families for students. Their major

challenges, although generally focused on specific students, are family challenges. The public school system, together with the PTA, is largely an untapped source of sponsorship for Family Cluster. Because a single Cluster consists of only four or five families, and many more families may wish to participate in Family Cluster than would constitute a single Cluster, it would be wise, if a school or school district wishes to sponsor Family Cluster, to conduct an initial demonstration Cluster before conducting more than one Cluster at any given time. Cluster can be held in a classroom in one school to begin with, and in several classrooms in several schools as the number of Clusters grows (and if leaders are available). However, care should be exercised to ensure that Cluster held in classrooms does not interfere with the arrangement of classroom furniture and wall and bulletin board space. If school equipment such as sports equipment, kitchen supplies, or audiovisual equipment is used, it should be left in the same condition in which the Cluster found it. If school supplies are used, they should be planned and arranged for well in advance of each Cluster session so school personnel can make them available for Cluster when needed. If publicity and pre-Cluster assessment are to take place, these should be worked out well in advance of the first Cluster session so families can be identified in advance of the beginning of Cluster and so arrangements can be made for home visits, completion of assessment instruments, payment for Cluster participation, custodial arrangements that are necessary before each Cluster session, and so on.

There are many details involved in the planning of Cluster. They involve lots of "little things." Anticipation of these "little things" can grease the way to effective Cluster sessions. Without anticipation of the many little details involved in Cluster planning, public school sponsorship of Cluster can disappear because of poor planning.

Colleges and universities often have family life education programs. The institution may wish to sponsor Family Cluster as part of its family life curriculum. This is the case at the university where I teach. There is a once-a-year Family Cluster practicum for both graduate and advanced undergraduate students. The university provides space in one of the preschool laboratories for Family Cluster. There is a kitchen nearby where refreshments and sandwich meals can be safely stored. There is a carpet on the floor so

Cluster members can sit on the floor during Cluster activities (Cluster often involves floor activities). Because the practicum is part of my teaching load, my salary compensates me as a trainer of leaders-in-training (LITs) for Family Cluster. I have access to all of the audiovisual resources at the university, including movies, videos, books, and audiotapes. Any college or university would have such resources available for Family Cluster if it decided to become a sponsor.

Families are the backbone of any community. When families are in trouble, so are communities. *Public service agencies* such as United Fund agencies and senior citizens' centers are primarily organized to assist families in need. Perhaps such agencies may sponsor Family Clusters for assistance in their stewardships to help families in the community.

Where Will Family Cluster Be Held?

Often a sponsor will provide the space needed for a Family Cluster. There should be a room large enough for four or five families to move about freely and a place for everyone to sit. Sometimes public schools, colleges or universities, YWCAs or YMCAs, churches or synagogues, or even family therapy or mental health clinics will sponsor Clusters by providing space, staff, and even funding for the Clusters.

Occasionally a Cluster can be held in a private home if *all* members of the Cluster can meet during each *entire* session in one place. It is not a good idea to send individual families off to separate rooms. This defeats one of the major purposes of Cluster, which is to provide affirmation and support for *every* member of the Cluster by other Cluster members.

Cluster sessions should be held in space where individuals are free to move around, play games, make things that are messy with clay, paints, and finger paints, put their "masterpieces" on the wall (with masking tape), and, where there is room, put up (with masking tape) signs printed on newsprint, computer paper, or butcher paper.

Occasionally, things can become a bit messy during Cluster. If finger paints are used, running water must be readily available to wash off messy hands, paper towels should be available to dry hands, wash cloths or sponges should be available to clean up spills, and so on. If clay is used, there should be wash cloths available and other items necessary to work with a "messy" medium. Work surfaces should be available for "messy" work. It won't hurt people to kneel while working at learning activities. Thus low tables or boards stretched between blocks or bricks can be effectively used during Cluster sessions. During summer, late spring, and early fall, Cluster sessions can even be held outdoors, but anticipate the numerous distractions that can occur when groups meet outdoors.

How Will Family Cluster Participants Be Selected?

Any family desiring educational enrichment is eligible for Family Cluster. Any family in the community is potentially eligible for Family Cluster.

The sponsor of Family Cluster, such as an employer or a religious congregation, might wish to make Family Cluster available to the families under its umbrella. In such a case, it is a good idea to work closely with someone in the sponsoring organization to select families, publicize Family Cluster, select a site for Cluster, select equipment, materials, and supplies that might be available in the sponsoring organization, and so forth.

What Materials, Supplies, and Equipment Are Required?

Before Cluster begins, the following should be obtained and be ready for any Cluster session:

—a roll of newsprint or butcher paper (rolls of newsprint can be obtained free of charge from printing establishments such as newspapers)
—a supply of varieties of colors of construction paper
—plain paper (end pieces from printing establishments or used computer paper)
—colored markers (a box of eight colored markers for each family included in the Cluster)
—a box of crayons

—plastic holders for markers and crayons such as used yogurt or cottage cheese containers
—pencils (no. 2), sharpened—enough for all Cluster members
—paste (such as library paste or homemade paste)
—containers for paste, such as used margarine or butter containers
—masking tape
—two or three pads of newsprint

You may think of other materials and supplies you need. For example, you may collect "beautiful junque" from around the house or old magazines from doctors' offices for cutting and pasting activities in Cluster. You might also want to make a collection of hand puppets for use in Cluster as well as children's storybooks, blocks, dolls, and stuffed animals for use in the play corner by children in the Cluster. Incidentally, if the Cluster has young children, blocks and books furnish the basic items in a *play corner* in the event the younger Cluster members need time out from regular Cluster activities. The "play corner" should not be so attractive that it vies with other Cluster activities. The equipment and supplies used in the play corner should be those that, when used, will not disturb other Cluster members participating in the regular activities of Cluster.

Chairs and tables are nice but not necessary. It should be possible for people to gather together while sitting on the floor and to spread out on the floor for Cluster activities.

The room should be well lighted. The temperature should be such that Cluster members can work comfortably in shirtsleeves.

If electronic equipment such as VCRs, audiotape recorders, and overhead projectors are required for Cluster sessions, they should be readily available along with necessary electrical outlets and a screen.

Cluster is something like camping, where everything has several uses, nothing is wasted, and fancy space and equipment are generally unnecessary. It is the activity, the togetherness, that counts.

What Financial Resources Are Available for Family Cluster?

Space, leader time, supplies, equipment, and materials cost money. The sponsoring organization of Family Cluster should be prepared and willing to provide the major financial resources required for Family Cluster. The sponsoring organization usually can provide space, equipment, and even some of the supplies and materials required for an effective Cluster.

Preferably, compensation for leader time should be a resource available from the sponsoring organization. Personnel expenses are usually the largest expense in any budget. Leaders are not inexpensive. Few families, however, can afford to pay what Cluster leaders are worth. Even with four or five families who are members of the Cluster contributing to the financial resources required by the Cluster, the expense of Cluster leaders probably would be beyond the means of any but the most affluent families.

With a rapidly fluctuating economy and pay-scale differences throughout the United States, I won't suggest what would be adequate compensation for Family Cluster leaders. I would suggest, however, that Cluster leaders find out how much other family life educators in their area (such as some marriage and family therapists) charge for conducting workshops and use those rates as guides when planning how much they will charge for service as a Family Cluster leader. Take into account the hours spent in planning and evaluating as well as those spent conducting Cluster when determining how much compensation they will seek.

How Many People Should Be in a Family Cluster?

A Family Cluster is composed of four or five families. Any more families may create an unwieldy group for leaders to lead.

How do you determine how many families should be in Cluster—four or five? That depends on the average size of families within the umbrella of the sponsoring organization. If Cluster is sponsored by an organization such as a United Fund agency that wishes to sponsor a Family Cluster for families where there are two or more preschool children and no children older than preschool, you may be able to cope with five families. There will be at least 10 preschoolers in such a Cluster and perhaps some toddlers (children between the ages of 12 months and 2½ years) and some infants (children between the ages of birth to 12 months). This, in addition to the 10 parents, would be a Cluster of 20-plus people.

However, if a religious congregation is sponsoring the Cluster, and the average size of families in the congregation is five children, then a Cluster of four families could have 20 children, plus 8 adults (parents), making a total of 28 people in the Cluster.

When you plan how many families to include in the Cluster, you should determine how many children with which you are capable of and willing to work. If you have lots of children in the Cluster, spread out over a wide age range, you may wish to reduce the age spread, the number of children, and the number of families.

There probably isn't an ideal number of people in a Family Cluster. The desired number of families depends on the number of children, the combination of their sexes and ages, and how the leaders feel about working with any given combination of age and sex.

How Many Times Should Cluster Meet?

Just as with the number of families in Cluster, there probably isn't an ideal number of sessions for a Family Cluster. Sawin (1979) suggests at least eight sessions. I have found this a good minimum number for Clusters I lead. This allows two sessions (the first two) for getting acquainted and determining Family Cluster ground rules. It also allows for one closing session, leaving five sessions in which to concentrate on family strengths selected by the Cluster families. I have found that eight sessions also allows Cluster families an opportunity to become well acquainted with one another, bonded to each other, and a true support group of families. Twelve to fifteen sessions for a Cluster is even better. It would provide more time for change to take place.

How Many Sessions per Theme Should Be Planned?

The curriculum for Family Cluster is drawn from the family strengths selected by the Cluster families, based on their responses to the Family Strengths Inventory (see Chapters 7 and 8). My experience tells me that any major category selected from the FSI, such as communication or commitment, requires, at the very least, three Cluster sessions. When a Cluster is new, I focus the first session on getting acquainted, the second and third sessions on determining Cluster rules and policies, and the last session on "saying good-bye" (termination). That leaves five Cluster sessions for a category or two related to family strength.

How Much Does Family Cluster Cost Each Family?

When I served my internship as a psychotherapist, I remember my mentor and supervisor advising me to charge each client what he or she could afford—charge each client *something*, even if the client was dirt poor—because people who pay for professional services they receive are more likely to be motivated to do whatever is necessary to make improvements in their lives. Dipping into one's pocketbook seems to motivate action related to the expenditure.

Similar advice would probably hold true for families in Family Cluster, even though the sponsoring organization such as a congregation or a business would be willing to pay the costs that would normally accrue to the family. Families should have the opportunity to contribute toward the Family Cluster by, at the very least, paying for the materials and supplies needed for the Cluster. In 1986 and 1987 I charged each family in Clusters I conducted $10 per family. This purchased paste, construction paper, crayons, colored markers, masking tape, and a couple of large newsprint tablets for use in Cluster. In 1988 I charged $15 per family for similar materials because prices had gone up on most of the materials and because I had had to take money out of my own pocket for materials and supplies the previous year.

Should Families with Special Challenges Be Included?

At one time I thought I would conduct some Clusters for stepfamilies and some for families where a member had experienced some form of catastrophic illness. I suddenly found myself focusing on the problems of stepfamilies and those of families where a member has experienced catastrophic illness. I had to remind myself that Cluster is not therapy. I can't make the assumption that stepfamilies need "fixing" (and, therefore, are eligible for therapy) any more than I can make that same assumption about families where one of the members has experienced catastrophic illness. Once the emphasis is on problems, we have entered the realm of therapy. Family Cluster is experiential education—an enrichment experience for everyone in its families. Making assumptions about the normality of any family will hinder our planning as Cluster leaders. The focus is on strength—on making what works work better.

It is not necessary for all families to be homogeneous (that is, all intact nuclear families, all Mexican American, all poor, and so on). It helps if the families share essentially the same values about work, responsibility, showing affection, honesty, and other basic values in our society. It is not necessary for them to share the same religious background any more than it is necessary that they all share a similar challenge or problem, such as being a stepfamily or dealing with catastrophic illness.

Should Leaders Make Home Visits Before Cluster Begins?

Though some leaders prefer to meet families for the first time at Cluster, important opportunities for answering questions, getting acquainted with families in their own homes, and obtaining family contributions to the Cluster experience are missed. Home visits are *very* important and should not be left out of planning for the first Cluster.

When I make a home visit, I first make a telephone appointment with the family. Sometimes I send a letter indicating a welcome to Family Cluster and when I will call for an appointment. I take with me a contract (see Exhibit 6A) for the family to sign prior to coming to the first Cluster session. The contract I use gives information about where the Cluster will be held, on what dates, and at what time. The contract also includes some other items to which the family members are committing themselves, such as arriving on time, bringing their own sandwich meal for each session (if there is to be a meal), wearing comfortable clothing, and handling emergencies when someone must be absent from Cluster. It also describes the purpose of Family Cluster. I have *each* member of the family sign the contract and provide an opportunity for family members to ask questions about Family Cluster. Visiting the home gives me an opportunity not only to get acquainted with the members of the family on a one-to-one basis but also to get a feeling, though somewhat superficial because the visit is not long, for the atmosphere in the home. I watch how family members interact, who does the talking, how they respond to each other and to us, their leaders. Sometimes family members wonder if Family Cluster is something like therapy with a different name, so the home visit gives me an opportunity to explain what Family Cluster is and to assure the family that therapy does not take place at Cluster, nor do we leaders analyze every movement of the family. We are in Family Cluster to affirm one another, to focus on our strengths, to discuss whatever seems important to us at the time.

When I make home visits, I also take enough copies of the Family Strengths Inventory composition form (FSI-CF) for each family member who can read (see Chapter 7). I hand out pencils to the family and wait for them to complete the FSI-CF (it doesn't take long; there are three to fourteen items in each of eight categories). Sometimes I send the FSI-CF copies in advance of our visit, pick them up later, and bring with me the inventory that is the result of the selections of Cluster families on the FSI-CF. Then during the home visit my coleader and I discuss how the inventory will be analyzed to determine the focus of our Cluster sessions and how the performance of the family, though confidential, will help us make the choice of focus for our Cluster sessions. The newly developed inventory has only 24 items, so we usually wait for family members to complete the inventory, just as we did before with the FSI-CF.

Before we leave the home, we usually collect a small fee to cover the costs of materials and supplies. Every family should feel it is pulling its own load economically in a Cluster. Perhaps leaders' compensation and rent for the space is out of reach for most families. However, the materials and supplies required in Family Cluster are relatively inexpensive and easily obtained. The cost probably should be borne by the families in the Cluster, even though the sponsoring organization might be able to provide such materials and supplies.

When we leave the home after our short visit, we leave a copy of the contract with the family (and keep a copy for our own files). At that point, we can call each person by name. We make a point of doing that in our farewell.

How Should Leaders Plan Cluster Sessions?

Using SMITTIs (single most important thing to improve) resulting from analysis of the completed Family Strength Inventories (FSIs), the Cluster leaders determine what the theme (or focus) of each Cluster session will be. Avoid planning a SMITTI theme for the first, second, or last sessions. The *first session* should be entirely devoted to getting acquainted and the *second session* should be devoted to planning the Cluster ground rules (or contract). The *last session* should be devoted to termination activities (see sample session agenda plans at the end of Chapter 8).

Setting the Stage for the First Cluster

After you prepare your session agenda plans (see Chapter 8), you will be ready for the "opening night" of Cluster. Maybe you are nervous and have worked your tail off getting ready. Provide the most comfortable and welcoming environment you can devise for the members of the Cluster you lead. Maybe you will want to have welcoming signs painted and posted for everybody to see. At the very least, have a place where Cluster members can sign in, where they can get acquainted in comfortable circumstances. And be ready for everybody to arrive at least 15 minutes before the session is due to begin. If no one arrives early, that is your time to relax and catch your breath. You should be relaxed and able to "hang loose" when the Cluster members arrive. When they arrive, your exclusive focus should be them, not you.

Bringing It All Together

There are many details that need to be dealt with before you hold the first Cluster session. I'm a detail person. Sometimes I get so carried away with the details of something in my task-oriented way that I forget that it is people I'm leading, ordinary mortals like myself. You can become a significant person in the lives of people in Family Cluster. You will set the model for effective family living in your preparation and your ability to relax and provide a comfortable atmosphere for those attending Cluster. When the first Cluster member enters Cluster, preparation time is over and the *real* Cluster has begun. Maybe the *real* you has begun, as well.

Case Study, Part A

Matthew Marshall, age 35 and a commercial artist, and his wife, Alice, age 33 and an elementary school teacher, live with their two children, Matt, Jr. (age 10), and Cindy (age 6) in a modest one-story, three-bedroom bungalow in a small midwestern city. Both are active in their local Protestant congregation. Last summer the Marshall family attended a family camp for a week in the woods a three-hour drive from their home, a camp sponsored by the district headquarters, where their congregation is located. The camp was a training camp for leaders of Family Cluster. Matthew and Alice were leaders-in-training at that family camp. They worked as a leader team. During training they planned and conducted together two Cluster sessions. During the two Cluster sessions their children joined another family.

Matthew and Alice's church encourages its members to hold a Family Together Night every Monday evening (or any other weekday evening of their choice, if Monday is not possible). Under the sponsorship of their congregation, Matthew and Alice will soon be conducting their first Family Cluster, the first for which they will be totally responsible as leaders. This will also be the first Family Cluster sponsored by their congregation. A room at church that is large enough for a Family Cluster, with restrooms and a kitchen nearby, has been made available for Family Cluster on Monday evenings. The church kitchen will be used for families to leave their sandwich meals, and small-scale food preparations can be made and needed water for Cluster activities can be obtained there. Tables and chairs are available for Cluster use, as are media equipment such as an overhead projector, slide projector, and VCR with TV monitor.

Recently Matthew and Alice notified the following four families in their congregation who had applied for Family Cluster that they had been selected to participate in Cluster and that Matthew and Alice would be making appointments soon for home visits before Cluster begins. The families are as follows:

The Kenyon Family
Chad, age 40, a distribution director
Mary, age 37, a homemaker
Ted, age 16

The Crowley Family
Mark, age 39, a professor
Ellen, age 36, a homemaker
Marni, age 15

Linda, age 13
Monica, age 10
Tami, age 7

Bill, age 13
Jimmy, age 9
Nathan, age 6
Sandy, age 3

The Dart Family
Bill, age 43, an insurance salesman
Susan, age 40, a social worker
Bill, Jr., age 17
Jared, age 14
Cam, age 11
Andrew, age 7

The Bradshaw Family
Ken, age 39, a carpenter
Ruth, age 36, a nurse
Robin, age 12
Danny, age 10
Matt, age 8

Thus the Cluster will have 16 children between the ages of 3 and 17 and 8 adults, or a total of 24 people.

The Marshalls have made arrangements with the secretary at church to send a letter to the Cluster families informing them of the date Cluster begins, the time, and the place, as well as how to complete the enclosed Family Strength Inventory composition forms (FSI-CF), and that Matthew and Alice will be telephoning soon for an appointment to get acquainted, to bring by the Family Cluster contract, to pick up the FSI-CFs, and to answer questions about Cluster. The Marshalls plan to make their last home visit to a Cluster family at least a week before Cluster begins. They have been collecting newsprint and miscellaneous end pieces of paper from a nearby newspaper plant. They have also purchased the necessary supplies for Cluster and plan to collect $20 from each family during their home visits to pay for the needed Cluster supplies.

The Marshalls have made a written agreement with the governing board of the church to conduct this first Cluster for a modest compensation to both of them because it is their first Cluster and the congregation sponsored their training as leaders the previous summer. Arrangements have been made for an increase in their compensation for subsequent Clusters. In the meantime, there are currently four families on a Family Cluster waiting list in the congregation.

Matthew is looking forward to using his skills as a commercial artist in preparing signs for Family Cluster. Alice, as an elementary school teacher, is an accomplished "printer." She will be the chief printer of signs for Cluster. They both are aware of how useful signs are during each Cluster session. They have stocked up on marker pens of all colors to make and "paint" signs for Cluster. In addition, they are looking forward to planning Cluster session agenda plans. They will score the FSI-CFs as soon as they pick them up from the families and make a Family Strength Inventory that is unique to their Cluster. They will arrange for the families to take the FSI and return it to them well before Cluster begins so they can analyze the FSIs, determine the SMITTIs for each family, and plan the educational focus of each Cluster session.

Alice and Matthew have already arranged with authorities in the congregation that they will lead 15 Cluster sessions in this first Family Cluster sponsored by their congregation. The Cluster members can determine later when they are well into their Cluster experience whether or not they wish to continue Cluster and hold more than the agreed-upon 15 sessions.

Alice's mother, a widow (Grandma Stubbs), lives in the same town and will be at home with the children when Alice and Matthew need to be at church attending to their Cluster responsibilities.

Reference

Sawin, M. M. (1979). *Family enrichment with family clusters.* Valley Forge, PA: Judson.

Exhibit 6A *FAMILY CONTRACT*

Family Cluster 19??
Brigham Young University
Leader: Dr. Barbara (Vance)
Family surname: ________________Date ____________________

We, the ________________family, promise to attend EACH of the following Family Cluster sessions, uniquely planned for our family and three or four other families, to be held in *Rm. 00 SFLC* on the Brigham Young University campus, on the following *MONDAY* evenings from *6:00 PM to 8:00 PM*:

January 26—Session 1

February 2—Session 2

February 9—Session 3

February 23—Session 4 (skip February 16 because of Presidents' Day Holiday)

March 2—Session 5

March 9—Session 6

March 16—Session 7

March 23—Session 8

We will arrive on time, bring our own sandwich meal, and participate in the activities of each Cluster session, dressing in casual, comfortable clothing so we can sit on the floor and participate in all activities with comfort and freedom.

We understand that the purpose of these Cluster sessions is to learn how to make things that work (that we like) in our family work better, based on our family scores on the Family Strengths Inventory. We also understand that Cluster activities will be planned so we can have lots of fun with our family and learn to support other families who are part of our Cluster.

We promise that if an emergency arises and any one of us is unable to attend a Cluster session, that person will be responsible for calling Dr. Barbara (office: ______________; home: ______________) to let her know of our absence BEFORE the Cluster session begins. Otherwise, the

Cluster can count on each of us attending Cluster and participating in the Cluster activities.

We also understand that if we wish to bring a guest we must receive PRIOR permission from Dr. Barbara to do so by calling her on the telephone.

(Signatures of family members)

____________________ ____________________

____________________ ____________________

____________________ ____________________

____________________ ____________________

____________________ ____________________

____________________ ____________________

____________________ ____________________

____________________ ____________________

____________________ ____________________

7. Planning Goals and Objectives for Family Cluster

If you don't know where you're going, any way will get you there. This applies to planning for Family Cluster. First, you have to know what your destination is—what your aim or goal is.

Because Family Cluster is not therapy but an education and enrichment experience designed to strengthen the family, the goals of Family Cluster relate to those characteristics of strong families discussed in Chapter 3.

It probably seems obvious to you that the planning process begins with the identification of those who will be in the Cluster. Once you know who the Cluster members are going to be, you need to have clearly in mind your purpose for gathering them together in Cluster. The purpose of this chapter is to provide you with information that will help you effectively and efficiently identify who your learners really are as well as identify your instructional purposes, goals, and objectives for your learners—the members of your Family Cluster.

Step 1: Identify the Target Population of Learners

Your target population of learners—the families in Cluster—may come from a variety of settings. A church in your community may want you to plan and lead a Cluster for families where there are adolescents or preschoolers or school-age children. A business or industry may sponsor a Family Cluster for their employees.

freshmen in each section, there is an approximately equal distribution of sophomores, juniors, and seniors. Students enroll in the course as an elective or as a required course in their undergraduate major. The average age of students in our parenting courses is 21, which is somewhat older than a group of students in a similar class distribution, who are taking other courses outside the department, would be. When asked what they expect from the course, most students answer, "To learn how to be a good parent."

The parenting course is one of a series of "functional" courses related to marriage and the family offered at the university. The idea of "functional" assumes that the course will focus on "how to" rather than on theory.

One of the challenges I face as an instructor of a "functional" parenting course is making the course relevant in the lives of a target population the members of which, by an overwhelming majority, are not currently parents, whose major concern is whether or not they will have a date Saturday night. Therefore, I approach the course in the same light as Guerney and Guerney (1981), who suggest that, when the target population is not currently acting in the roles discussed during instruction, it is more effective to focus the instruction on the roles the students currently play relative to the roles they will play in the future. For example, high school students enrolled in a parenting course would more likely benefit from a course focusing on their relationships with their own parents and including opportunities to transfer such learning to their future roles as parents.

Because students who enroll in my parenting course generally are not even close to being parents, I focus my instruction on where they are in life and relate it, by analogy, to where they will be one day as parents.

The members of Family Clusters are currently involved as members of their own families. Therefore, what they experience in Cluster can have immediate application/implementation in their own families.

Once you have determined the needs of your Cluster members, you are ready to determine the expected learner results in the Cluster relative to your mastery model.

Determine expected learner results. The dictionary defines *result* as anything that comes about as the consequence of some action or process. At this stage in planning you are ready to state the desired consequences in the learner (Cluster member) from exposure to your Cluster (that is, learner results). These consequences are the aims or *goals* of your program. Such results, aims, or goals are stated in relatively general, nonspecific terms. *Determining specific learner objectives is a later step in the planning process.*

Given the characteristics of my Cluster members and their needs relative to the mastery model, I designed one Cluster program to focus on the following desired learner results (aims or goals):

> By the end of Cluster, members will (a) participate in the determination of Cluster rules; (b) frequently express appreciation to individual members of the Cluster; (c) feel a close emotional bond with each Cluster member; (d) exhibit adaptability when participating in Cluster experiences; (e) exhibit a sense of commitment to Cluster by following Cluster ground rules; (f) converse openly and honestly with family and Cluster members, frequently sharing feelings as well as ideas; (g) cope effectively with crisis and stress; and (h) enjoy spending time with Cluster members.

These goals are directly related to the mastery model for Cluster. Their achievement can be observed in Family Cluster. However, the *real* achievement of these goals is their implementation in the home with members of the family. The FSI can measure change in the family following Cluster experience.

It is easy to skip the process of determining goals when planning Cluster. You need to know what your goals are for your Cluster members before you move on to the next stage in Cluster planning, that of planning objectives for Cluster.

Planning Objectives for Family Cluster

Once you have determined your goals for Family Cluster, which are general and difficult to observe individually, you can determine the learning objectives of Family Cluster.

Objectives should be stated in terms that indicate *observable behavior* on the part of the learner (Cluster member). However, learning objectives suitable for Cluster differ from learning objectives suitable for the typical classroom. The focus of instruction in a classroom setting is generally the individual, whereas the focus of instruction in Cluster is the family. This is not to suggest that individuals are not doing the learning. However, members of Cluster live in primary social groups called families. They interact with other members of their families on a daily basis. Family strength is based on ways that members of families interact on a social basis. Interaction is usually based on the way a person *feels* about another person. The typical classroom, on the other hand, focusing on the individual learner, provides instruction designed to help the learner *think* and *reason*. That is, the focus of the content of classroom instruction is *cognitive* content, not emotional or *affective* content. The focus of instruction and, therefore, learning in Family Cluster is affective content called *insight*. Though mental processing is used, the focus of the education experiences in Cluster depends on one's feelings, especially as they relate to interactions with family members.

Insights

Insights are those components of subject matter that answer the question: "How does this have value for me in my life?" For example: "I can see now that no one can fill my needs but myself";

or

"I can see I don't like to do X, so I will do Y, which makes me happier and gives me a greater sense of accomplishment";

or

"I can see that when I accuse X of causing my feelings, she becomes defensive, so I will own my own feelings";

or

"I can see that I haven't been successful because I haven't been clear in the past about what I want to do, so I will clarify my intentions."

Insights most likely grow out of principles. That is, something has value in one's life when one can see a cause-and-effect relationship between conditions, methods, and outcomes. (At the very least, one can see a correlational relationship between conditions and outcomes, a relationship that has value in one's life.)

At this point, it is a good idea to back up and explore the meaning of *principle* because insights are based on principles.

Principles

Principles are those components of subject matter that answer the question: "What outcome seems to occur when outcome X occurs?" For example, What changes in school behavior tend to occur in children when their parents divorce? What is the nature and frequency of aggressive behavior in children who watch very little TV? What are the typical interaction patterns of happily married couples (*correlational relationships*)?

A *correlational principle* is a prediction of why things happen in the world. It is a correlational relationship that is used to interpret events or circumstances (Merrill, 1983). A correlational principle is represented by the following model:

> Given X (*conditions*), if Y_1 (*outcome*) occurs then Y_2 (*outcome*) also tends to occur.

A *cause-and-effect principle*, on the other hand, asks the question: "What causes something to happen and why does it happen?" For example, What causes behavior in children to increase in frequency? Decrease in frequency? Why do some families have frequent gestures of affection toward one another and frequent praise and encouragement of one another (*cause and effect relationship*)?

A cause-and-effect principle is represented by the following model:

> Given X *conditions*, if Y (*method*[*s*]) happens it will cause Z (*outcome, result, or consequence*) to occur.

A *cause-and-effect principle* is an explanation of why things happen in the world. A cause-and-effect relationship is used to interpret events or circumstances (Merrill, 1983). "*Principles* are explanations or predictions of why things happen in the world. Principles are those cause-and-effect or correlational relationships that are used to interpret events or circumstances" (Merrill, 1983, p. 288). Reigeluth (1983, p. 14) further defines a principle:

> A principle describes a relationship between two actions or changes. This relationship may be *correlational*, in which case it does not state which action influences the other, or it may be *causal*, in which case

> it does state which action influences the other. . . . It also may be *deterministic*, in which case the cause sometimes (or often) has the stated effect. Finally, the term *principle* is used here regardless of the degree of certainty of the relationship. Hence, it includes everything from pure conjecture or hypothesis (having little or no evidence for its truthfulness) to scientific law (having much evidence for its truthfulness).

This may still sound too abstract to apply to the planning of objectives for Family Cluster. Try it this way: A principle is always made up of three elements—the event(s), the happening(s), and the result(s). The *event(s)* describe the situation or condition; the *happening(s)* describe what occurs with the event(s); and the *result(s)* describe the outcome of the interaction between the event(s) and the happening(s). Here is an example of a *correlational principle* derived from a study by Heinicke, Diskin, Ramsey-Klee, and Given (1983):

Events: Mothers at mid-pregnancy . . .

Happenings: . . . who are warm and outgoing, high in ego strength (i.e., highly adaptive and who have high self-esteem), and are confident in visualizing themselves as mothers . . .

Results: . . . are later found to be highly sensitive and responsive to their infants' needs throughout the first year.

The next two examples of *correlational principles* are also derived from research. (Incidentally, one effective way to read research is to derive such principles and then evaluate the methods and results of the research.)

Events: Mother-infant interaction

Happenings: Sensitive mothers who often talk to their infants and stimulate their curiosity . . .

Results: . . . tend to produce infants who

a. have secure emotional attachments,

b. have exploratory competence,

c. grow intellectually, and produce children who, at ages 2 and 3, have greater skill in problem solving and peer relationships (derived from Ainsworth, 1979, and also from Belsky, Goode, & Most, 1980).

Events: Parent-child interaction

Happenings: *Authoritative* parents (i.e., those who direct the child's activities in a rational manner, encouraging verbal give and take, providing reasons behind policies, and displaying a high degree of warmth) are more likely than either authoritarian or permissive parents . . .

Results: . . . to have preschool children who are

a. friendly and cooperative with peers and adults;
b. socially responsible;
c. self-reliant; and
d. interested in achievement (derived from Baumrind, 1971, 1977).

Corollary Principle No. 1

Events: Parent-child interaction

Happenings: *Authoritarian* parents (i.e., those who severely restrict the child's autonomy, use arbitrary or irrational methods of control, and are rather hostile with their children) tend to have . . .

Results: . . . children who are:

a. surly;
b. defiant;
c. uncomfortable in social situations; and
d. lacking in independence.

Corollary Principle No. 2

Events: Parent-child interaction

Happenings: *Permissive* parents (i.e., who do not demand much of their children, do not discourage immature responses, do not actively encourage self-reliant behavior) tend to have . . .

Results: . . . children who are

a. selfish;
b. rebellious;
c. aggressive;
d. rather aimless; and
e. quite low in independence and achievement ("spoiled-brat" syndrome).

The following is an example of a *cause-and-effect principle*:

Events: In a family atmosphere of acceptance and openness . . .

Happenings: . . . whatever any family member thinks and feels can be honestly expressed to any or all members of the family . . .

Results: . . . resulting in

a. an increased sense of self-worth in family members;

b. responsibility of parents for their children and accountability of children to their parents;

c. trust in self and others by all family members;

d. increased ability by individuals and the family as a group to choose effective/functional behavior to cope with strong feelings and stressful situations;

e. self-reliant problem solving by family members;

f. frequent gestures of affection toward one another by family members;

g. frequent and spontaneous acts of service by all family members toward each other and toward those outside the home;

h. frequent times together as a family in enjoyable activities;

i. frequent praise and encouragement of family members by one another.

Although principles basically have cognitive content, they form the basis for the insights that Cluster members can develop as a result of their Cluster experiences.

Insight (continued)

An insight is a selected piece of knowledge that a person applies to his or her personal life after having had a deeply personal experience with that knowledge at an intuitive level. This piece of knowledge looks like it could have special value in the person's life. The person sees that, if this knowledge is put to work, it could prevent something from occurring that the person does not want to happen, or it could enhance the person's life in some worthwhile way. The continued application of the insight would give the person a clearer understanding of self (Mace, 1981). An insight is represented by the following model:

Given X conditions, if I do Y, then Z (*something worthwhile*) will happen.

or

Given X conditions, if I do Y, then Z (*something undesirable*) will *not* happen.

Making such a change in a person's actions, however, always involves a risk. It is always a step into the unknown (Mace, 1981). An example of *insight*, stated in the "I" form of a principle, is

Event:	In a conflict situation . . .
Happening:	. . . when I level (give a direct message) with the other person . . .
Result:	. . . I feel less defensive and more open to the other person's point of view; I'm more willing to accept information from the other person; the other person is more likely to imitate my leveling response; thus there is greater likelihood of our feeling a closer bond and solving the problem to our mutual satisfaction.

It is important that *you* know what insights you wish Cluster members to develop as a result of their learning experiences in Cluster. However, because insights are individual and personal (because they are determined by what is of value to the individual), it probably is not a good idea to share such insight objectives with members of the Cluster.

It is a good idea, however, to determine two or three objectives that *can be shared* with Cluster members at the beginning of each Cluster session. These objectives should be *short*, *related to the experience of Cluster during the session*, and stated in terms of *observable behavior*. For example, here are some behavioral objectives that could be shared with Cluster members (written in big black letters on a large piece of newsprint) related to the Cluster goal of "participate willingly in family celebrations of special occasions":

1. Help your family decide how many jelly beans are in the glass.
2. Participate with your family in making "un-birthday gifts" for members of another family.

3. Participate in the Cluster discussion of special occasions that make us happy.
4. Smile!

Each of these objectives (a) is short, (b) is related to the activities planned for Cluster, and (c) specifies observable behavior.

It is important to determine the goals or aims of learning in Family Cluster; that, however, is not enough. The learning objectives of Family Cluster must be derived from the goals or aims. Objectives in Family Cluster are based on insights, which are personal and are often not articulated. However, insights are derived from principles, which are general statements indicating the relationships to be expected between or among events (correlational principles) or explaining why events occur (cause-and-effect principles). Families become strong families according to principles that can be stated explicitly. Insights can be derived from those principles. Objectives, which are specific and observable, can be derived from those insights. The activities of Cluster are designed to help Cluster members achieve the insights derived from principles related to the development of family strengths.

Once the objectives of Family Cluster have been determined, the next step is to plan each Cluster session agenda. It is easy to skip the planning of goals and objectives, but they are *essential* to the planning of appealing Cluster experiences that are also effective learning experiences (that is, the learners, or Cluster members, achieve the desired learning outcomes or insights).

Case Study, Part B

Matthew and Alice, once they selected, on a first-come first-served basis, four families who applied for Family Cluster from their congregation, made appointments with each family to deliver the Family Strengths Inventory composition form (FSI-CF). At each home they arranged for the family to meet together and complete the form while the leaders waited. They also had the family members sign a Cluster contract (they left a copy for each family), answered questions about Cluster, and collected $20 from each family to cover the supplies that would be needed in Cluster.

A 24-item Family Strengths Inventory (FSI) was later developed unique to that Cluster based on family selections from the FSI-CF, which included three items from each of the eight categories of family strength in the FSI-CF. This new FSI was typed, copied, and delivered to each family during a second quick visit. Each family delivered their FSIs to Matthew and Alice before church services the following Sunday.

On Monday and Tuesday evenings of that week Matthew and Alice compiled the data on the FSIs, item by item, and ranked the FSI items for each family. They then selected the top-ranked three items from each family (that is, items needing the most improvement as perceived by the families—SMITTIs). They were struck by the fact that the families, on the average, perceived themselves as close to ideal on each of the items on the FSI. The lowest average rating in any of the four families (out of a possible −21 or +21) was a −7 on Item 5 in the communication category: "Conversations in our family show lots of caring for one another." The next lowest ranking was a −5.8 for Item 10 relating to the family strength of appreciation: "In our family, we do things for each other that make us feel good about ourselves" (see Exhibit 7A for a sample FSI family profile).

The next task for Matthew and Alice, once they analyzed and ranked the data on the FSIs, was to determine the items for focus during Cluster (that is, those needing most improvement), the themes related to the items, and the dates of Cluster for focus on those themes. They expected some overlap in items needing improvement, which was, indeed, the case on the cohesion item (Item 11): "Family togetherness is very important to us in our family." However, they didn't need to go beyond the three SMITTIs from each family because of the themes related to each and the number of Cluster sessions the families had agreed should be held for this first Cluster experience, which was 15 sessions.

Alice and Matthew knew that three sessions would be devoted to other than FSI items: The first session would be devoted to getting acquainted, the second to determining the Cluster contract or ground rules, and the last session to terminating Cluster activities. That left 12 Cluster sessions that would be devoted to the SMITTIs from the FSIs the family members had completed. Matthew and Alice then planned the following items and themes for the Cluster, which was scheduled to begin the following Monday evening. (These are not in order of their ranking on the FSI.):

Item 1. (Adaptation) In our family, we shift household responsibilities from person to person.
Theme: Doing What Needs to Be Done in Our Home

Item 9. (Adaptation) In our family, parents and children discuss punishment together.
Theme: Punishment Is a Family Affair

Item 2. (Appreciation) In our family, we say things to each other that make us feel good about ourselves.
Theme: Expressing an Attitude of Gratitude

Item 10. (Appreciation) In our family, we do things for each other that make us feel good about ourselves.
Theme: Giving and Receiving in Our Family

Item 3. (Cohesion) We feel closer to one another in our family than we do to people outside our family.
Theme: To Be a Part or Apart?

Item 11. (Cohesion) Family togetherness is very important to us in our family. [Each of two families had this as one of their SMITTIs.]
Theme A: When I Need to Be Alone
Theme B: Having Fun as a Family

Item 5. (Communication) Conversations in our family show lots of caring for one another.
Theme: Talking *with* Instead of *to* Another

Item 6. (Coping with Crises and Stress) We unite as a family to face stress or crisis.
Theme: When the Going Gets Tough, the Tough Get Going

Item 14. (Coping with Crises and Stress) In time of crisis or stress, we communicate to solve our problems.
Theme: When the Going Gets Tough

Item 23. (Time Together) We spend one-on-one time with members of the family.
Theme: Do I Really Know You?

Item 19. (Commitment) In our family, we have traditions, things we always do to celebrate special days.
Theme: Birthdays and Other Special Occasions

These 12 themes (derived from family profiles on the FSI—see Exhibit 7a) will form the basis for the planning of objectives and learning experiences for the 12 Cluster sessions. The first session will be a get-acquainted session, the second will be devoted to developing a set of Cluster ground rules, and the last session will be a special termination session. This will bring the total to 15 sessions for which the Cluster has contracted. Matthew and Alice will use these themes and guides for the remainder of their planning for Cluster sessions.

Notes

1. Information about the Family Strengths Inventory composition form (FSI-CF) can be obtained from the author, together with prices for forms, computation and analysis of the forms, information about preparation of unique Cluster Family Strength Inventories, and ways to use the inventory, by writing to the author as follows:

Dr. Barbara Vance
Professor of Family Sciences
Brigham Young University
Provo, UT 84602

2. I acknowledge the assistance of Dr. Philip B. Daniels, Professor of Psychology at Brigham Young University, who introduced me to the idea of SMITTIs in the use of rating scales such as the Family Strengths Inventory.

References

Ainsworth, M. D. S. (1979). Attachment as related to mother-infant interaction. In J. S.Rosenblatt, R. A. Hinde, C. Beer, & M. Busnel (Eds.), *Advances in the study of behavior* (Vol. 9). New York: Academic Press.

Baumrind, D. (1971). Current patterns of parental authority. *Developmental Psychology Monographs*, 4(1, Pt. 2).

Baumrind, D. (1977, March). *Socialization determinants of personal agency*. Paper presented at the biennial meeting of the Society for Research in Child Development, New Orleans.

Belsky, J., Goode, M. K., & Most, R. K. (1980). Maternal stimulation and infant exploratory competence: Cross-sectional, correlational, and experimental analyses. *Child Development, 51*, 1168–1178.

Guerney, B., Jr., & Guerney, L. F. (1981). Family life education as intervention. *Family Relations, 30*, 591–598.

Heinicke, C. M., Diskin, S. D., Ramsey-Klee, D. M., & Given, K. (1983). Pre-birth parent characteristics and family development in the first year of life. *Child Development, 54*, 194–208.

Mace, D. (1981, October). The long, long trail from information-giving to behavioral change. *Family Relations, 30*(4), 599–606.

Merrill, M. D. (1983). Component display theory. In C. M.Reigeluth (Ed.), *Instructional-design theories and models: An overview of their current status*. Hillsdale, NJ: Lawrence Erlbaum.

Reigeluth, C. M. (1983). Instructional design: What is it and why is it? In C. M.Reigeluth (Ed.), *Instructional design theories and models: An overview of their current status*. Hillsdale, NJ: Lawrence Erlbaum.

Exhibit 7A. Family Strengths Inventory Family Profile

Family Name KENYON Date October 0000

Attached is a bar graph illustrating the Change Index for each of the items on the Family Strengths Inventory for your family. The CI (Change Index) is the Much/Little Average multiplied by the Importance Average. Each bar on the graph represents the CI for your family on that item only. The possible extremes of the CI are +21 (too much) and -21 (too little). The farther the CI to either extreme (+21 or -21), the more important the family thinks that item is and the more improvement they think that item needs. The closer to the center, the less improvement is perceived to be needed by the family as a whole. If the CI has a minus sign, that means the family perceives itself as having too little of that item. If the CI has a plus sign, that means the family perceives itself as having too much of that item. The rank means how the family views the need for improvement in this item compared to the other 23 items on the inventory. The higher the rank (i.e., 1, 2, 3) the more improvement is perceived by families to be needed. The lower the rank (i.e., 22, 23, 24) the less improvement is perceived by family members to be needed.

Adaptability

1. In our family, we shift household responsibilities from person to person.

   Much/Little Avg. -.27 Importance Avg. 4.18 CI -1.13 Rank 17

9. (Item printed)

   Much/Little Avg. -.91 Importance Avg. 4.64 CI -4.22 Rank 2

17. (Item printed)

   Much/Little Avg. -.36 Importance Avg. 4.91 CI -1.77 Rank 9

Appreciation

2. In our family, we say things to each other that make us feel good about ourselves.

   Much/Little Avg. -.64 Importance Avg. 5.36 CI -3.43 Rank 4

10. (Item printed)

   Much/Little Avg. -.09 Importance Avg. 5.91 CI -.53 Rank 22

15. (Item printed)

   Much/Little Ave. -.09 Importance Avg. 6.35 CI -.57 Rank 20

Cohesion

3. We feel closer to one another in our family than we do to people outside our family.

Much/Little Avg. -.27 Importance Avg. 6.00 CI -1.62 Rank 11

11. (Item printed)

Much/Little Avg. -.45 Importance Avg. 5.73 CI -2.58 Rank 6

18. (Item printed)

Much/Little Avg. -.45 Importance Avg. 4.91 CI -2.21 Rank 7

Commitment

4. In our family, the family comes first.

Much/Little Avg. -.36 Importance Avg. 5.36 CI -1.93 Rank 8

12. (Item printed)

Much/Little Avg. 0 Importance Avg. 6.64 CI .00 Rank 24

19. (Item printed)

Much/Little Avg. -.27 Importance Avg. 5.00 CI -1.35 Rank 15

Communication

5. Conversations in our family show lots of caring for one another.

Much/Little Avg. 0 Importance Avg. 5.67 CI .00 Rank 23

13. (Item printed)

Much/Little Avg. -.27 Importance Avg. 5.45 CI -1.47 Rank 14

20. (Item printed)

Much/Little Avg. -.27 Importance Avg. 5.64 CI -1.52 Rank 13

Coping with Crises and Stress

6. We unite as a family to face stress or crisis.

Much/Little Avg. -.27 Importance Avg. 5.82 CI -1.57 Rank 12

(Coping with Crises and Stress, cont'd)

14. (Item printed)

Much/Little Avg. -.18 Importance Avg. 5.64 CI -1.02 Rank 18

21. (Item printed)

Much/Little Avg. -.55 Importance Avg. 5.36 CI -2.95 Rank 5

Spiritual Wellness

7. In our family, we have a sense that a power greater than ourselves guides our lives.

Much/Little Avg. -.18 Importance Avg. 6.82 CI -1.23 Rank 16

22. (Item printed)

Much/Little Avg. -.09 Importance Avg. 6.35 CI -.57 Rank 21

24. (Item printed)

Much/Little Avg. -.64 Importance Avg. 5.45 CI -3.49 Rank 3

Time Together

8. We have meals together often as a family.

Much/Little Avg. -.36 Importance Avg. 4.82 CI -1.74 Rank 10

16. (Item printed)

Much/Little Avg. -.09 Importance Avg. 6.36 CI -.57 Rank 19

23. (Item printed)

Much/Little Avg. -.91 Importance Avg. 6.09 CI -5.54 Rank 1

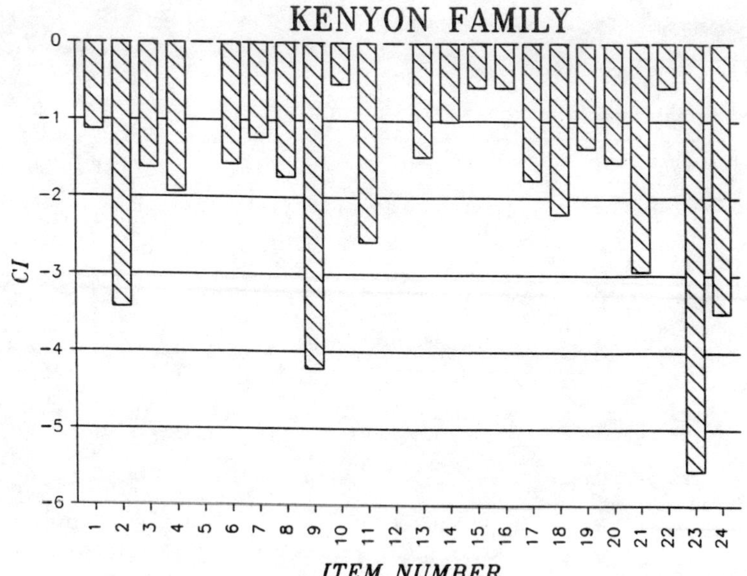
KENYON FAMILY
0
-1
-2
-3
-4
-5
-6
CI
1
2
3
4
5
6
7
8
9
10
11
12
13
14
15
16
17
18
19
20
21
22
23
24
ITEM NUMBER

8. Planning the Cluster Session Agenda Plan

In education classes, they call it a lesson plan. In Family Cluster, I call it a session agenda plan.

A *session agenda plan* is a detailed plan for each session of Family Cluster. It includes the session theme, the principle on which the insight focus of the session is based (see previous chapter on goals and objectives), and the objectives for the session, as well as detailed instructions for each activity on the agenda for the session.

I ask the LITs I train to write very detailed session plans. (I have included several such examples of Cluster session plans at the end of this chapter—see the exhibits.) I would not expect such detail in writing for every Cluster session led by Cluster leaders. Sometimes just a simple listing of Cluster activities, together with the timing of each and the necessary materials, equipment, and supplies, is all that is necessary to assist Cluster leaders in making appropriate preparations and to remind Cluster leaders what is coming up next. However, the leaders of the Cluster with less detailed agenda plans in writing should make sure they discuss the specific agenda items of each session in enough detail that each knows exactly what the outline for the agenda means and which leader will be doing what on the agenda plan outline.

The following is a suggested agenda schedule for a weekly Cluster session lasting one and one-half hours (90 minutes). This period of time does not allow for a meal:

15 minutes—gathering activities designed to involve each Cluster member immediately upon arrival

20 minutes—Cluster meeting to discuss what has been going on during the week and to engage in some weekly Cluster rituals such as singing

10 minutes—game time, which involves all Cluster members and increases the energy level following the Cluster meeting

40 minutes—theme activity, family activities focusing on the theme; includes processing (see Chapter 13)

5 minutes—closure, ending the session, singing

(Refreshments served at end of Cluster session)

If a meal is included in the Cluster session agenda plan, the following schedule (now a two-hour—or 120-minute—schedule) is recommended:

15 minutes—gathering activities as Cluster families arrive

30 minutes—meal

20 minutes—Cluster meeting

10 minutes—game time

40 minutes—theme activity including processing

5 minutes—closure

(Refreshments served at the end of the Cluster session)

The remainder of this chapter discusses each of the major items on the Cluster session agenda plan.

Objectives

The previous chapter discussed the idea that Cluster focuses on insight through experience. Insight is based on principle. Given a principle (e.g., about self-esteem or communication), you plan two or three objectives related to the experiences of Cluster that you will share with the Cluster members, that is, specific behaviors that you expect to be accomplished during the session's activities. These objectives should be printed on a large piece of paper (newsprint is good, or butcher paper, although it is far more expensive) tacked or taped to a wall or door along with the session agenda outline and gathering instructions, so Cluster members can see them immediately upon entering Cluster.

Gathering (15 minutes)

In general, not all families arrive at Cluster at the same time. People tend to wander in when they arrive, seemingly somewhat tentative about what they should do when they arrive. It takes a few minutes to make the adjustment from "not-Cluster" to Cluster activities. The gathering is designed to accomplish this adjustment in as painless and fun a fashion as possible.

Gathering can capture the interest of each person when it is something related to the theme and yet is simple and relatively nonthreatening and is expected of each Cluster member once he or she arrives. This can be as simple as handing each person 10 beans and requesting everyone to mill around chatting with one another asking questions of one another. The point of the gathering experience is for each person to collect as many beans as possible by getting people to answer "yes" to some questions. A person must give up a bean every time he or she says "yes."

Gathering is an opportunity for leaders to be creative with ideas about how to capture the interest of Cluster members as they arrive. Ideas that at first may seem poor may turn out to be Cluster favorites. The focus should be appeal and ease of activity, something that *each* Cluster member can do and might wish to do for a little fun.

For instance, the members in Clusters I have led get a big kick out of making name headbands, usually out of computer printout paper. They are instructed to make a headband (using computer printouts and masking tape) and to write their names on the headband. That is where the fun begins. Each name, when it is written on the headband, should be preceded by an adjective that describes the person and begins with the first letter of the first name (such as Mighty Matt, Dancing Donna, Little Liza), or the first name should be printed on the headband with another word that rhymes with the first name (such as Dizzy Lizzy or Silly Willy). Later, as the Cluster gathers in a big circle on the carpet, we play the Name Game, where each person says his or her own name out loud and then names each person who has come before in the circle by the name written on the headband (see sample agenda session plan for the first session of Cluster at the end of this chapter). This is not only a fun way to get acquainted but some of the name combinations are never forgotten during Cluster. Sometimes we call one another by the two names when we greet each other outside of Cluster (e.g., "Caring Claude"). It helps to bond us together as well as to know one another's names.

Gathering experiences should be simple, "do-able" for every Cluster member, and possible to be cut off quickly for the next activity on the agenda. One time I made the mistake of having Cluster members make hats out of newspapers and computer printouts and decorate them any way they wished. Valentine's Day was later that week, so I had red and white construction paper plus any other "beautiful junque" I could find in my office and at home to give a Valentine motif to hats. Cluster members became so engrossed making their "chapeau creations" that they didn't want to stop for the next activity. Cluster ran overtime that evening (which is unacceptable). But, more important, a perfectly wonderful activity was used at the wrong place in the agenda plan for the Cluster session (it could have been a very effective theme experience later).

Meal (30 minutes)

If the Cluster includes a meal (and, therefore, is a two-hour—120-minute—session), the meal should follow the gathering.

Why a meal? It isn't necessary to have a meal together to have an effective Cluster. However, there are a couple of reasons why I have included a meal in our Clusters. First, when people eat together, they usually relax and enjoy the bonding fellowship that comes from "breaking bread" together. Generally, many of those times in the lives of families and friends that carry the fondest memories are those where they have shared a meal together, whether a special celebration such as an anniversary, a holiday picnic such as the Fourth of July, a wedding feast, or two friends sharing a lunch together after weeks or months of separation.

Second, having a meal together in Cluster can avoid the last-minute panic of getting the family fed before Cluster begins. That is the primary reason I decided it would be a good idea for our Cluster to have a sandwich meal. We hold our Cluster sessions at the university on Monday evenings because the major church in the area encourages and sponsors family home evening on Monday evenings. That is a good time for our Cluster to meet because Monday evening is usually set aside for family home evening in most homes in the area. Cluster is a superb way for the family to be together during that special family together time. However, our past experience has indicated that some of the families in our Clusters arrived late because they were hurrying to complete the evening meal. Now our Cluster families bring a sandwich meal with them to each Cluster session. We encourage them to pack simple foods. In addition, each family takes turns with the other families bringing refreshments for everyone. Refreshments are served at the end of Cluster, not at the end of the meal. We have noticed the families are more relaxed during Cluster, possibly because orchestrating the busy schedules of family members to fit in an evening meal before Cluster is no longer the problem it once was.

It is important, however, that rituals become a part of the meal at Cluster. For instance, all our Cluster families are of the same religious faith. It is customary in that faith to say grace before the meal begins. Sometimes we sing a short song before one of our Cluster members says grace. It takes about five minutes at the end of the meal for us to clean up and get settled in a circle for the next activity on the agenda.

We sit on the carpet in a big circle to eat our meals together. This, we found, allows more conversation between people across families. When we used tables for the meal, we discovered that families were sitting in exclusive family groups. As a matter of fact, they were becoming very possessive about their table space, making it difficult to get people to move from space to space during the remaining activities of the Cluster session.

This means that people should come to Cluster dressed for sitting on the floor, which usually means jeans or slacks for the women. Clothes that restrict activity are not appropriate for Cluster.

Once the meal is over, the Cluster meeting can begin.

Cluster Meeting (20 minutes)

It is not necessary to hold a Cluster meeting. However, I have found that Cluster members like to meet for a few minutes to talk informally about some things not particularly related to the session theme. They like to sing songs, as well, and this is a good time to sing. If all members share the same religious faith, and a meal is not eaten together earlier, Cluster meeting is a good time to have a prayer together.

Cluster meeting is a time to talk about special events that have occurred since the last Cluster session in the lives of Cluster members, such as birthdays, wedding anniversaries, new jobs, or high school or college graduation. The father in one of our Clusters had lost his job and missed one of our Cluster sessions while visiting another state for job interviews. When he returned with the good news that he had been offered and had accepted the position, Cluster meeting gave us a chance to congratulate him and support the family in the move they would make soon after our last Cluster session.

One of our Cluster fathers told us about a fire he had helped fight during the preceding week, a spectacular fire that was in the news for several days afterward. The TV news had reported the daring rescue of someone in the building by one of the firemen. Our Cluster father was that man (he is a fireman and paramedic). He gave us details we never would have heard on TV or read in the newspaper.

We have a ritual at the end of Cluster meeting that all of us enjoy and look forward to. During the first Cluster session, I had read *The Warm Fuzzy Tale* (Claude Steiner, 1977) to the group. I discovered this little picture book at a professional conference and decided to share it with Cluster because the focus of Cluster is relationships and affirmation of one another. I also made some "Warm Fuzzies" out of colored pom-poms, felt, and eyelets I had purchased from a craft shop. I randomly handed out about 10 Warm Fuzzies after the story to Cluster members, "just because." A ritual relating to Warm Fuzzies during Cluster meeting developed after that. I made a whole bunch of Warm Fuzzies and gave four to each family each week to give to anyone in Cluster they wished. I also gave four each week to Cluster members in addition to the ones I handed to a parent in each family. Now the giving of Warm Fuzzies is an important ritual in our Cluster meetings.

Singing is an important part of Cluster. There is the adage that "the family that prays together, stays together." Maybe a new adage could be "the family that sings (or attends Cluster) together, stays together." Our songs are simple and sometimes accompanied by guitar or uke. The Cluster meeting is an opportunity for us to sing our favorite songs. It helps to bond us together.

It is amazing how little some families converse with one another. Conversations in too many families consist of parents "commanding" their children to do something. The Cluster meeting allows leaders to model how conversations can begin. For instance, a simple question like "Has anyone had something special happen this week?" can lead to sharing by several Cluster members and the acknowledgment of such sharing by Cluster leaders. Such acknowledgment models reinforcement of statements by others that generate relaxed conversation. Such conversation time during Cluster meeting also helps children to recognize that what they say in Cluster is just as important as what the adults say.

Game (10 minutes)

A game following Cluster meeting is generally an effective way to make the transition from Cluster meeting to the theme experience. It also changes the energy level, which may be desirable following Cluster meeting.

The game should be closely tied to the theme for the evening and should be short, simple, fun to play, and possible for all Cluster members to play.

A word of caution: Sometimes adults and older children get so enthusiastic about playing a game that they forget the smaller children in their midst. This frightens some children and can result in tears, which can dampen the spirits in a Cluster, to say the least! People have a tendency to get so competitive in games that they forget themselves. Sometimes stopping the game and gently reminding them of the smaller children is all that is necessary. Cluster, including game time, is for *everybody* in Cluster. Games should be planned to include and involve everyone.

Theme Activity (40 minutes)

The activity of Cluster reaches a climax during the theme activity, the longest item on the session agenda, the one focusing on the theme for the session, the one designed to prepare participants to achieve major insights related to the theme principle (see sample agenda session plans at the end of this chapter).

Although the theme experience is the major learning activity for the session, it should not become a "tell and regurgitate" activity, with the leaders telling Cluster members what they should be learning and Cluster participants, in turn, repeating what they have learned. Instead, this should be a carefully planned experience focusing on the theme, where Cluster families have the opportunity to work on an interesting activity that is later "processed" through a series of questions by one of the leaders (see Chapter 13). Processing is designed to help Cluster members recognize ways they can apply the theme principle in their own families (insight).

Theme experiences should be appealing, unusual, and planned to involve each family at a maximum level. This is a time for Cluster leaders to stretch their imaginations and become creative with new possibilities for family involvement with an important principle of relationship—the theme.

For instance, during one Cluster session I conducted, we (coleaders) handed each family a large paper bag in which were leaves, pieces of colored construction paper, long pieces of string, paste, and a variety of other miscellaneous materials that might be used to make leis for other members of the Cluster. Inside each bag was a card with the family name of one of the other Cluster families, the names of the individuals in that family, and instructions to make a lei for each person in that family. Until a later signal, each family was instructed not to reveal for which other family they were making leis. The theme was nonverbal communication. Families were instructed to spend five minutes planning how they were going to make the leis. Then they had fifteen minutes to make the leis—in silence.

At the end of the lei-making period, families, with guidance from the leader of that Cluster activity, presented leis silently to those for whom they had made them. This was the fifth session of the Cluster. Cluster members were well acquainted with each other. This experience of communicating nonverbally was touching and poignant for everyone in the Cluster. Tears were freely shed.

During processing, after all the leis had been presented, people responded to questions often with tears in their eyes and lumps in their throats. It was difficult for people to articulate insights that grew from this bonding, affirmative experience. They were still too close to it. Sometimes our greatest insights cannot be explained but, nevertheless, affect our future behavior in ways difficult to imagine. After this particular Cluster session it was more difficult than usual for Cluster members to say good-bye after closure and refreshments. They seemed to hunger more for the bonding—the togetherness—than for the refreshments. I'm sure there were many conversations in Cluster families that following week about what they had experienced in Cluster during the theme experience with the leis.

Role-playing, family sculpting, puppets, drawing life-size silhouettes, viewing a videotape, listening to an audiocassette tape, sculpting with clay, reading picture books out loud, engaging in group imagery experiences, making cards to give to others, reading poetry, miming, and singing songs are just a few of the activities that can be focused on any given theme. Sawin (1979) includes many additional activities appropriate for theme experiences.

A *play corner* for the younger children in the Cluster might be used during the processing of a theme experience. This should be a quiet place where young children (toddlers and preschoolers) can slip away to play with dolls, stuffed animals, "squeezy" toys, dress-up clothes, crayons and paper, and picture books. It should not interfere with other Cluster activities, including discussions, but should be a place for children to "get the wiggles out" and enjoy activity away from the Cluster group. Agreement should be reached during the discussion of Cluster ground rules (probably in the second session) about how the play corner will be used, including who will use it and how it will be supervised.

The last 10 minutes of the theme experience should be reserved for processing the experience (see Chapter 13). This is the opportunity for Cluster members to explore the meaning of the activity just experienced and to derive insights they can implement when appropriate in the future. Processing is *very important*, possibly the most important experience of the Cluster session. Some leaders might want to skip this very important segment of the theme experience because they have had little experience leading discussions and because families might be so involved in a given activity for the theme experience that they won't want to quit. A Cluster theme experience is incomplete without processing. Processing allows Cluster members to achieve closure relative to the theme for the session.

Closure (5 minutes)

Closure is the opportunity to summarize what has happened during the session, for leaders to give additional affirmation to

Cluster members, and to review something to be thought about, discussed, or accomplished during the week in each family. If "homework" should be assigned (such as Cluster members bringing self-portraits of themselves at the beginning of the next Cluster session—see sample session agenda plan for Sessions 1 and 2 at the end of this chapter), closure is the time to make the homework assignment and to discuss and clarify it. It is also the time to sing a favorite song, engage in a favorite "good-bye" ritual, and perhaps have a closing prayer (if all members desire it and it is included in the Cluster contract or ground rules).

Refreshments

Refreshments can be served immediately at the end of the Cluster session. Then the family assigned cleanup duty can clean up while Cluster members take their leave.

I have noticed that the better acquainted Cluster members become and the more time in Cluster they experience together, the longer it takes them to say good-bye to one another. This is valuable time. It should not be hurried. At the same time, leaders need to consult with each other immediately following the session to evaluate the session and to plan the next session (see Chapter 15 on Cluster evaluation). It is difficult to do this when Cluster members want to talk. Don't expect them to read your mind. Let them know during one of the Cluster meetings early on what needs to be done when everyone is gone. Usually people will accommodate your plans if you let them know what goes on behind the scenes.

It also might be a good idea to have a colorfully wrapped (old shoe box) suggestion box by the door, with a pencil and sheets of plain paper nearby. Encourage Cluster members to write (unsigned) suggestions for making a more effective Cluster and drop their suggestions through a slot in the suggestion box. During Cluster meeting, if any suggestions involve changes in ground rules or Cluster agenda, these need to be discussed in Cluster until consensus is reached. Avoid making decisions that should be made by the Cluster as a whole. Cluster members may learn some important lessons about open communication, decision making, and commitment when such negotiation occurs in Cluster.

One of the reasons it is so difficult to evaluate effectiveness of Family Cluster is because each Cluster has a unique program. Indeed, each Family Cluster is unique, not like any other Cluster. This is as it should be.

Each Cluster session agenda should be planned with the needs of that particular Cluster in mind. Family Cluster provides unusual freedom of choice and possibility for creativity for leaders to plan and provide experiences for families to grow stronger and more effective in their relationships with one another.

I frequently remind those I train to plan well the "geography" of each Cluster session. It isn't enough to have a general idea of what should be done. Details are important. It is important to know exactly what materials and equipment will be required when, and what each leader will be doing during each activity on the session agenda. It's also important to have a picture in your mind of the geography of activity in the Cluster room. You should have a good idea of what people will be doing and where, as well as how long it will take them.

Undoubtedly there will be some stress involved in planning and conducting Family Cluster, especially when doing it for the first time. No matter how well we know the members of our Clusters, there is always something unexpected that will happen. The best rule of thumb is to expect the unexpected. Whatever happens during Cluster, it can become a much more satisfying experience for leaders and Cluster members if the session agendas are well planned to meet the perceived needs of the members of the Cluster.

References

Sawin, M. M. (1979). *Family enrichment with family clusters*. Valley Forge, PA: Judson.

Steiner, C., with pictures by Dick, J. A. (1977). *The original Warm Fuzzy tale*. Rolling Hills Estates, CA: JALMAR. (Available from JALMAR Press, 45 Hitching Post Dr., Bldg. 22B, Rolling Hills Estates, CA 90274)

Exhibit 8A *FAMILY CLUSTER SESSION AGENDA PLAN*

Session 1
FSI Item: None (this is the first session of Cluster)
Theme: Beginnings (Getting Acquainted)
Principle: When people in a group know each other and experience affirmation consistently, they are more likely individually to develop a sense of acceptance in, belonging in, and commitment to the group.
Objectives (to share with our Cluster):

1. Learn the name of each person in our Cluster.
2. Learn something about each family.
3. Share information about yourself and your family with other members of the Cluster.

Leader Instructions—Before Cluster Begins
Materials and supplies needed:

Butcher paper to make three signs and a family shield for each Cluster family

Newsprint to print songs, signs, and instructions

Paper to make name tags

Masking tape strips to attach name tags to blouses/shirts

Colored markers to make name tags (three sets of colored markers: one for name tags, one for use on the Family Cluster Map, and one for signing in at Our Family Cluster)

Scissors to cut name tags

Leaders should be in the Cluster room to set up for the session at least one hour before the Cluster session begins. Plan the "geography" of the session well in advance and then set up the room according to the plan. Families often arrive early, so everything should be in readiness at least 15 minutes before the designated time for the beginning of the Cluster session.

Before coming to the Cluster room to set up, the following signs should be made. *First*, a large sign on butcher paper titled "Our Family Cluster" should be made that has the name of each family in our Cluster printed in large letters followed by a space under each family name for each member of the family attending the Cluster to sign in.

A *second sign* should be made on butcher paper that shows a representation map of the areas from which the families come so each family can draw an X and the name of the family in the appropriate "city."

A *third sign* can be printed on newsprint. This is the instruction sign for the gathering experience as the families enter. The sign should read as follows:

Instructions for Family Cluster Members

Please do the following as soon as you arrive:

1. Go to the "Name Tag" table and do the following:
   a. Select a sheet of paper and a marker pen
   b. Cut or draw or tear the paper to show something you like to do
   c. Put on the paper in large letters the name you like to be called
   d. Attach your name tag to your blouse or shirt with a piece of masking tape
2. Go to "Our Family Cluster" sheet and sign your name under your family name
3. Go to "Our Family Cluster Map" as a family, mark an "X" in the area where you live, and print the last name of your family by the "X"
4. Introduce yourself to as many members of the Family Cluster as possible by what you had for breakfast this morning (such as, "Hello, I'm orange juice and corn flakes")

A *fourth sign,* in newsprint, should show the objectives for the session and the session schedule.

A *fifth sign,* in newsprint, should have the words to the "Whobody Song" as follows:

Who is a whobody right here?
Who is a whobody we'll cheer?
(Say name)
Somebody special,
Somebody rare,
Somebody for whom we can care.

A *sixth sign,* in newsprint, should have the words to the "Family Song" as follows:

Sometimes we go left,
Sometimes we go right,
Sometimes we are happy,
Sometimes we're up tight!

Figure 8.1. Music for the "Family Song" (Richard Nystrom)

Chorus:
But we're a family, yes we are, yes we are.
But we're a family, yes we are!

Sometimes we are scared,
Sometimes we're o.k.
Sometimes it's like night,
Sometimes it's like day.
(Repeat chorus)

Sometimes we are cold,
Sometimes we are hot,
Sometimes we are loving,
Sometimes we are not.
(Repeat chorus)

Sometimes we're together,
Sometimes we're apart,
Sometimes we are foolish,
Sometimes we are smart!
(Repeat chorus)

In addition, a shield should be drawn on a piece of butcher paper, one for each family in the cluster. This prepared butcher paper will be used during the theme activity. Also required for that same activity will be scissors, paste in small plastic containers (one for each Cluster family), colored marker pens, and a variety of old magazines that can be cut up.

The Cluster room should be set up so that the carpet is cleared almost entirely for floor activity. The sign with the Cluster session objectives and schedule should be taped to one side of the chalkboard, and the signs with the words to the two songs should be taped to the right side of the chalkboard, with the "Whobody Song" taped over the "Family Song" so it can be lifted back easily. The instructions for gathering should be taped to the easel near the entrance so they will catch the eye of Cluster members as they enter the room. "Our Family Cluster" should be on a low table so children can sign it as easily as adults. A container of marker pens should be on the table with this sheet. Another low table should have the family map, with some marker pens on the same table. A third table should be designated the "name tag" table and should contain sheets of colored construction paper cut in sizes approximately 4 × 6. There should also be marker pens, scissors, and strips of masking tape with which people can tape the name tag to the shirt or blouse.

A place for Cluster families to leave their sandwich meal should be prepared before Cluster begins so families can store their meal items quickly and easily and then immediately get involved with gathering activities.

Leaders should be ready to greet family members at least 15 minutes before Cluster is scheduled to begin. As family members enter, leaders can assist them in hanging up wraps, reading the instructions, signing the Family Cluster map, making name tags, and introducing themselves.

Leaders start the introduction part of the gathering by shaking hands with each Cluster member and introducing themselves by what they had for breakfast that morning (e.g., "Hello, I'm orange juice and cracked wheat," "Hello, I'm nothing," and so on). Leaders establish the energy level at the beginning of the Cluster. Enthusiastic team leaders will result in enthusiastic Cluster members.

SCHEDULE

GATHERING (6:00–6:30 P.M.)

Name tags
Our Family Cluster Map
Our Family Cluster—sign in

SANDWICH MEAL (6:30–6:50 P.M.)

All members of the Cluster get their food and sit in family groups to eat their sandwiches together. This can be done while seated on the floor picnic-style. Chairs can be made available for those who prefer to sit on chairs.

CLUSTER MEETING (6:50–7:20 P.M.)

Song: "New River Train" with adaptations
Introduce people who signed "Our Family Cluster"

Locate each Cluster family on "Our Family Cluster Map"
Discuss what we are grateful for tonight
Read *A Warm Fuzzy Tale*
Presentation of Warm Fuzzies (this will become a Cluster meeting ritual)

Leader Instructions for Cluster Meeting
Materials and supplies:

Baritone uke or guitar
About 10 Warm Fuzzies
The picture book: *Warm Fuzzy Tale* (Steiner, 1977)

As people complete their sandwich meal, a leader with a baritone uke or guitar sits on the floor and begins to strum chords and sing the words of the following song:

New River Train
We're waiting for the New River train;
Waiting for the New River train;
The same old train that brought us here
Will be taking us home again.

As people gather around on the carpet, the leader asks individual Cluster members to name "exotic" forms of transportation (e.g., a pink elephant, a yellow albatross, a fat ostrich, a three-wheelie, a blue Cadillac, a helicopter) and uses that form in the song, such as

We're waiting for the new pink elephant;
Waiting for the new pink elephant;
The same pink elephant that brought us here
Will be taking us home again.

The other leader then brings "Our Family Cluster" sheet over to the chalkboard. The leader conducting this part of the session then asks each family on the chart to stand up, family by family, and then each person in the family is introduced (everybody repeats the first and last name of each person; this assists in the learning process by adding sight of the written name with the sight of the person and the spoken name of the person).

The "Our Family Cluster" sheet is then attached to the wall with masking tape and "Our Family Cluster Map" is brought to the front of the group by the other leader. A representative of each family shows where each family lives on the map.

Next, the leader reads *The Warm Fuzzy Tale*. It probably is best to sit on a low chair so all can see as the leader turns the pages and reads the book. Ask members to talk about what they heard in the story, what they liked most about it, what message they got from the story, and so on (that is, process the book).

Show the Cluster a Warm Fuzzy. Indicate that it represents something each of us has plenty of inside ourselves—love. Then hand out the Fuzzies to members of the Cluster, telling each person who receives one something positive you have noticed about that person (e.g., "You helped __________ take off her coat and find a place to hang it up"; "You worked really hard trying to get acquainted with the members of the Cluster"; "You had a smile on your face when you entered Cluster tonight"; "I felt good when you gave me a cheerful hello tonight"; and so on).

Tell the Cluster that each week there will be a few Warm Fuzzies distributed to each family. Each family will be able to hand out their Warm Fuzzies as they wish to other Cluster members. It isn't always necessary to tell others why they are getting Fuzzies, just as it isn't always necessary to tell someone why we are giving them a big hug. Warm Fuzzies represent the warm feelings we have for others. They represent something we *always* have inside of us.

GAME (7:20–7:30 P.M.)

Zip-Zap [game]

Leader Instructions for Game

The "Zip-Zap" game is a circle game designed to assist Cluster members in learning one another's names. All Cluster members stand in a circle holding hands. Once the circle is formed, everyone drops hands to the side.

One person is "it" and quickly goes from person to person pointing and saying either "Zip" or "Zap" before quickly counting to 10. If he or she says "Zip," the person pointed to must name the person on his or her *right*. If "it" says "Zap," the person pointed to must name the person on his or her *left*. If "it" finishes counting to 10 before a correct response, the person in the circle becomes "it." The game continues for approximately 10 minutes (or less if people begin to tire of it). One of the challenges is for each new "it" to learn the names of the persons to the left and right when he or she gets a new place in the circle.

It's a good idea for the leader in charge of the game to model how to play the game. Otherwise, Cluster members may "drag their feet."

Cluster members are just getting acquainted with each other and may be reluctant, at first, to play. The model established by the leader will help to set the energy level for this activity. Cluster members have just finished sitting during the Cluster meeting. They may be reluctant to move. This "inertia" may occur at any change in activity. It is up to the leader to change the energy level for each Cluster activity.

THEME ACTIVITY (7:30–7:55 P.M.)

Our Family Values Shield

Processing of Theme Activity

Song: "Whobody Song"

Leader Instructions for Theme Activity

Materials and Supplies:

A piece of butcher paper, with a shield drawn on it, for each Cluster family

A box of colored markers in a container for each family (container can be an empty plastic cottage cheese container or something similar)

A bunch of old magazines that have pictures of all kinds (sometimes these can be gathered from the offices of local MDs and dentists)

Paste in a container for each family

Newsprint sheet with "Whobody Song" printed on it

Hand out to each family a piece of butcher paper on which has been drawn a shield. Instruct each family to use the markers and magazines to create representations on their shield of the values that are important to the family (such as sports, love, responsibility, kindness, travel). Allow 10 minutes for families to make their shields. Give them a one-minute warning before a quick cleanup (the major cleanup can be done at the end of the session).

When the shields are ready, have individual families volunteer to describe their shields. As each family completes the description, sing the "Whobody Song" to the family and everybody clap for the family (set the model).

Families likely will be reluctant to stop the shield-making activity. Recognize this difficulty, and give the families a two-minute warning when cleanup time is approaching. Help to set the energy level for the change to sitting in a large group again to describe each shield.

Process what has happened after the families have described their shields. Start the discussion by asking such questions as the following:

1. How did your family go about making the shield? How were assignments made? How did you decide what values you wanted to portray on the shield?
   (Identify phase)
2. What did you like about making the shield?
   (Analysis phase)
3. What were you feeling as you made the shield?
   (Analysis phase)
4. What did you learn about yourself as you made the shield?
   (Generalize phase)
5. What did you learn about your family as you made the shield?
   (Generalize phase)

Don't rush this process. Accept the statements as they are made (i.e., restate them in your own words or ask clarifying questions to provide affirming experiences for those volunteering information). It might then be appropriate to ask families to share what they have learned about other families in the Cluster that will help them to feel closer to them.
CLOSURE (7:55–8:00 P.M.)

Song: "Family Song"
Homework assignments

Leader Instructions for Closure

Closure provides an opportunity for the Cluster to draw together in a unifying experience that brings the Cluster to a close. Talk about some of the things that have been learned about families tonight and how each family can be lots of things and yet it is OK to be whatever they are. Then sing the "Family Song" and encourage the Cluster members to join in. (The "Whobody Song" should have been lifted up and away from the "Family Song" before this song is sung.)

Then talk about preparations for the next Cluster. Ask each member of the Cluster to take a piece of paper home and draw a self-portrait and bring it to the next Cluster session. Also ask each family to make a list of all the names of the people in the Cluster they can remember and bring the list with them to the next Cluster.

Exhibit 8B *FAMILY CLUSTER SESSION AGENDA PLAN*

Session 2
FSI Item: None (must develop a Cluster contract before focusing on FSI items)
Theme: The Rules We Live by (Developing a Cluster contract/set of ground rules)
Principle: When people in a group help determine the rules they live by, the rules are posted where everyone can see them, and each person in the group commits him- or herself to those rules, there is greater likelihood that the members will take responsibility for their actions, will enjoy the group experience together, and will keep the rules to which the entire group is committed.
Objectives:

1. Learn the name of each person in the Cluster.
2. Assist in developing a set of Ground Rules for our Cluster.
3. Commit yourself to the Ground Rules by any form of signature you and your family choose.
4. Participate in all Cluster activities during the session.

SCHEDULE

GATHERING (6:00–6:20 P.M.)

1. Self-portraits to (Name of Leader) [number each on front with the name of person in pencil on the back]
2. Headbands [with your first name and a word that describes you beginning with the first letter of your name, such as "Mighty" Matt, "Adorable" Ann, or an adjective that rhymes with your first name, such as "Dizzy Lizzie"—print name at least one inch high with dark-colored marker on headband; put the headband on your head]
3. Get-Acquainted Circle [each person tells own name, with adjective or rhyme, and names each person named before him or her, including the appropriate adjective or rhymed word; when the last person names self and everyone in group, then person who started the game names everyone in the group]

SANDWICH MEAL (6:20–6:45 P.M.)

All Cluster members sit in family groups to eat their sandwich meal together.

Before meal begins, group sings a song of grace before the meal.

CLUSTER MEETING (6:45–7:05 p.m)

1. "Warm Fuzzies" (storybook)—ask questions about specifics in the book and what "Warm Fuzzy" means
2. "Warm Fuzzies" for Cluster members (by team leader)—sing "Warm Fuzzy Round" from last week
3. Songs: "Family Song" [from last week]

"Whobody Song" (sing to each *family* rather than each individual, as was done last week)

Ask, "Who is a Whobody?" Reply: "I am!" [everybody together]

"Magic Penny" [new song: teach; printed on newsprint]

[Describe the agenda for this session—announce that next week Cluster activities will begin focusing on themes that Cluster families perceived needed improvement after completing the Family Strengths Inventory]
Game (7:05–7:30 P.M.)

Self-portraits (leader needs a master sheet listing each person in Cluster with numbers of portraits listed on the sheet beside each person's name) [each person needs a game sheet and a pencil]

THEME EXPERIENCE (7:30–7:55 P.M.)

Discuss what it means to make a promise.

Discuss what it means to keep promises.

(Show family contracts; who signed; what each family member who signed promised to do)

Areas where we need rules: use of bathroom [where it is and when we can go, especially little ones]; arriving on time and leaving on time [so leaders can have a meeting right afterward, so assigned family can clean up, so all can get to bed on time, and so on]; what children should call adults, and so on; how to make suggestions [suggestion box? how to tell someone—don't just complain]; Cluster dates coming up and what the themes will be; child tending [who is responsible]; use of quiet corner [play corner] for children; any problems that have already come up

Each family makes its own list of suggested Cluster rules (give each family a marker and a large piece of newsprint); then read each family's rules, write the rules on a large piece of newsprint or butcher paper, and agree by consensus on the rules after each family's suggested rules are read

CLOSURE (7:55–8:00 P.M.)

"Alice's Camel"
"Family Song"

Exhibit 8C *FAMILY CLUSTER SESSION AGENDA PLAN*

FSI Item (Cohesion): Family togetherness is very important to us in our family.
Theme: When I Need to Be Alone (first of two themes related to this FSI item)
Principle: When people openly and honestly experience their own space and time alone when they desire and need it, they are less likely to interrupt others without asking permission, are more likely to provide space and privacy to other individuals when they need it, and are more likely to feel close to other members of the family and enjoy being with family members.
Objectives:

1. Recognize the times when you need time and space alone.
2. Recognize that other people need space and time in their own individual ways.
3. Allow others to have privacy, to have times alone and space alone.

Before Cluster members arrive, hang on the wall a large banner with the words: DO YOU NEED YOUR SPACE?
GATHERING (6:00–6:15 P.M.)
Cluster activities:

Name tags
"Outer-space" hats

Leader instructions:

Name tags: Have colored paper, paper plates (the least expensive kind), and glue as well as gummed stars and yarn cut in two-foot lengths (as many pieces as there are Cluster members) spread out on a table before Cluster members arrive. Have each Cluster member write his or her name on a paper plate and decorate the paper plate. Hang the paper plate around each person's neck like a giant necklace by punching two holes in it and attaching the yarn through the holes. (Paper punch should be handy for use in punching holes in paper plates.)

Outer-space hats: Provide small paper cups, styrofoam balls (very small), pipe cleaners, glitter, gummed stars, curling ribbon (like Christmas wrapping ribbon), or yarn cut in two-foot strips on a separate table from the name tag table. Help Cluster members, using the materials on the table, each attach outer-space-looking headgear by using the materials provided. Each member should tie on the "hat" with the ribbon or yarn. Use a paper punch to punch holes through the paper cups. Paper cups can be the "ears" of the "outer-space" headgear. Pipe cleaner can be strung out of the end of the cup, to which is attached a styrofoam ball. [It might help Cluster members if a sample "outer-space hat" were available as a model.]

Gathering ends when each person has a "paper-plate" name tag and an "outer-space" hat.

SANDWICH MEAL (6:15–6:45 P.M.)

Everyone eats their sandwiches together.

CLUSTER MEETING (6:45–7:00 P.M.)

Cluster Activities:

- Transition Song (Cluster or leader choice)
- Warm Fuzzies
- Games
- Space Stations (make)

Materials and supplies:

- About 12 Warm Fuzzies to hand out to the families [4 to each family]
- Guitar or baritone uke
- Balloons (one each) tied with a length of yarn or string
- Play-dough (salt-flour clay: 3 parts flour to 1 part salt, mixed with water and food coloring to make a soft claylike dough); enough dough (about the size of a large grapefruit) for each family
- Transition song printed on newsprint and posted for all to see

Instructions: As the families finish their meal, begin the Cluster Transition Song (see Chapter 9 for suggestions), with someone playing the guitar or autoharp. Encourage Cluster members to sing along with the person accompanying and singing the song (song words should be printed on newsprint and displayed) and to gather together on the rug around the leader who started singing. When everyone is gathered together on the rug, have families give Warm Fuzzies to whom they choose (give four Warm Fuzzies to each set of parents to distribute among the family). Then ask if anyone noticed the banner reading DO YOU NEED YOUR SPACE? Ask for people to give their ideas about what this might mean. However, do not spend lots of time on this. More about this later.

GAMES AND THEME ACTIVITIES (7:00–7:50 P.M.)

Materials and supplies:

- A balloon for each person in Cluster, blown up and tied with a piece of string about three feet long

Play-dough or salt-flour clay in about a grapefruit-sized lump for each family

A piece of cardboard for each family on which to build something with the "clay"

The Transition Song (see Chapter 9 for suggestions) printed on newsprint and displayed where everyone can see it

A tape of easy-listening music for the Gravitational Pull game

A tape player to play the audiocassette tape

Games:

Meteor Shower: Have each member of Cluster tie a filled balloon with a string around it to one of their ankles. As soon as everyone is ready, shout "Go!" while everyone attempts to break the balloons of other people without getting their own popped. This can get lively. Be cautious about young children so they don't get trampled or frightened.

Gravitational Pull: This is a game something like "musical chairs." While some recorded music plays, or someone sings, people should mill around together. Then someone appointed by the leader calls out a number like "Two," "Three," "Four," "Five," "Six." When the number is called out, everyone tries to get into a group of people that size. If anyone cannot get into a group with that number, he or she is "lost in space." The last two people remaining are the winners.

Space Station: Give each family a clump of play dough or salt-flour clay about the size of a grapefruit and a piece of cardboard on which they can build their "dream space station." Give each family five minutes to discuss how their space station will be built. Then give them 10 minutes to build the space station in silence. There should be no talking during the "building" of the space station. (This is the major theme activity for later processing.)

Asteroids, Asteroids: This is a transition experience to get everyone settled on the floor for processing following the building of their space stations. This is something like "Ring Around the Rosies." Everyone stands up, forming a big circle. Then everyone joins hands and walks around the circle singing (to "Ring Around the Rosies"):

Ring around the asteroids,
Pocket full of stars.
Meteors, meteors, we all fall down.

Process the activities, focusing on experiences we all had where people got in our way, times we needed more space but didn't have it, what it felt like to remain silent while building our "space stations," and how we communicate our needs when we don't or can't verbalize them. Refer to the banner, "Do you need your space?" Now discuss what this means. Help Cluster members discuss experiences outside of Cluster when people get in their way and when they would like to be alone and not talk to others. Discuss what it feels like to have someone else enter your "personal space" or your "territory" when you don't invite them to do so. Discuss ways to communicate our needs for space to others. Perhaps do some role-playing. Ask Cluster members what they have learned from this experience together that they can apply at home with the family.

CLOSURE (7:50–8:00 P.M.)

Activities:

"Whobody" Song

Other songs Cluster members wish to sing

Exhibit 8D *FAMILY CLUSTER SESSION AGENDA PLAN*

FSI Item (Commitment): In our family, we have traditions, things we always do to celebrate special days.
Theme: Birthdays and Other Special Occasions
Principle: In the family that has a rich repertoire of rituals and traditions to celebrate birthdays and other special occasions, there tends to be unity and commitment in the family, and family members enjoy being with one another.
Objectives:

1. Participate in all the "un-birthday party" activities of Cluster during this session.
2. Participate in the discussion of rituals and traditions in our families.
3. Help your family "costume" one member of the family.

Because the focus of this session of Cluster is on rituals and traditions in the family, this will be a "generic party." That is, the experiences of Cluster during this session can be applied to a variety of events in the family when celebrating special occasions. The leaders should dress in generic black and white to add to the focus of the session.
GATHERING (6:00–6:15 P.M.)

Materials and supplies:
Colored construction paper
Scissors
Colored markers or crayons
Blocks to be used in building towers (each family should have the same kind and number of blocks)
A jar filled with jelly beans (counted, for a contest)
A large banner printed on newsprint with the word: TRADITION
Strips that are the names of special occasions, such as
- Birthday
- Baptism
- Graduation
- Wedding anniversary
- Confirmation
- Bar Mitzvah
- Bat Mitzvah
- The Fourth of July
- Thanksgiving
- Valentine's Day

Birth of a baby
Marriage
Etc. (others you can think of)

(The banner and the signs should be posted around the Cluster room)

Masking tape for name tags

Sign with the following instructions printed for Cluster members:

INSTRUCTIONS FOR FAMILY CLUSTER MEMBERS:

1. GO TO NAME TAG TABLE AND MAKE A NAME TAG, ANY WAY YOU WISH, THAT BEST DEPICTS THE MONTH IN WHICH YOU WERE BORN.
2. GET TOGETHER WITH YOUR FAMILY AND GUESS THE NUMBER OF JELLY BEANS IN THE JAR. GIVE *(leader)* YOUR GUESS.
3. WITH YOUR FAMILY AND USING ONE OF THE PILES OF BLOCKS ON THE FLOOR, MAKE A TOWER AS HIGH AND AS ATTRACTIVE AS YOU CAN.

Leader Instructions:

Hang the banner (TRADITION) and ritual and tradition strips around the room where all members of the Cluster can see them. On one table, place the construction paper, the scissors, the colored markers (or crayons), and the masking tape so members can make their name tags. Put enough blocks in as many different places on the carpet as there are families in the Cluster so the members in each family can build the family "tower." One of the leaders should have a pencil and a piece of paper on which to record the guesses of the Cluster families as to the number of jelly beans in the jar. These should be counted in advance. The jar full of jelly beans should be prominently displayed somewhere separate from other Cluster activities so family members can see it clearly and make their guesses.

Before the gathering ends, the leader conducting the gathering helps the Cluster members determine who has built the tallest tower and also the most attractive tower. Everyone gives a big hand, not only for the winners, but for everyone who participated.

SANDWICH MEAL (6:15–6:45 P.M.)

Each family eats its own meal, previously prepared, after everyone has made a name tag and each family has guessed the number of jelly beans in the jar and built their tower.

GAME: (6:45–7:00 P.M.)
Materials and supplies:

- A straw for each member of Cluster
- A piece of Kleenex cut in quarters
- A long, narrow balloon for each Cluster member (Cluster members can blow them up themselves, or this can be done in advance)

Straw and Paper Game: Hand each person in the Cluster a straw; demonstrate how to suck into the straw and pick up the piece of Kleenex from a hand. Organize the Cluster into three or four teams, mixing ages and sex and families as much as possible. The objective of the game is to pass the Kleenex on a straw from person to person in the team, beginning and ending with the same person. Demonstrate how to do this and then cheer the teams on their way.

Balloon Game: Hand each person a balloon. When the balloons are blown up and tied (by tying them at the end), show Cluster members how to bend them into animals. Then challenge the Cluster members to make an "animal" out of each balloon. It might be a good idea to have some "balloon animals" on display so the Cluster members can see what is possible.

THEME ACTIVITY (7:00–7:55 P.M.)
Materials, supplies, and equipment:

- A short piece of rope (about a foot long), with the ends frayed
- A large brown grocery bag for each Cluster family, containing items that can be used to "costume" someone, including newspapers, paper plates, cups, crepe paper, colored paper, yarn, string, and large pieces of fabric
- Videotape of *Alice in Wonderland*—cued to the "un-birthday party"
- Videocassette playback equipment, including VCR and a television set
- Audiocassette of *Fiddler on the Roof*, cued to the fiddler on the roof playing the theme
- Audiocassette playback equipment

Instructions:

(1) Introduce the theme by drawing the attention of Cluster members to the banner and to the tradition signs displayed around the room. Lead a brainstorming session, where Cluster members tell what traditions they have in their families. Discuss why families have traditions and what their favorite traditions are.

(2) Ask if anyone has noticed that the leaders are wearing black and

white and why they might be doing this (because this is a "generic party," providing ideas for ways to celebrate any number of special occasions in the family).

(3) Have Cluster members demonstrate some of their special talents for the Cluster (perhaps some are painters, musicians, gymnasts, instrumentalists). This should be planned and arranged in advance. Don't "surprise" Cluster members at this point.

(4) Give a bag full of items for costuming to each family. Instruct the families, first, to choose a member of the family whom they will costume with items in the bag. Then give each family about 15 minutes to costume that person. At the end of the interval, have the costumed members of the families parade around the Cluster so all can see them.

(5) Show the "un-birthday party" on the *Alice in Wonderland* video.

(6) Announce the winning family in the "guess-how-many-jelly-beans" contest. The prize? The jar of jelly beans.

(7) Play the *Fiddler on the Roof* theme on the audiocassette playback equipment. Process these experiences in terms of the traditions that were exhibited, how they could be used to celebrate special occasions in the family, and what new traditions families might wish to develop.

CLOSURE (7:55–8:00 P.M.)

Sing some favorite songs

Exhibit 8E *SAMPLE SESSION AGENDA PLAN: FINAL CLUSTER SESSION*

FSI Item: None (This is the closing Cluster session)
Theme: Endings
Principle: Terminating the Cluster experience often brings sadness and a form of grieving. The last Cluster experience can ease the grief and sadness by celebrating our time together when Cluster members engage in activities and rituals designed to help us let go of weekly activities and associations together in Cluster.
Objectives:

1. Participate in decisions about which Cluster items to keep and which ones to dispose of.
2. Participate in and enjoy activities that help us say farewell to our experience in Cluster.
3. Write or draw those "thank you's" or special things remembered about friends in Cluster.

Schedule/Instructions

A large sign on newsprint should be made and posted where all can see:

WELCOME TO OUR LAST CLUSTER SESSION

GATHERING (6:00–6:15 P.M.)

Activity: Make "treasure bags"

Materials and supplies: Paste, scissors, colored construction paper, colored markers, enough large brown grocery bags so each person in Cluster can have one

Leader Instructions:

On a "Treasure Bag" table in the room have a stack of large brown grocery bags, colored markers, scissors, paste, and crayons. Prepare on a sheet of newsprint the following instructions:

INSTRUCTIONS

PUT YOUR POTLUCK ITEMS IN THE KITCHEN AND GO DIRECTLY TO THE "TREASURE BAG" TABLE. MAKE YOURSELF A TREASURE BAG BY:

1. SELECTING A BAG FOR YOURSELF.
2. PRINTING YOUR FIRST NAME ON THE BAG IN LARGE LETTERS.
3. DECORATING THE BAG SO IT SUITS *YOU*.

MEAL (6:15–7:00 P.M.)
Potluck
Leader Instructions:

Tables should be set up in the room ready for the potluck dishes before the gathering begins ("Our Gourmet Garden").

Invite Cluster families to put their food dishes on the "Gourmet Garden" tables.

Then invite Cluster members to begin the food line.

Have chairs, large and small, set up in the room and some small tables arranged so people can sit at the tables, if they wish.

CLUSTER MEETING (7:00–7:20 P.M.)

Warm Fuzzies (leaders hand out to families before the meeting begins).

Sing: "Family Song" (printed on newsprint and posted on chalkboard) and "Whobody Song" (see Chapter 9)

Determine what to do with

1. Our Cluster Ground Rules
2. Our Family Cluster sign-in sheet
3. Our Family Cluster map
4. Items gathered from previous Clusters (portraits, family collages, etc.)

   (Discuss idea that this is one way to say good-bye to Cluster)

Four fathers, previously assigned, share their brief comments or perceptions of Cluster.

GAME/THEME ACTIVITY (7:20–7:55 P.M.)

1. Cluster Pursuit

Materials needed: Game board (prepared by leaders, based on the game "Trivial Pursuit," one die, game piece for each family, game cards with questions [created following each previous Cluster session])

__________will explain and conduct the game.

2. Filling our "Pots"

   Materials and supplies: Story about filling the "pot" from Virginia Satir's *Peoplemaking* (1972, pp. 20–21), "treasure bags" made during Gathering, pencils, pads for everyone (with enough sheets in each for each member of the Cluster)

Everyone sits in a big circle on the floor

Leader tells the story of filling the pot (from Virginia Satir's *Peoplemaking*)—describes the treasure bags made earlier in Cluster session as our "pots" to be filled

One-by-one each person in Cluster sits in the center of the circle on the floor with his/her "treasure bag"

Hand out pads and pencils

Each person in circle writes what he/she likes about the person in the center or a special thank you or other short message and folds the sheet and puts in the bag (signatures not necessary)

While each person sits in the center, sing "Whobody Song" while people are writing (children can draw something)

CLOSURE (7:55–8:00 P.M.)

Post on chalkboard a sign with the words printed to "God Bless This Special Family" (to the tune of "Israel, Israel, God Is Calling")

Stand in a big circle—each family, one by one, goes into the center while Cluster sings "God Bless This Special Family" (guitars: leaders)

God, Bless This Special Family
(To: "Israel, Israel, God Is Calling")
God, bless this special family,
All together now, as one.
Several families have been sharing
Joys and care and love and fun,
Which have held us close in family feeling
Since this Cluster was begun
Help us share our love with others,
So all families may be one.

9. Selecting Music for Family Cluster

Family Cluster without music is like a sandwich without the middle.

It has been said that music is the universal language. It is a language everyone can speak, whether young or old or in between. In Family Cluster, music helps bond people together and provides memories that can nourish the Cluster members all their lives.

But what kind of music is appropriate for Family Cluster? All kinds. This chapter will focus on the selection of songs for Cluster.

Selecting Songs for Cluster

Listen to young children singing jingles to commercials on television and you will get some idea of what might work in Cluster. I'm not suggesting that you sing TV commercials in Cluster. However, children sing what they like and what comes easily to them. They quickly learn to sing commercials they've heard on TV, probably before they have any idea what the words they are singing mean. The songs generally

(1) are repetitive,
(2) have melodies that are easy to sing,
(3) have words that are intriguing yet interesting to say, and
(4) are of short duration.

These are the characteristics to search for in songs you might sing in Cluster.

Sometimes you or members of Cluster might make up words to songs already written. You may want to use songs from movies and Broadway musicals. Or you may wish to select songs that were composed exclusively for Family Cluster.

There are some songs Cluster members might wish to sing over and over again, perhaps at every Cluster. This means the songs should be taught during the early sessions of Cluster so they can be included in later sessions. Some songs can be introduced for theme experiences during Cluster and perhaps sung only during the Cluster sessions in which they are introduced.

When I had my training sessions as a Cluster leader, several of us (LITs and family members alike) brought our favorite camp, gospel, and group songs and our instruments (four guitars and one baritone uke). We had a ritual of singing songs in every Cluster session. We had so much fun singing in Cluster, we decided to have a sing-in outside of Cluster one afternoon. All the LITs and Cluster family members arrived. We recorded our sing-in on someone's portable tape recorder. Originally we had planned the session for one hour—but it wasn't long enough. We were having too much fun to stop at the end of one hour. We had some words printed up (contributed by LITs and families) so everyone could sing along, even when the songs were new. The providers of the new songs taught them to the rest of us. When we got good with each song, we recorded it. The sing-in tape was duplicated for each LIT and Cluster family. Today, years later, we keep in touch with one another and still listen to the tape and remember that sing-in. It touched and, perhaps changed, our lives. We'll never forget that experience as we sat on the floor of a museum by a lake in the Midwest on a hot August afternoon and sang until we were hoarse.

The major purpose of Family Cluster is to affirm one another, to support one another, to encourage one another in growth. To help us in this process, Clusters I lead always begin with the "Whobody Song." We sang this song at the Cluster where I received my training.

A Whobody is somebody who is special—not just anybody, but a special Whobody. Everybody is special and important to somebody. The members of Cluster are special and important to one another. Therefore, when we sing this song, we usually sing it first to each person in the group, then to each family, and finally to

Figure 9.1. Music for the "Whobody Song" (Margaret Sawin)

ourselves. We always ask the question at Cluster meeting, "Who is a Whobody?" Of course, the answer is "I am!" Here is the song:

Who is a Whobody right here?
Who is a Whobody we'll cheer?
[Name of person, family, and so on]
Somebody special, somebody rare,
Somebody for whom we can care.

Another song that helps us to affirm one another is "Magic Penny." The words are easy to learn, and the melody is catchy. When we have learned this song in Clusters I have led, I've often heard Cluster members (including children) hum the tune while they were engaging in other Cluster activities. Any song that is often sung by the group can be heard as a humming accompaniment to one's activities, both inside and outside Cluster. I have taught this song to my college students just because they have heard me humming and singing it when I enter class and have wanted to learn it.

There are many other sources for songs. For instance, there are songs from movies and Broadway musicals that lend themselves beautifully to Cluster. Some of my favorites are the following:

From *Snow White*, movie:
"Whistle While You Work"
"Heigh-Ho"
"The Dwarf's Yodel Song"

Figure 9.2. Music for "Magic Penny"

"With a Smile and a Song"
"Bluddle-Uddle-Um Dum"
From *The Sound of Music,* movie and Broadway musical:
"Do-Re-Mi"
"My Favorite Things"
From *South Pacific,* movie and Broadway musical:
"Happy Talk"
From *The King and I,* movie and Broadway musical:
"Getting to Know You"

These are just a few of the many songs in the movies and in Broadway musicals that might be appropriate for Family Cluster. Songbooks with the words and music to these songs are available wherever sheet music is sold.

Because Warm Fuzzies are so much a part of the ritual of Family Clusters I lead, there are Warm Fuzzy songs we like to sing. An entire songbook of Warm Fuzzy songs (including Cold Prickly songs) are available in the *Warm Fuzzy Song Book* (1979, ISBN 0–915190–14–1, JALMAR Press, 45 Hitching Post Drive, Bldg. 22B, Rolling Hills Estates, CA 90274). Also available through this same publisher is *All About Your Feelings—Songs of the Warm Fuzzy,* a record album of the songs now contained in the *Warm Fuzzy Song Book.* All of the songs on the record and in the songbook are appropriate for Family Cluster.

A song activity that Cluster members enjoy is singing old favorites, such as "Row, Row, Row Your Boat," leaving off one word each time it is sung.

Another song activity is chanting poems, such as "Jay Bird" (Agard, 1977)[1], in a singsong rhythm:

> Way down yonder not so very far off,
> A jay-bird died of the whooping cough;
> He whooped so hard with the whooping cough;
> That he whooped his head and his tail right off.
>
> [Say in rhythm]
> Same song, second [third, and so on] verse,
> A little bit louder and a little bit worse.
> [Repeat the poem]

"Alice's Camel" is a circle-song that almost everyone loves to sing, especially the children (they often requested it in the Cluster where I received my training). Everyone stands in a big circle. Each person holds up all 10 fingers to begin singing the song in a kind of chant form. As each verse is sung, everyone eliminates one finger. Toddlers and preschoolers get all mixed up trying to hold up the correct number of fingers, but they get a big kick out of participating and trying the finger motions. A word of caution: This song gets vigorous at the end of each verse ("boom, boom, boom") as people bounce their hips from side to side. Care should be taken not to overlook and overwhelm the little ones with this.

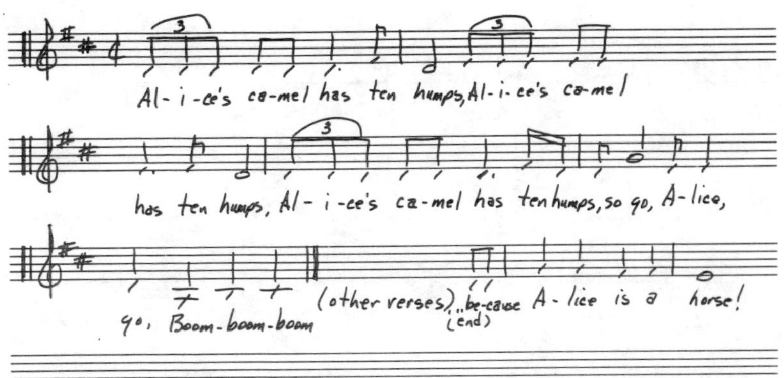

Figure 9.3. Music for "Alice's Camel"

They should be included but watched carefully; if it is too overwhelming for any child, it should be stopped immediately.

> Alice's camel has 10 humps [9 humps, 8 humps, and so on, for each successive verse]
> Alice's camel has 10 humps,
> Alice's camel has 10 humps,
> So, go, Alice, go
> Boom, boom, boom [bump hips from side to side].
> [Go to next verse, same as before but with one fewer hump].
>
> [Last verse]
> Alice's camel has no humps,
> Alice's camel has no humps,
> Alice's camel has no humps,
> Because Alice is a HORSE!

A song for closure that is effective is "He's Got the Whole World in His Hands" (a popular folk song), using the names of the people in Cluster ("He's got Laura and Jared . . .").

During a Cluster session focusing on "family fun," the leaders asked one of the families to teach us one of their favorite songs. Suddenly, everybody had a favorite song they wanted to teach so, family by family, we had a spontaneous "sing-in" as we learned favorite songs from family members. It was one of those joyful

Figure 9.4. Music for the "Transition Song" (Lynette Carver)

times we'll always remember. Even Cluster members who tended to be typically somewhat passive during Cluster activities blossomed during that session.

Sometimes Cluster members or leaders make up songs for Cluster. Figure 9.4 is a transition song created by one of the LITs I trained.

There are favorite gospel, camping, school, and folk songs that can be shared in Cluster. The only limitation is your own imagination.

Note

1. Used by permission.

Reference

Agard, B. (1977). *Family cluster resources*. (Available from the Department of Christian Education, The Evangelical Covenant Church of America, 5101 No. Francisco Ave., Chicago, IL 60625)

10. Selecting Books and Stories for Family Cluster

Everybody likes a good story. Note how popular television is. Television tells stories.

People tell stories, too. We've almost lost the knack of telling stories. It is so much easier to plop down in front of the TV to be entertained. But parents and grandparents still tell stories to their children and grandchildren before tucking them into bed at night. Or they read them stories from favorite books.

Family Cluster provides all kinds of opportunities to tell stories and read books. Any stories or books in Cluster should focus on the theme for the session. Other characteristics to look for in stories or books that might be effective in Cluster are the following:

(1) The telling/reading of the story should take no longer than 10 or 12 minutes. Young children, especially, begin to lose interest if the story is too long. If they are interested in a story, their interest can be maintained for about 10 to 12 minutes.

(2) The plot should capture the interest of the audience immediately. The basic plot should become apparent in the first minute of the telling (the first couple of paragraphs, if the story is being read to the group). Some conflict should be introduced, but not so much tension that people lose interest. If the plot becomes too complicated, such as too many things going on at once, the audience will lose interest, especially the young children.

(3) The words should be appropriate for the story and understood by the audience. Children, especially, love to roll words

around on their tongues, especially if they are repeated over and over, such as "Hundreds of cats, thousands of cats, millions, and billions, and trillions of cats," in Wanda Gag's (1928/1977) classic children's book, or "big" words that fit so beautifully into a story such as "screamed after him the most odious insults that came to her mouth," or "Caleb went crashing into the forest by their house, pondering why he had married such a cantankerous hoddy-doddy; but after he'd walked a while, his fury faded and he couldn't remember what it was they had quarreled about," in William Steig's (1977) *Caleb and Kate*.

(4) If a picture book is used, the illustrations should tell the story, as well as the words, and should be large and clearly distinguish figure from ground. The illustrations need not be in color. However, they should be clear enough that it is easy for young children to see immediately what the story is talking about. The illustrations should be large enough that all members of the Cluster can see them from where they sit without having to sit right next to the storyteller.

You can think of other important characteristics of effective books and stories for Family Cluster. But *do* read to Family Cluster members and tell them stories. Not only do you share *yourself* when you do so, but you set a model for conversing in the home.

With the prevalence and popularity of TV and movies, family members converse with one another all too infrequently. Several years ago a friend of mine, then a principal in an elementary school, told me of a study she conducted about conversations in the families of a small sample of children in her school. Dinner table conversations were recorded on tape. The major finding? Adults spent most of their "conversation time" at the dinner table telling children what to do or criticizing them (e.g., "Get your elbows off the table!" "Quit slurping your food!" "You didn't make your bed this morning!" "You haven't done your homework yet!").

As you read books and tell stories in Cluster, both children and adults hear your voice, hear a model of conversational tone and words, and receive interesting and necessary information in very palatable form.

This chapter focuses on the selection of picture books. The books described here are only to whet your appetite for searching for more. Hopefully, you will be curious enough to delve into the shelves of picture books available at your local library and to chat with a librarian, especially a children's librarian, when you need some suggestions for storybooks appropriate for Family Cluster themes. You may want to get a copy of *The Read Aloud Handbook* by Jim Trelease (1985) to find out what's available that might be appropriate for Cluster.

You probably have heard stories all your life. Now is a good time to start collecting your favorites. If they can be told with simple flannel-board figures (or even figures drawn on a chalkboard or pasted on a long sheet of newsprint or butcher paper) or objects, all the better.

Here I will share with you some picture books I've used or have seen used in Family Cluster. These are just a few teasers so you'll get started on your own collection. I'll give the title, author and illustrator, approximate reading time, publisher, the ISBN number (if available), and a description of each, similar to the way Trelease (1985) does. I'll also suggest some possible Family Cluster themes for which these stories might be appropriate.

Caleb and Kate (about 12 minutes; William Steig, author and illustrator; 1977, Farrar, Strauss, & Giroux, New York)
—Possible themes: Quarreling, dealing with conflict, commitment, when I'm feeling sorry

Caleb, a carpenter, and his wife Kate, a weaver, have a quarrel. Caleb angrily stomps out of the house and into the woods nearby. Feeling sorry about the quarrel, he continues into the woods, looking for oak trees to cut down and take to the mill later. But he grows tired, and curling up to sleep on the forest floor, he slips into a "green sleep." The witch Yedida, who lives in a hidden cave in the same forest, happens upon the sleeping Caleb. She tests a new spell Cousin Iggdrazil taught her and succeeds in turning Caleb into a dog. Caleb later wakes up surprised to find himself a dog. He goes home, attempts to tell Kate who he is, can only manage a bark, and later becomes a trusted pet, sleeping in the bed with Kate where Caleb (now "Rufus") once slept. One night, many months later, thieves break in and Caleb, attempting to protect Kate, is wounded on the very spot where the witch cast her spell. The spell is undone. Caleb the dog becomes Caleb the man. Now Caleb can tell his devoted wife of his love, how sorry he is they quarreled, and what happened when he stomped off into the woods many months before.

Alexander and the Terrible, Horrible, No Good, Very Bad Day (about 8 minutes; Judith Viorst, author; Ray Cruz, illustrator; 1972, Atheneum, New York)
—Possible themes: Solving problems, when everything goes wrong, when I've had a bad day

Alexander, age anywhere from 6 to 12, wakes up with gum in his hair and trips over his skateboard getting out of bed. Alexander knows he's going to have a terrible, horrible, no good, very bad day. And he does. Nothing goes right for him. He even has to sit in the middle of the backseat in the car on the way to school, and no one hears that he might get carsick if he doesn't sit by a window. His teacher likes someone else's picture better than Alexander's "invisible castle." Things get worse. His best friend tells him he is his "third best friend" after two other friends. After school his mother takes Alexander to the dentist along with his two siblings, and Alexander is the only one with anything wrong—a cavity that must be fixed next week. He knocks over everything on his father's desk at the office without even trying when he goes with his mother to pick him up after work. Then he has lima beans for dinner, sees people kissing on TV, and even has to wear the pajamas he hates to bed that night. Several times he threatens to go to Australia. His mother tells him that even in Australia people have terrible, horrible, no good, very bad days.

Badger's Parting Gifts (about 6 minutes; Susan Varley, author and illustrator; 1984, Lothrop, Lee & Shepard Books, New York)
—Possible themes: Death, dealing with strong feelings

Helpful, dependable, reliable old Badger, beloved by his many animal friends, was so old he knew he must soon die. He knew almost everything. He wasn't afraid of death but was worried how his friends would feel when he was gone. He tried to prepare them by telling them that one day soon he would be going down the Long Tunnel, hoping they wouldn't feel too sad when he died. One day, while watching Mole and Frog have a race, he felt especially old. He wanted to race with them, but his old legs wouldn't let him. When he arrived home that night, he wished the moon good night, closed the curtains on the world outside, had his supper, sat down at his desk to write a letter, and then fell asleep in his rocking chair by the fire in his home deep underground. He dreamed that he was running down a long tunnel without his cane. The next morning his friend, Mole, announced to the other animals that Badger had died during the night. Mole read them the farewell letter Badger had left them. They all missed him terribly, especially Mole. They missed him through the long winter months and often reminisced about the things he had taught them. Each could remember something special that Badger had taught him. These shared memories brought joy to them all. When the last snows had melted and spring came, Mole went walking on the hillside, looked up to the sky, and thanked his friend, Badger, for his parting gifts of love, especially the memories of all he had taught his friends before he died.

Frederick (about 4 minutes; Leo Lionni, author and illustrator; 1967, Pantheon, New York, ISBN 0–394–81040–6)
—Possible themes: Being an individual, self-worth/self-esteem, being oneself

Frederick is a field mouse who lives in the old stone wall by the meadow with his family. Winter was not far off. While his four brothers and sisters gathered corn, nuts, wheat, and straw, Frederick gathered "sun rays for cold dark winter days," colors "for winter is gray," and words for the many long winter days when they ran out of things to say. But was Frederick really working, even though he said he was? When the snows came, the mouse family had plenty to eat, but eventually nibbled up almost all the food as they told stories to each other. Then they realized how cold and bleak it was in their stone home and remembered Frederick gathering sun rays, colors, and words while they gathered food. Through the avenue of their imaginations, Frederick helped them to feel the warm rays of the sun and to see the colors of the world about them in the not-winter world outside. Then he shared with them a poem he had made up. After applauding their brother, they said, "But, Frederick, you are a poet!" To which Frederick shyly replied, "I know it."

The Original Warm Fuzzy Tale (about 8 minutes; Claude Steiner, author; JoAnn Dick, illustrator; 1977, JALMAR Press, 45 Hitching

Post Drive, Bldg. 22B, Rolling Hills Estates, CA 90274, ISBN 0–915190–08–7)
—Possible themes: Loving others, sharing, affirming others

Tim and Maggi were very happy with their two children, John and Lucy. In those days everyone received a soft Fuzzy Bag at birth. Whenever a person reached inside the bag, he or she was able to pull out a Warm Fuzzy, which made him or her feel warm and fuzzy all over. No matter how many Warm Fuzzies a person gave away, the bag was always full. If a person ever wanted a Warm Fuzzy, all he or she had to do was ask. One day a bad witch, whose business selling potions and salves was very poor because nobody was buying, planted the idea in Tim and Maggi's minds that Warm Fuzzies were not as plentiful as they thought. The idea spread. People became afraid that their supplies of Warm Fuzzies might run out. They began to hoard their Fuzzies, and people started to die for lack of Warm Fuzzies. Dead people can't buy potions and salves. So the bad witch gave everyone a bag similar to that with the Warm Fuzzies, only it had a counterfeit, Cold Pricklies. Cold Pricklies prevented people from dying, but didn't make them happy. One day, the Hip Woman came to town, started passing out Warm Fuzzies like they would never run out, and convinced the children to do the same thing. A law was passed that Warm Fuzzies could not be given away freely. But the children ignored it. And the struggle to ask for and give Warm Fuzzies freely and to be loving and healthy goes on.

Moths and Mothers, Feathers and Fathers: A Story About a Tiny Owl Named Squib (about 5 minutes; Larry Shles, author and illustrator; 1984, Houghton Mifflin, Boston, ISBN 0–395–36695-X)
—Possible themes: Feeling warm and fuzzy inside, loving others, my parents and others I love

This black-and-white illustrated book is about a tiny owl, Squib, and his life with his mother and father. It is the first in a series of three books about Squib currently in print, although it is projected that the series will have ten books. This book begins the adventures of a tiny, vulnerable owl. Squib tries to name the feeling he has when he is around either or both of his parents. They play with him. They hold and cuddle him. They tell him stories before he goes to bed. They take him soaring with them in the sky. They rescue him when he ventures too far from the nest or gets in trouble with his friends. He looks into his mother's eyes and sees the same thing reflected in her eyes that he feels for her. At last he is able to give words to his feeling. Softly, he whispers to his mother, "I love you." Squib represents the vulnerability in all of us, especially as we struggle with our emotions.

Hoots & Toots & Hairy Brutes: The Continuing Adventures of Squib (about 9 minutes; Larry Shles, author and illustrator; 1985, Houghton Mifflin, Boston, ISBN 0–395–36556–2)
—Possible themes: Being oneself, self-esteem, being an individual, developing one's own talents

This is the second in the series about the little owl. Squib can toot, but he can't hoot the way a "real" owl does. He can't get his parents or his friends to listen to him. When he plays "owlpile" with his friends, he always ends up on the bottom. Not even when he perches on the ear of a sleeping cat can he manage anything more than a weak "toot," not even enough to wake the cat. Then he hears about the Hairy Brute who stalks the forest and kills for no reason at all. Squib tries to find out about the Hairy Brute, but adults and children become quiet when Squib asks about him, so Squib is left to his own imagination to figure out what the Hairy Brute looks and sounds like. Squib takes lessons to learn how to toot so that he can deal with the Hairy Brute some day. He even wishes *he* were the Hairy Brute so others would think he is big, powerful, and feared. Then he wouldn't be ignored any more. He is tired of being ignored. His mother took him to an orthodontist, who fitted him with special headgear, thinking perhaps Squib's problem was an "overbeak." When the headgear came off, poor Squib's toot had become "thooth." A "psychowlogist" said Squib was too tense. Learning to relax, Squib ended up saying "Shoosh" because he was so relaxed he didn't "give a toot." Finally, Squib's mother hired a tutor. Squib thought he needed a hooter, not a tooter. But Squib's "hoot tutor, who was cuter and astuter than most hooters, launched him into his lessons." Alas, Squib ended up saying, "Froot," not "hoot." "The tutor had done nothing more than turn Squib into a frooty tutee." Realizing he would never be able to hoot, Squib wandered off into the forest and found himself at the very place where his parents searched for food. Suddenly he saw the Hairy Brute! His parents were in danger! Squib prayed he would be able to let out a hoot to warn them. Instead, Squib could only give a toot; but what a toot! "It was . . . the most remarkable toot you'd ever want to hear. It wasn't loud, but it was crystal clear and pure." His parents heard Squib's toot and were able to soar to safety. From then on, Squib's life changed. He was no longer ignored. He became the hero of his part of the forest. "Squib now knew that his toot could be worth as much as any hoot in the world."

Hugs & Shrugs: The Continuing Saga of a Tiny Owl Named Squib (about 9 minutes; Larry Schles, author and illustrator; 1987, JALMAR Press, 45 Hitching Post Drive, Bldg. 22B, Rolling Hills Estates, CA 90274–4297, ISBN 0–915190–47–8)
—Possible themes: Showing affection to others, being myself, loving others

This is the third in a series of black-and-white illustrated picture books about the little owl Squib. This time, Squib has lost a piece of himself, right in the center of himself. He finds no joy in anything. His mother tries to feed him some pieces, but they aren't what Squib needs and they don't plug the hole left by the missing piece. So he goes in search of the missing piece. Not far away he happens upon an owl who smells like "the entrance to a cave." The poor owl's skin oozed constantly. The owl begged for a hug, but Squib was too anxious to continue his search for the missing piece. He had neither the time nor the inclination to give such a "remolting creature" a hug. So on he goes. He meets the challenge of climbing a mountain for a while. Then he finds a friend, a female owl as tiny as Squib, who gives him lots of affection, but Squib knows he must get back home. On the way, he begs for a hug from a vulture, a bat, a hummingbird, a hawk, even a snake. For one reason or another, hugs just don't work out. At last he meets again the "remolting creature," the molting owl with the oozing skin. Squib feels strangely drawn to the terrible creature, who continues to want a hug. So Squib does just that. Squib discovers that the missing piece of himself "resurfaced from within." Crawling up the creature's wing, Squib perches on his shoulder. "Sensations of freedom and exaltation lingered and consumed him in warmth and light. . . . Squib's journey had brought him to the loftiest perch he could ever know. He was home."

Gorky Rises (about 12 minutes; William Steig, author and illustrator; 1980, Farrar, Strauss, and Giroux, New York, ISBN 374–42784–4/0370)

—Possible themes: Using one's imagination, fantasy versus reality

Gorky is a frog. All of the "people" in the town where he lives are animals. Here the prize-winning author and illustrator of children's books, William Steig, takes us into the imagination of a child. What child hasn't dreamed of floating up in the sky, able to see everything below, while perfectly content with his or her newfound ability to float. That's exactly what happens to Gorky. As soon as his parents kiss him good-bye and leave the house, Gorky goes to work in his kitchen "laboratory" to mix a magic potion. He mixes a little of this and a little of that. But it is his mother's perfume that makes Gorky's mixture just right. So he takes the magic potion, in his mother's perfume bottle, outdoors and says magic words over the potion. Then he heads for Elephant Rock to wait for further developments. It is such a beautiful day that Gorky gets tired on the way and lies down in the green grass of spring to have a nap. Next thing Gorky knows, he is floating over the village and nearby farms. Everyone sees him float by. He floats into a big storm, but floats above the clouds into the sun again. Night comes and passes and morning is about to dawn. Gorky discovers he can get back down to earth by letting out some of the liquid in the bottle filled with the magic potion. He has been holding on to the bottle all along. By pouring out a drop at a time, Gorky gradually lowers himself to earth. He finds himself back at Elephant Rock with just one drop left. He drops that on the rock, which then turns into a real elephant. Gorky returns home riding on the elephant's back and finds his parents frantically searching for him. He tells them his strange adventure and takes them to Elephant Rock in an attempt to convince them the rock became a real elephant as a result of being touched by the magic potion. Surprised, Gorky's parents just stare at the space where Elephant Rock used to be. Finally, Gorky's father says, "Well, son, you must be tired after all that flying. Let's go home and get some sleep."

Jennifer and Josephine (about 10 minutes; Bill Peet, author and illustrator; 1967, Houghton Mifflin, Boston, ISBN 0–395–18225–5)
—Possible themes: Commitment, dealing with crisis

Jennifer is an old automobile; Josephine is a cat. This is a tale of their adventures together. It all starts in a junkyard where Jennifer has landed. Josephine raises a litter of kittens in Jennifer's backseat. The kittens grow up and wander away. A traveling salesman buys Jennifer at a cheap price. With Josephine in the backseat, off they go, through the busy city streets and out into the country. Mr. Frenzy (the name Josephine gives the salesman) drives Jennifer much too fast. Impatiently, he even tries to pass a big red truck on a hill when an oncoming truck forces them off the road, through a rail fence, across a field, and back onto the road when the right rear tire blows out. Mr. Frenzy replaces the blown-out tire with the spare and hurries on again, beating a train to a rail crossing. He stops at a service station for gas at night and drives Jennifer down a muddy road and over an embankment before deserting her to walk back to the nearest town. Josephine, in the meantime, half scared out of her mind, finds a boy feeding his cats in a nearby barn the next morning and leads him to Jennifer. The boy gets his father, who also brings along a team of horses, which pulls Jennifer out of the ditch and up to the barn. Mr. Frenzy never returns for Jennifer so the farmer drives Jennifer once in a while, at her favorite speed, 20 miles an hour. Josephine, of course, goes along for every ride, never deserting her friend, Jennifer.

Where the Wild Things Are (about 3 minutes; Maurice Sendak, author and illustrator; 1963, Harper & Row, New York)
—Suggested themes: Imagination, dealing with fear, when I'm feeling helpless

Maurice Sendak, who won the coveted Caldecott Award in 1964 for the Most Distinguished Picture Book of the year for this book, has created a book of monsters that almost every child will be able to identify with because the monsters are probably just what they imagine them to be. Along comes Max, who is sent to his room without his supper for doing what he wasn't supposed to in his wolf costume. His room becomes a jungle bordered by a sea that has a boat with Max's name on it. So Max sailed off "through night and day and in and out of weeks and almost over a year to where the wild things are." In spite of their terrible roars and gnashing of teeth and rolling of eyes and showing their terrible claws, Max tells them to "BE STILL!" He performs a magic trick of staring without blinking into their yellow eyes and is made king of all wild things because he is the "most wild thing of all." Max and his new friends march through several pages of a "wild rumpus." Then Max stops the rumpus and discovers he is lonely and can smell good things to eat, so he gives up being king and sails back home to "his very own room where he found his supper waiting for him."

Granpa (about 2 minutes; John Burningham, author and illustrator; 1984, Crown, New York, ISBN 0–517–55643-X)
—Possible themes: Our relatives, being a family, when death comes to those we love

This book is a series of comments and questions between Granpa and his little granddaughter. There is no plot, just the comments and questions. The illustrations tell the story. In the last illustration, there are no words, just Granpa's granddaughter sitting on a chair staring at the empty, green easy chair that was where Granpa used to sit.

Mr. Gumpy's Outing (about 2 minutes; John Burningham, author and illustrator; 1970, Holt, Rinehart & Winston, New York, ISBN 0–03–089733–5)
—Possible themes: Who our friends are, when we do what we're not supposed to do

Mr. Gumpy lives in a house by the river and has a boat. One day he takes his boat out for a ride. The children, the rabbit, the cat, the dog, the pig, the sheep, the chickens, the calf, and the goat ask Mr. Gumpy if they can go along. He allows them all to have a ride, but admonishes each, in turn, not to do some specific thing that could result in trouble for everybody. For instance, the children are cautioned not to squabble. They all have a happy ride together for a while. But then, one after another, the riders do what they were told not to do and the boat tips over. So they all swim to the bank and walk home across the fields. But first they stop for tea at Mr. Gumpy's house. And there they all are on a wordless page, seated around a big table having tea. Then they all go home and Mr. Gumpy invites them to "come for a ride another day."

These are just a few of the many storybooks that are available for use in Family Cluster. You will find others. For example, there are Walt Disney and Golden picture books that are appropriate and relatively inexpensive.

Books, including picture books, are expensive. If the organization that sponsors the Family Cluster does not have a picture book library, or a budget for one, use the local children's library.

If children enjoy the story, so will adults. I have been in church congregations, for instance, where someone at the pulpit has told an illustrated story (using a flannel board) to the children in the congregation. The adults in the congregation have been just as involved in the story being told as the children. If the story captures the interest of the children in Cluster, it will capture the interest of the teenagers and the adults.

Many stories are appropriate for Family Cluster, even if they are not illustrated like a storybook. I remember the telling of Saggy Baggy Elephant in a Cluster during a session focused on self-esteem. To this day, the members of that Cluster talk about the Saggy Baggy Elephants in their lives. The Cluster leaders had drawn representations of an elephant out of construction paper. They also had sketched some background "scenery" for the story with colored markers on a large sheet of butcher paper. Adults and children probably will never forget their experience with that simple story.

You don't have to be an artist in order to tell a story. However, any story you tell Cluster should be illustrated, even with stick figures drawn on a chalkboard. Expand the world of your story possibilities in Family Cluster by carefully investigating the possibilities of stories not written in storybook form.

References

Burningham, J. (1970). *Mr. Gumpy's outing*. New York: Holt, Rinehart & Winston.

Burningham, J. (1984). *Granpa*. New York: Crown.

Gag, W. (1977). *Millions of cats*. New York: Coward, McCann. (Original work published 1928)

Lionni, L. (1967). *Frederick*. New York: Pantheon.

Peet, B. (1967). *Jennifer and Josephine*. Boston: Houghton Mifflin.

Schles, L. (1984). *Moths and mothers, feathers and fathers: A story about a tiny owl named Squib*. Boston: Houghton Mifflin.

Schles, L. (1985). *Hoots and toots & hairy brutes: The continuing adventures of Squib*. Boston: Houghton Mifflin.

Schles, L. (1987). *Hugs & shrugs: The continuing saga of a tiny owl named Squib*. Rolling Hills Estates, CA: JALMAR.

Sendak, M. (1963). *Where the wild things are*. New York: Harper & Row.

Steig, W. (1977). *Caleb and Kate*. New York: Farrar, Strauss, & Giroux.

Steig, W. (1980). *Gorky rises*. New York: Farrar, Strauss, & Giroux.
Steiner, C. (1977). *The original Warm Fuzzy tale*. Rolling Hills Estates, CA: JALMAR.
Trelease, J. (1985). *The read-aloud handbook*. New York: Penguin.
Varley, S. (1984). *Badger's parting gifts*. New York: Lothrop, Lee & Shepard.
Viorst, J. (1972). *Alexander and the terrible, horrible, no good, very bad day*. New York: Atheneum.

11. Selecting Games and Activities for Family Cluster

To lots of people, playing a game means competition. People play games to win. Victory is the end goal. Maybe that's why some people play "war games" (somehow, those words seem contradictory to each other!). The object is to win. And when someone wins, someone else loses.

Winning is not the point of playing games in Family Cluster. Being together, having fun together, is the point. Everybody wins.

Obviously, people enjoy the competition games provide. In addition, they enjoy the skill required to play the game. However, when the motive is winning, then such a game should not be included in Family Cluster.

Games have rules. That's part of the fun of playing games, keeping the rules while enjoying being with others in the process.

Games are excellent equalizers. That is, adults are no longer adults; kids are no longer kids. Age and developmental differences are erased if the members of Cluster are enjoying a game. Everybody is a somebody, a special individual.

Because games can be great fun and because they can be equalizers of people, they can be very effective resources for discovering some important truths about relationships with others—in and out of the family. The learning that takes place seems incidental, or even accidental, but wise leaders plan games to fit the theme for the session and establish the environment for each game so that desired learning can occur.

Activities, such as theme activities, are gamelike experiences for members of Cluster that are designed to build the strengths of families and individuals in the Cluster, to educate and enrich. Though they are not always used for the same purposes as games, they, nevertheless, are important experiences for Cluster members in the process of achieving Cluster objectives.

Your creativity can have full expression when planning games and activities for Cluster. Games you have enjoyed all your life can be adapted for use in Cluster. Almost any game, whether it is a card or other table game, a small group or large group game, can be adapted for use in Cluster. I never cease to be pleasantly surprised at what LITs I train create for the Cluster sessions they lead. Some of the games in this chapter have been derived from their creative efforts.

This chapter will introduce you to a variety of games and activities that are appropriate for use in Family Cluster. However, these games and activities should not be considered the only ones appropriate for Cluster. These should get your own creative ideas going. Stretch yourself and branch out from this beginning.

Get-Acquainted Games and Activities

The first order of business when the Cluster is new is getting acquainted with each other. This should be lots of fun and informal. The following activities have proved to be fun and effective get-acquainted activities in Family Clusters.

Stems

This activity (Benson & Hilyard, 1978) is an effective and fun way for families to get acquainted with each other and to work together as families. It is probably best used as a gathering activity. Families can do this activity when they arrive at Cluster.

Materials and supplies: Large sheets of newsprint (or newsprint sheets from newsprint pads) or butcher paper and colored markers or crayons.

Instructions: If you are using newsprint with colored markers, be sure that each piece of newsprint has another sheet behind it to soak up the marker and prevent marking the wall behind it. Before the Cluster members arrive, tape sheets to the wall with the following stems (the sheets should have enough room that each family or individual can complete the stem):

We are (write your name)
I like to . . . .
I am feeling . . . .
I dream about . . . .
I am wondering about . . . .
Draw a funny face:
Things people like about me:
Ways in which I am like my family:
Ways in which I am different from my family:

As people arrive, ask them to complete *each* stem, with older people assisting the younger ones as needed. Other stems can be used, depending on the Cluster session's theme.

Information from the stems should be acknowledged sometime during the session, such as during the Cluster meeting.

Cluster Hunt

This activity (Benson & Hilyard, 1978) is an effective gathering activity, probably best used for gathering at the second or third Cluster session after Cluster members have had an opportunity to find out who the members of the Cluster are. It is a good "mixer." Cluster members during the first Cluster session may be reluctant to mix outside their own families because they don't yet know the routine of Cluster or what might be expected of them during Cluster. In other words, they probably don't yet feel a sense of "inclusion."

Materials and supplies: Pencils and enough copies of "Cluster Hunt" for each member of the Cluster.

Instructions: As each Cluster member arrives, hand that person a pencil and a "Cluster Hunt" sheet of paper. Instruct that person to find a Cluster member who *best* fits each description. Ask that person to sign his or her name by the side of the description. At the end of the gathering, include in the Cluster meeting an opportunity for Cluster members to share what they have learned about each other. The discussion can be generated by asking such questions as

(1) Did any of you discover someone who is like you?
(2) Did any of you meet someone new?
(3) Did any of you find some surprising discoveries about others in our Cluster?
(4) What do you want to do with your discoveries?

Cluster Hunt List

Instructions: Find someone in our Cluster who matches as many of the following descriptions as possible. When you find someone who matches a description, have that person sign on the line by that description. Get as many different signatures as possible.

1. Find someone who attends school (preschool, elementary school, junior high school, high school, or college)

   ____

2. Find someone who has the same color eyes you have

   ____

3. Find someone who was born in another state

   ____

4. Find someone who was born in the same town as you were

   ____

5. Find someone whose first name begins with the same letter yours does

   ____

6. Find someone who has been to Disneyland ______________
7. Find someone who likes something you do ______________
8. Find someone who has two or more sisters ______________

9. Find someone who speaks another language ______________

10. Find someone who has a pet ______________

11. Find someone who plans to go to college ______________

12. Find someone who plays a musical instrument ______________

13. Find someone who has read a book just for fun during the last three months

    ____

14. Find someone who has lived all of his or her life in this town

    ____

15. Find someone who has slept in a tent this year ______________

16. Find someone who likes yogurt ______________

17. Find someone who subscribes to a magazine ______________

18. Find someone who would like to be a space traveler ______________

19. Find someone who has acted in a play ______________

20. Find someone who has a bike or motorcycle ______________

21. Find someone who has a job ______________

22. Find someone who has done volunteer work in the community

    ____

23. Find someone who has broken an arm or a leg ______________

24. Find someone who has never had to go to the emergency room in a clinic or hospital

    ____

25. Find someone who has traveled outside the United States

    ____

Hand Stacking

This activity (Benson & Hilyard, 1978) is an effective way to get Cluster meeting started at the end of the gathering.

Instructions: (1) Gather everybody together in a tight circle because they will need to be close together so they can stack hands. (2) Then have each person in the circle say his or her name and put his or her right hand in the middle of the circle (you may have to divide the Cluster into two or three groups or have a small circle—about 10—in the center surrounded by the other Cluster members). As each person says his or her name, he or she puts one hand on the stack in the center. (3) When the right hands are stacked, have people begin stacking their left hands on the same stack, each time completing one of the following stems:

"My favorite food is . . ."
"I like to . . ."
"My favorite TV program is . . ."
"I would rather do __________ than anything else."

You can do this several times until all the stems are used (you can make up stems). (4) Then have everyone in the circle close his or her eyes and take turns naming everyone in the circle (they don't need to be named in any kind of order).

Circle Game

This game (Benson & Hilyard, 1978) is a good way to begin or end Cluster meeting during the second or third Cluster session.

Instructions: (1) Gather everyone into a big circle. (2) One by one, ask members of the Cluster who fit each of the following descriptions to stand in the center of the circle:

Everyone who goes to school . . .
Everyone who has green eyes . . .
Everyone who has brown eyes . . .
Everyone who has blue eyes . . .
Everyone who is five or under . . .
Everyone who weighs 100 pounds or over . . .

Everyone who has a dog (or cat, or whatever) for a pet . . .
Everyone who plays the guitar . . .
Everyone who is hungry . . .

(3) Name those who respond to each item on the list; have them go into the center of the circle. (4) Call out as many descriptions as there are on the list, including others you may think of, or until interest or energy begins to diminish. Use this as a transition to the next activity.

Family Interviews

This activity (Benson & Hilyard, 1978) may be an effective activity for Cluster meeting during the first session or during the theme activity for the first session. No materials or supplies are needed.

Instructions: (1) Pair the families and ask them to interview each other. Here are some possible interview questions you may wish to print on a sheet of paper for each family to give them some idea how to conduct the interview:

- What are the names and ages of the family members?
- What are the talents, skills, and interests of the members of the family?
- What is the family looking forward to in Cluster?
- What are some of the favorite sports, foods, hobbies, and talents of family members?
- What makes your family different from any other family you know?

(2) Have the families introduce each other, using the information they gleaned from the interviews. (3) As the Cluster sits in a big circle, ask such questions as the following to help them reflect on their experience with the interviews and learning about each other:

- What did you learn about yourself?
- What did you learn from other members of your family?
- What did you learn about the families in this Cluster?
- How is your family like other families in the Cluster? How is it different?

- What would you like to do with the information you have just learned about one another?

Flower Garden

This activity (Benson & Hilyard, 1978) can be used as a theme activity during one of the early Cluster sessions to help Cluster members get better acquainted with each other.

Materials and supplies: Colored construction paper (variety of colors), scissors, markers, glue, a long strip of butcher paper.

Instructions: (1) Prior to the session, pin or tape a long piece of butcher paper or newsprint to the wall or to a long table on its side in front of the group. Draw a stem with two leaves for each person in the group, putting the stems together in family groups and labeling them by the name of the family. (2) Ask each Cluster member to pick a piece of construction paper that is his or her favorite color. (3) Each Cluster member should then be instructed to make a flower to go at the top of his or her stem. The flower should be identified with that person's name written in colored marker on the front of the flower. (4) When the "flowers" are completed, ask each family to go up to the "flower garden" and paste/tape their flowers on the stems where the family name is listed. (5) Ask each family to choose someone to describe their family flowers to the other members of the Cluster. (6) Process this experience by asking such questions as

(a) What do you see in the flower garden that tells you how the families are alike in our Cluster?
(b) What do you see in the flower garden that tells you how the families in our Cluster are different?
(c) What does this garden tell you about our whole Cluster?
(d) What else did you learn about members of our Cluster that you didn't know before?

Building Our Home

This get-acquainted activity (Benson & Hilyard, 1978) involves some family "art" work.

Materials and supplies: Crayons, colored markers, large piece of newsprint or butcher paper for each family in the Cluster.

Instructions: (1) Hand out a piece of butcher paper/newsprint and either crayons or colored markers to each family. (2) Ask each family to draw their home any way they like. Ask each person to be thinking about their favorite room in the home and why. (3) When all the homes are drawn, ask each family to show their home, and ask each person in the family to describe their favorite room in the house and why it is their favorite room. (4) When each family has finished describing their home, process the experience together by asking such questions as the following:

(a) What did you discover about us that makes us alike?
(b) What did you discover about us that makes us different from one another?
(c) How did you feel while you were drawing your home? What does that tell you about the experiences you might have in Cluster?

Junque Bag Construction

Some people call the odds and ends we find around the house "beautiful junque." This activity (Benson & Hilyard, 1978) is an opportunity for you to gather together some of that "beautiful junque" you've been wondering what to do with and use it in Cluster.

Materials and supplies: A paper bag for each family filled with odds and ends from around the house, such as plastic food cartons, tin cans, string, yarn, school scissors, crayons, colored construction paper, toilet-tissue rollers, facial tissue, crepe paper, paste, pieces of fabric, and old magazines.

Instructions: (1) Give a paper bag with "beautiful junque" items to each family in the Cluster. (2) Instruct the families to look in the bag and to discuss what they want to build with the materials in the bag that will be a reflection of their family. (3) Give the families 15 minutes to construct their family "creations." (4) When the "creations" are done, ask each family to describe their "creation" and how it is representative of the family. (5) Process the experience by asking the Cluster members what they have learned about each other through this experience. Allow those who have questions for individual families to ask questions.

Name Tags

This activity (Agard, 1977)[1] probably should be used as the gathering activity for the first or second Cluster session.

Materials and supplies: Colored markers, scissors, a variety of colors of construction paper, masking tape or pins (for taping or pinning on name tags).

Instructions: (1) As people enter, instructions on a piece of newsprint should direct them to the name tag table. These instructions should include the following: "Select a color you like. Write your name at the top of the paper with a marker. Then write or draw six things you like to do that end in '-ing' (for example, 'reading, skating, skiing'). Attach your 'name tag' to your shirt or blouse and mingle with the other members of Cluster, reading their '-ing' interests. Try to find others who have the same '-ing' interests that you do." (2) When people have finished their name tags, have them sit in a big circle on the floor. (3) One person begins by sharing his or her name and one "-ing" interest; the next person to the right says that person's name and one "-ing" interest, then tells his or her own name and one "-ing" interest on his or her list; then the next person to the right repeats the first two names and interests, adding his or her own name and one "-ing" interest; continue this way around the circle until everyone has been introduced.

Gathering Games and Activities

Many of the get-acquainted activities just described can be effectively woven into the Cluster gathering. The following activities are simple, fun, and are good starters for people as they enter Cluster one by one. These are gathering activities and games primarily to be used when Cluster members are acquainted with each other.

Fantasy Names

This activity should be held after the Cluster members have had at least a couple of Cluster sessions to get acquainted with each other.

Materials and supplies: Before Cluster begins, have as many fantasy names as there are Cluster members printed individually in large marker letters on sheets of paper. Have masking tape cut in strips so the names can be attached to the backs of people as they enter Cluster. (Don't let the individuals see the names you are pinning on their backs.) The following are some possibilities to get you started naming some "fantasy" figures:

Snow White
Cinderella
Snoopy
Charlie Brown
The Wizard of Oz
Big Bird
Santa Claus
(Names of favorite sports figures)
Garfield (the cartoon cat)
(Names of well-known TV actors)
Queen Elizabeth
Prince Philip
(Name of the current U.S. president)
Bambi
Dumbo
The Cookie Monster
Mrs. Claus
(Names of favorite music figures)
Dr. Zhivago

And the list goes on and on—add/replace with your own ideas.

Instructions: (1) As each Cluster member arrives, attach a name to his or her back with a piece of masking tape. (2) Instruct each person to mill around the room asking questions about who they are that can be answered only "Yes" or "No" (e.g., "Am I a living person?" "Am I a cartoon character?" "Am I a character in a book?" "Am I a TV personality?"). (3) As soon as each person finds out who he or she is, the person should continue to play the game by helping others find out who they are. (4) Call time when the gathering needs to come to an end or when interest begins to fade. Some people still might not know who they are when you end the game. Perhaps they can stand in the middle of the Cluster just at the beginning of the Cluster meeting and fire lots of questions at Cluster members until they find out who they are.

Family Portraits

This activity should be planned well in advance so that, in the preceding Cluster, members can be given the assignment to bring individual portraits of themselves that they have sketched in pencil. You might even wish to hand out the sheets of paper on which you want the portraits drawn.

Materials and supplies: You will need a sheet of paper, for each person entering Cluster, that has the name of each person in the Cluster listed, with a space at the side to write in a number. Enough pencils for all Cluster members should also be available.

Instructions: (1) As Cluster members enter the room, instruct them to go to one of the leaders and hand in their self-portrait (if they forgot, hand the person a pencil and sheet of paper and instruct the person to go off someplace private and draw his or her self-portrait). Each person should also be given a sheet of paper containing the names of each person in the Cluster and a pencil. The leader collecting the portraits should put a number in pencil on the front of each "portrait" and write the name in pencil of the person on the back of each portrait. The number should be recorded on a master "key" kept by that leader (on one of the lists with all the names). (2) The portraits should be tacked or taped to the wall where they are clearly visible to everyone, including the children. (3) Instruct everybody to look at the portraits and write down the number at the side of each person on the list whose portrait they think they recognize. (4) When everyone has had a chance to view and ponder the portraits, call time and suggest everyone sit on the floor in a circle. The other leader should remove the "portraits" from the wall. (5) One of the leaders should hold up each portrait and identify it by name and number.

Keep the portraits and tape them to the wall at the beginning of the next Cluster so Cluster members can view them again when they enter Cluster.

Family Cheers

Materials and supplies: A large piece of newsprint and a colored marker for each family.

Instructions (1) As each family enters the Cluster room, hand the family a large piece of newsprint and a marker and instruct them to go off by themselves and create a cheer and write it on the newsprint. The cheer can be in prose or poetry. It need not be long, but should be descriptive of the family. (2) When every family has arrived and had an opportunity to prepare a cheer (it takes an average of 10 minutes for families to make up their cheers), gather in a big circle. (3) One by one, have the families perform their cheer for everyone in the Cluster. At the end of each "performance," encourage lots of clapping and cheering from the group.

Theme Games and Activities

The following games can be used for a variety of themes. The suggested theme for each is indicated. However, each game can be adapted for themes other than the one indicated.

The Human Knot

This is an effective group activity (Fluegelman, 1976)[2] at the beginning of the theme activity for the Cluster session. This can be the "game" that precedes the theme activity(ies) for the Cluster session.

Suggested themes: Cooperation, our dependence on one another.

Instructions: (1) Everyone in the Cluster stands in a big circle, shoulder to shoulder. (It might be a good idea to divide the Cluster into two groups in the beginning. Have about 10 people in each group. Each group should have some adults and some children—a good combination of each.) (2) While Cluster members are standing shoulder to shoulder, instruct them to "begin forming the knot by first placing your hands in the center. Now everybody grab a couple of hands." (Make sure that no one holds both hands of the same person or holds the hand of a person right next to him or her.) "Now untangle yourselves without letting go of hands. However, you may climb under or go over or do whatever else is necessary to untangle yourselves. Just make sure you don't let go of hands." You may need to instruct them to analyze what's going on. If a group gets hopelessly tangled, suggest "emergency 'knot-aid': Break hands momentarily. Then go back to work." (Note: Children love this activity and often come up with the best suggestions for how to get untangled. However, little ones should be watched carefully. If they seem too small to engage in the activity, perhaps they can stand nearby and suggest ways for the group to become untangled. This gives them an opportunity to become part of the group without getting lost in the shuffle—or even hurt by the scramble of bodies.) This can get noisy as people laugh, giggle, and call out directions in an attempt to be heard by the others.

Red-Handed

This game (Fluegelman, 1976) can be played right after the Cluster meeting to introduce the theme activity(ies) for the Cluster session.

Suggested Themes: Honesty, open communication of feelings and ideas.

Instructions: (1) Form a big Cluster circle. (2) One person, "it," stands in the center of the circle. (3) While "it" closes his or her eyes, other players pass a small object (such as a small stone) from person to person. (4) "It" signals and opens his or her eyes; then "it" tries to guess who has the object. If "it" is unsuccessful, keep going until the person holding the object is found. That person becomes "it." In the meantime, everybody tries *fake passes* to decoy "it."

Stand Up

This is another game (Fluegelman, 1976) that can be used immediately following the Cluster meeting to "get the wiggles out" and introduce the theme for the Cluster meeting.

Suggested Themes: Cooperation, supporting one another.

Instructions: (1) Everybody chooses a partner. (2) Partners sit on the floor, back to back, knees bent and elbows linked. Then they attempt to stand up together. Variations: Try in trios, then quartets, then the whole group.

Musical Hats

This activity (Agard, 1977) can be used at the beginning of the Cluster meeting or as one of the games during the session.

Materials, supplies, and equipment:

- A collection of old caps and hats of any kind. There should be enough hats so that each person in the Cluster can use one for this activity/game. Families can contribute caps and hats they may have at home. The Salvation Army or a similar organization in your community may have some you can borrow.
- Music to play on the piano or a tape or record and a tape recorder or record player or piano to play the music during the activity.

Possible Theme: Enjoying being together as a family (family togetherness).

Instructions: (1) Everybody gather together in a big circle. (2) Give each person in the circle, except one, a hat. (3) Instruct people to march around in a circle to the right while music is played on a piano, a tape player, or the like. While the music is playing, each person takes the hat off the head of the person in front and places it on his or her own head. Keep doing this until the music stops. (4) When the music stops, the person without a hat steps outside the circle. (Watch out! There may be a mad scramble for a hat when the music stops or as people anticipate the end of the music.) (5) Remove a hat from someone in the group and continue until only one person is left in the circle. (6) Process the game appropriate to the theme for the Cluster session.

Birdie on the Perch

This game (Agard, 1977) can get noisy but is a great mixer. Be especially watchful of little children (preschool age and younger).

Suggested theme: Family togetherness.

Supplies and equipment: Music to play on a piano or from a tape or record to be used during the activity. A piano, tape player, or record player.

Instructions: (1) Instruct everybody to find a partner. (2) Form two circles. Each circle will have an inner circle (one of the partners must be in this inner circle) and an outer circle (the other partner will be in the outer circle). (3) Play music on a piano or electronic device (such as a record player or tape player). While the music is playing, the inner circle walks around in one direction and the outer circle walks around in the opposite direction. (4) When the music stops the partners find each other. The partner from the inside circle sits on the knee of the partner in the outside circle. The last couple to get together is eliminated. (5) Continue until only one couple is left. (6) Process this experience to fit the theme for the Cluster session.

Fruit-Basket Upset

This is another noisy, scramble game (Agard, 1977). It can be used to introduce the Cluster meeting, as a game after Cluster meeting, or during the theme activity.

Suggested theme: Family togetherness.

Equipment: There should be enough chairs for Cluster members to sit on in a big circle.

Instructions: (1) Make a circle of chairs, one less than the number of people in this Cluster session. (2) Give the name of a fruit to each person (such as apple, orange, grapefruit). Use the names of at least three fruits. Several people should end up with the name of the same fruit. (3) Have the Cluster members sit on the chairs in the circle. Someone should be appointed "it" to stand in the middle of the circle of chairs. (4) "It" calls out the name of a fruit; when people with that fruit name have their name called, they should get up and change seats; in the meantime, "it" rushes to find a chair. The person without a chair becomes "it." (5) Remove a chair and continue the game until only one person is left. Variations: Play the game with the names of family members such as father, mother, daughter, brother, sister. (6) Process this experience to fit the theme of the Cluster session.

Telephone

This is a circle activity (Agard, 1977) most of us have experienced in school, if not during another social activity.

Suggested themes: Family communication, rumors.

Materials and supplies: None needed.

Instructions: (1) Everyone should sit in a circle on the floor, close enough so they can whisper to each other. (2) Whisper a message into the ear of one of the Cluster members. That person whispers it into the ear of the person next to him or her, and so on to the last person in the circle. (3) The last person tells the group out loud what message he or she heard. (4) You may wish to send another "whisper" message and perhaps even a third message. (5) Process this experience according to the theme focus of the Cluster.

Puzzle Rotation

This is a table game (Agard, 1977) that can be played by almost anyone of any age.

Suggested themes: Family togetherness, family fun.

Materials, supplies, and equipment: A simple puzzle for each family in the Cluster. (Note: These should not be complicated jigsaw puzzles with lots of pieces. It should be possible to complete the puzzles in 10–15 minutes at the most.) A card table for each family on which each puzzle can be placed.

A bell to signal when it is time for teams to change tables.

Instructions: (1) Have each family sit at a card table; put a puzzle on each table. (2) Have each family begin to build the puzzle. (3) Ring the bell when the families have a good start on their puzzles. Each family, at the sound of the bell, must move to another table and continue building the puzzle on that table. All should rotate to the next table in the same direction. (4) Ring the bell when the families again are working hard on the new puzzle. All families change tables again, rotating in the same direction as before. (5) Allow the families to complete the puzzle at the table where they are now sitting. Have the families raise their hands when they complete the puzzles. (6) Process the experience to fit the theme for the Cluster session.

Continuation Story

Variations of this activity (Agard, 1977) have been played by almost everyone in the Cluster.

Suggested themes: Family togetherness, family fun, talents.

Materials and supplies: None required.

Instructions: (1) Instruct everyone to sit in a big circle on the floor. (2) Tell one person to begin a "once-upon-a-time" make-believe story and continue to tell the story until you call time. (3) The next person in the circle continues the story until you call time. Continue the story until the last person in the circle ends the story. (4) Process the experience to fit the theme for the Cluster session.

Riddles and Jokes

This activity is one in which school-age children usually shine because they usually are "into" jokes and riddles.

Suggested themes: Family togetherness, family fun.

Materials and supplies: None required.

Instructions: (1) Everyone sits in one big circle on the floor. (2) The object is to tell a favorite joke or riddle. Tell one person to begin and continue around the circle until each person has told his or her favorite joke or riddle. (3) Process the experience to fit the theme for the Cluster session.

Edible Treats

This is an activity that everyone should be involved in and everyone will enjoy because almost everyone loves to eat.

Suggested themes: Family togetherness, family fun, special occasions and celebrations, ending Cluster.

Materials, supplies and equipment: Whatever is needed to prepare the edibles for everyone in the group.

Instructions: (1) (This should be planned well in advance of the Cluster session and discussed with the families so they can assist in bringing what is needed.) Make popcorn together, or have a taffy pull, or make ice cream sundaes. (2) Process the experience to fit the theme of the Cluster session.

What Is Special About You?

This activity (Agard, 1977) is difficult for some people because they are embarrassed to talk about the things they like about themselves. However, Cluster focuses on our strengths, not on our weaknesses.

Suggested Themes: Self-esteem, affirmation.

Materials, supplies, and equipment: Music for the piano or a tape or record. A piano should be available on which to play or a tape recorder to play the tape or a record player to play the record.

Instructions: (1) Divide the members of Cluster into two groups with the same number of people. (2) One group should go in an inside circle and one in an outside circle. (3) Begin playing the music and instruct the people in the circles to move while the music is playing. The inside circle should move in the opposite direction to the outside circle. (4) When the music stops, each person on the inside circle turns to the person in the outside circle and shares "what is special about me" with that person. Then the person in the outside circle does the same to the person on the inside. (5) Begin playing the music again, while both circles walk in opposite directions. When the music stops each person does as before, sharing "what is special about me." (6) Continue this activity as long as you like. (7) Process to fit the theme of the Cluster session.

Hope Chest

This activity (Agard, 1977) builds self-esteem and also may be an effective activity for the closing session of Cluster.

Suggested themes: Self-esteem, affirmation, saying good-bye (last Cluster session).

Materials and supplies: A piece of 8½ × 11 paper for each person in Cluster with a hope chest drawn at the top of the paper; a pencil for each person in Cluster.

Instructions: (1) Hand each person a piece of paper with a hope chest drawn on it and a pencil; instruct each person to print his or her name on the hope chest. (2) Have the members pass the papers around the group, with each person putting something in each person's hope chest (such as drawing a picture or writing a message, wish, or hope for that person). It is not necessary to sign one's name after each item put in the hope chest of each person. (3) When each person receives his or her hope chest, this time filled, have the Cluster members examine the "gifts" in their hope chests. Have a few members share what they feel are their most important gifts and what they felt when they examined their "gifts." (4) Process this experience to fit the theme of the Cluster session.

Who Am I?

This activity (Agard, 1977) focuses on a person's strengths, not weaknesses.

Suggested themes: Self-esteem, affirmation, talents.

Materials and supplies: Enough sheets of paper for all Cluster members with the following stems printed with enough space so that each person can complete the stem (and a pencil for each Cluster member):

My personality is unique because . . .
A talent I have is . . .
Something different/special about my looks is . . .
Something that has helped me to feel good about myself is . . .

Instructions: (1) Hand each person a pencil and a paper with the stems and instruct each person to complete the stems. (2) When the Cluster members have completed their stems, have as many as possible share their stems with the rest of the Cluster. (3) Process this experience to fit the theme for the Cluster session.

Personal Profiles

This activity (Agard, 1977) will cause many Cluster members to reach down inside themselves to find out who they really are.

Suggested themes: Self-esteem, affirmation, talents.

Materials and supplies: A pencil and a sheet of paper for each Cluster member with the following printed on it:

Talker ______________________ Listener
Doer ______________________ Thinker
Right Now ______________________ Tomorrow
Spender ______________________ Saver
Giver ______________________ Receiver
Optimist ______________________ Pessimist
City Person ______________________ Country Person
Leader ______________________ Follower
Day ______________________ Night
Pioneer ______________________ Settler
Active ______________________ Shy

Instructions: (1) Hand each Cluster member a pencil and a sheet of paper including the characteristics drawn in continuum lines. Instruct each person to indicate for each two characteristics where on the line he or she thinks he or she fits. (2) Have as many members of the Cluster as possible share their profiles with other members of the Cluster. (3) Process to fit the theme for the session.

Unwrapping Treasures

This activity (Agard, 1977) focuses on a "treasure" theme but can be adapted for a "values" theme.

Suggested themes: Treasures, values.

Materials, supplies, equipment:

- Several packages of candy wrapped in wrapping paper (you can use funny papers, newspaper, or leftover wrapping paper from birthday parties, Christmas, and so on)
- Several cardboard boxes
- A hat, a pair of gloves or mittens, and a scarf for each of the cardboard boxes
- As many packages of candy as there are boxes (perhaps six of everything; put one package of candy, a hat, a scarf, and a pair of mittens or gloves in each cardboard box)
- Music to play on the piano, tape, or record together with a piano, tape player, or record player to play the music.

Instructions: (1) Have everyone in Cluster sit in a big circle on the floor. Hand a box to each of six people (or to as many people as there are boxes). (2) Have people pass the boxes around the group while the music plays. (3) When the music stops, each person holding the box should put on the hat, gloves, and scarf and begin opening the package of candy. Just as the first person begins to tear away the wrapping on the candy, begin playing the music again. Each person holding a box must then take off the hat, gloves, and scarf, put them back in the box and pass the box on. Continue playing the music until the boxes have all been passed from person to person several times. (4) Stop the music and do as before. Do this as many times as necessary. When the packages of candy are finally opened, the persons opening them share their candy with others in the Cluster. (5) Process this experience to fit the theme for this Cluster session.

Spatial Communication

This is a series of activities (Benson & Hilyard, 1978) designed to explore communication from a variety of positions in space.

Suggested theme: Communication.

Materials, supplies, and equipment: There should be enough chairs for each person in Cluster.

Instructions: (1) Arrange the Cluster in pairs, preferably adult-child pairs. (2) Explain to the group that this will be a series of exercises exploring the effects of physical position on communication. *Exercise a*: Ask each child to stand on a chair and his or her partner (an adult) to kneel beside the chair. Instruct them to converse with each other by sharing with each other what they have done during the day and how they feel about it. After a minute or so, have each set of partners get themselves in a comfortable position and talk about how they felt conversing with each other with one standing on a chair and the other kneeling on the floor. *Exercise b*: Have each pair sit back-to-back on their chairs. Have them begin a conversation on any subject they wish. After a minute or so, have them move their chairs a few feet apart and continue the conversation. Have them move their chairs apart again, until they can't hear each other without shouting. Then have each pair get in a comfortable position and discuss their feelings during this experience. *Exercise c*: Have each pair sit facing each other, just a few inches apart and begin a conversation about anything they like. After a minute or so have them move farther apart. Continue to do this until the partners have lost contact with each other. Then have them get in a comfortable position and discuss how they felt during this exercise. (3) Process this experience to fit the communication theme of the Cluster session.

Design-a-Game

This family activity (Benson & Hilyard, 1978) allows the family to explore the ways it communicates with each other, both verbally and nonverbally.

Suggested theme: Communication.

Materials and supplies: A pencil and a piece of paper for each member of the Cluster. A bag of materials for each family (including colored construction paper, other kinds of paper, paste, colored markers or crayons, masking tape or Scotch tape, wrapping ribbon, sheets of paper, small objects like checker pieces, dice, colored game pieces, or dry beans).

Instructions: (1) Give a pencil and a piece of paper to each Cluster member and a bag full of materials to each family in the Cluster. (2) Instruct each family to design a game, using the materials in the bag for the game, and to determine the purpose of the game and the rules for playing it. (This should take 15 to 20 minutes.) (3) After the games have been designed, have each family share their game with the rest of the Cluster. (4) If there is time, have the Cluster play each family game. (5) Process the experience to fit the communication theme of the Cluster.

Silent Construction

This activity (Benson & Hilyard, 1978) provides an opportunity for families to explore nonverbal communication in the family.

Suggested theme: Nonverbal communication.

Materials and supplies: Prepare a bag of materials for each family, including such things as pieces of colored construction paper, plastic food cartons, paste, scissors, crayons or colored markers, pieces of string or yarn or wrapping twine, Scotch or masking tape, and so on.

Instructions: (1) Have the Cluster members get together in family groups. (2) Hand a bag of materials to each family in the Cluster and ask them to construct something *without talking to one another*. (3) Process the experience to fit the theme of the session.

Picture Description

This activity (Benson & Hilyard, 1978) allows each family to explore how clearly they send their verbal messages.

Suggested theme: Verbal communication.

Materials and supplies: Simple outline pictures for each set of partners in the Cluster. Paper and a crayon for each set of partners in the Cluster.

Instructions: (1) Have the members of the Cluster get together in partners. (2) Hand to one partner in each group a simple outline picture and instruct that person not to show it to his or her partner. (3) Hand the other partner a piece of paper and a crayon. (4) The object of this activity is for the partner with the picture to describe the picture in his or her hand well enough that the other partner can draw it. Partners are not allowed to describe what is in the picture or to name anything in it. (5) When the partner drawing the picture has completed his or her picture, have him or her share it with his or her partner and compare it with the outline picture that the partner used to describe how to draw the picture. (6) Process this activity to fit the theme for the Cluster session.

Life-Size Figures

This activity (Benson & Hilyard, 1978) allows individuals in the Cluster to explore how they feel about themselves.

Suggested theme: Self-worth.

Materials and supplies: Butcher paper or newsprint cut to the size of each person, colored markers or crayons, and scissors.

Instructions:(1) Ask the members of the Cluster to get together in pairs (perhaps this is a good time for children to work with adults from other families). (2) Hand two pieces of newsprint or butcher paper to each pair, together with a pair of scissors and some colored markers or crayons to write on their life-size figure later. (3) Instruct the Cluster members to spread the newsprint or butcher paper flat on the floor and to draw pictures of each other by lying flat on the sheets of paper, with the partner tracing around the person to make a life-size drawing of that person. Trade positions and tasks.

(4) Instruct the participants to write the answers to the following questions on the part of the body indicated:

Some of the things I can do (on the right arm).
Some ways I am like my family (on the left arm).
Some ways I am *not* like my family (on the torso).
Some things people can learn from me (on the head).
Some things I like to do (on the right leg).
Some things I *don't* like to do (on the left leg).

Have members of the Cluster share with the other members of the Cluster their life-size drawings and what they have written on them in answer to each item. (5) Process the experience to fit the theme for this Cluster session.

Family Rules

This experience (Benson & Hilyard, 1978) allows the families in Cluster to examine their family rules.

Suggested theme: Our family rules.

Materials and supplies: For each Cluster member, a paper that has space to complete the following:

Our Family Rules:
Our bedtime rules:
Our eating rules:

Our play rules:
Our cleanup rules:
Our rules about playmates:
Other rules in our family:

and a pencil.

Instructions: (1) Have Cluster members get together in their family groups. (2) Hand a pencil and a paper with "Our Family Rules," above, to each Cluster member, instructing each person to write the rules he or she believes exist in the family about each of the items on the paper. (3) Have each member of the family share with the other members of the family what he or she has written on his or her rule sheet. Other family members may only ask clarifying questions. This is not a time to decide whether family members agree or disagree about family rules. It is a time for people to list their *perceptions* of the family rules. Perceptions just are—they are neither good nor bad. (4) Distribute to each family a sheet that has the following questions from Satir's *Peoplemaking* (1972). Ask each family to discuss their family rules, using these questions as a guide to their discussion:

- How are the rules made in our family? (Does just one of us make them? Is it the person who is the oldest, the nicest, the most handicapped, the most powerful?)
- Does our family get our rules from books? from the neighbors? from the families where the parents grew up? Where do they come from?
- What has our family worked out for making changes in the rules? Who is allowed to ask for changes?
- The legal system of our country provides for appeals. What is the appeal system in our family?

(5) Process this experience to fit the theme for this Cluster session.

Pot Filling

This experience (Benson & Hilyard, 1978) provides an opportunity for members of the Cluster to affirm one another and to say good-bye to each other. This is best used during the last session of the Cluster.

Suggested themes: Saying good-bye, self-worth.

Materials and supplies: A large grocery bag for each person, crayons, small pieces of paper (each person needs a packet of paper equal to the number of people in the Cluster), pencils.

Instructions: (1) Invite the members of the Cluster to sit in a big circle on the floor. (2) Tell the story of the old iron pot (Satir, 1972, p. 20). (3) Give each person a paper bag and the instruction to decorate it with his or her name and any designs or symbols he or she wishes. Hand out pencils and crayons for decorating and writing. (4) When the bags are labeled and decorated, instruct the group that the Cluster members will now help "fill the pot" of each other member. (Hand out the packets of papers at this point.) One by one, each person sits in the center of the circle. Each Cluster member writes a special message of appreciation or thank you to the person in the center and puts the note in that person's bag or "pot." (Note: Young children can draw pictures.) This is also the time to give hugs as desired. (5) Hearts (and perhaps eyes) may be full at this time, so processing is not necessary.

Miscellaneous Games and Activities

Now it's your turn to figure out how a game could be used in Cluster. The following games have no suggested themes. Use your imagination and decide how many themes could be used for each of the following games.

Islands

This game (Fluegelman, 1976) can be used as a gathering activity, as a game following Cluster meeting, or as a game to be used as part of the theme activity for the Cluster session.

Themes? ______________________________

Instructions: Place a few Frisbees on the floor or ground, while everybody prances around them, chanting or singing. When the leader signals "Islands," everyone runs to touch a Frisbee without touching one another. The last person to touch a Frisbee is out (sits down). Reduce the number of Frisbees as the group gets smaller and smaller. If any two people touch while scrambling for the Frisbee, they are both out of the game.

Bug Tug

This is another game (Fluegelman, 1976) that can be used as a gathering activity, as a game following the Cluster meeting, or as part of the theme activity for the Cluster session.

Themes? ______________________________

Instructions: (1) (This is an adaptation of "tug-of-war" without a rope.) Mark a line on the floor with masking tape. Then choose partners. (2) Partners stand back-to-back on either side of the line. (3) Both bend forward, reach between their legs, and grab each others' wrists. (4) Process to fit the theme for the Cluster.

Pina

This game (Fluegelman, 1976) originated with the Nootka Indians of the American Northwest.

Themes? ______________________________

Instructions: (1) Everyone stands in a circle. (2) People take turns doing the following—take a deep breath and walk around the circle, tapping each person on the head and saying "Pina" (pronounced PEEnah). (3) The idea is to get back in place without taking a breath. Success depends as much on the size of the circle as the size of the lungs. (4) Process to fit the theme for the Cluster session.

Prui

This game (Fluegelman, 1976) is pronounced PROO-ee.

Themes? ______________________________

Instructions: (1) Everyone stands up in a group, closes his or her eyes, and starts milling about. (2) When a person bumps into someone else, he or she shakes hands and asks, "Prui?" If the other person answers, "Prui?" then you haven't found the Prui. (3) While people are milling about, the leader whispers to one of the players that he or she is the Prui. That person opens his or her eyes, but must remain mute. When someone bumps into him or her, that person remains mute. (4) Hold one hand of the Prui.

When someone bumps into you, take that person's hand, and that person becomes part of the Prui. Form a line of Pruis with a free hand at both ends. (5) When there are two or three wandering around trying to find the Prui, tell them to open their eyes. Give a big cheer for the Prui.

Hagoo

This game (Fluegelman, 1976) originated with the Tlinget Indians of Alaska.

Themes? ______________________________

Instructions: (1) Two teams face each other, about three feet apart. (2) Two players, one on each team, at opposite ends of the line, are challengers. The two "challengers" step forward and face each other, then bow to each other, say "Hagoo," and walk toward each other without breaking eye contact or reserve (don't smile). They pass in the center, continue to the end, and take each other's former place at the end of the line. The gauntlet, in the meantime, engages in any form of facial calisthenics or titillating hullabaloo that might crack up the challengers. If a challenger is successful, the person who smiles or laughs while running the gauntlet goes to his or her own team. If not, the challenger must join the other team. (3) Game ends when one team has everybody or when everyone has run the "giggle gauntlet."

Song Scramble

This activity (Heaton, 1971) is a good mixer and lots of fun.

Themes? ______________________________

Materials and supplies: Songs written on sheets of paper and cut into numbered strips, line by line, and put in a basket or bag for people to reach in and select.

Instructions: (1) Hand out slips of paper with the words to a song written on them, one line at a time. You can use any song, such as "My Favorite Things" (from *The Sound of Music*) or "Whistle While You Work" (from *Snow White*). (2) The idea is for the Cluster members to find others who have lines from the same song. (3) Then each group puts together the complete song and sings it to the entire group. (4) Process to fit the theme of the Cluster session.

Over and Under

This is a relay game (Agard, 1977) that almost everyone has played at one time or another.

Themes? ______________________________

Materials and supplies: A ball (such as a basketball, soccer ball, tennis ball, beach ball) for each team of seven or eight people (there should be three teams).

Instructions: (1) Divide the members of Cluster into three or four teams of seven or eight people each. Each of the teams lines up one in back of the other. (2) Give a ball to the first person in each team. (3) Instruct the teams to pass the ball from one person to the next. The person in front passes the ball over his or her head to the person in back. That person passes the ball under his or her legs to the person in back. The third person passes the ball over his or her head. The fourth person passes under his or her legs. This continues to the end of the line. (4) The last person runs to the front and the relay starts all over again. (5) The first team to pass the ball down the entire line *four* times (or as many times as you decide) wins the game. (6) Process the experience to fit the theme for the Cluster session.

TP Sculptures

This activity (Agard, 1977) is a variation of an activity often done in neighborhoods. Sometimes a family will wake up to discover that one of the trees in their yard has been "TPed."

Themes? ______________________________

Materials and Supplies: A roll of toilet paper for each family in the Cluster.

Instructions:(1) Have the families get together in their own family groups. (2) Hand each family a roll of toilet paper and instruct them to "sculpture" a member of the family with the TP, using their creativity as they desire. (Note: Preschoolers and younger children generally make poor subjects for such "sculpting." They move around so much it is almost impossible to sculpt. Some may even become frightened of the experience. However, they have good ideas and may enjoy assisting in the sculpting process if someone else in the family is the "sculptee.") (3) Call time when the "creations" are finished. Have each family discuss their sculpture, describing what it means to the family and what it is. (4) Process to fit the theme of the Cluster session.

These games and activities should get your own creative juices going. It is amazing what kinds of activities you can create once you put your mind to it.

Games and activities should fit the themes you select for Family Cluster and be the types of activities in which all members of the Cluster can engage.

Explore the games in game books. Not only might you get ideas for games but you might also come up with ideas for theme activities. Modify games any way you wish to fit a theme and the needs of the Family Cluster.

It is *very* important to process experiences following games and activities. Instructions to most of the games and activities in this chapter include processing. Be sure to read Chapter 13 on processing Cluster experiences, including processing "how to's."

Notes

1. This activity and the others from Agard (1977) are used by permission.
2. The Fluegelman books are excellent sources for Cluster games. They can be ordered as follows:
   YMCA Program Store
   Box 5077
   Champaign, IL 61820
   (217) 351–5077

References

Agard, B. (1977). *Family Cluster resources*. (Available from the Evangelical Covenant Church of America, Department of Christian Education, 5101 No. Francisco Ave., Chicago, IL 60625)

Benson, J., & Hilyard, J. L. (1978). *Becoming family*. Winona, MN: Saint Mary's Press, Christian Brothers Publications.

Fluegelman, A. (Ed.). (1976). *The new games book*. Garden City, NY: Dolphin/Doubleday.
Fluegelman, A. (1981). *More new games*. Garden City, NY: Dolphin/Doubleday.
Heaton, A. (1971). *Party starters and quiet games*. Salt Lake City, UT: Bookcraft.
Pappas, M. G. (1980). *Prime time for families*. Minneapolis, MN: Winston.
Satir, V. (1972). *Peoplemaking*. Palo Alto, CA: Science & Behavior Books.

PART III

Conducting a Family Cluster

The architect makes the plans and specifications for a building but does not build it. He or she works closely with the building contractor to make sure the building is built according to the plans and specifications.

Unlike the architect, the Family Cluster leader implements his or her own plans and specifications (session agenda plans) during the Cluster sessions. In order to do this, the leader must understand the dynamics of that unique social group called Family Cluster and how to accommodate those dynamics while processing the learning activities that take place in Cluster. The Cluster must be organized. Once it begins, the leader fills a number of roles that require practice so they can be implemented successfully during Cluster, such as telling stories, reading picture books out loud, conducting activities, teaching and leading games and music, evaluating the effectiveness of Cluster experiences, and deciding whether or not to continue Cluster sessions once the original contract comes to an end. Part III provides some "how tos" for the Cluster leader who is implementing his or her session agenda plans with real families.

12. Conducting Family Cluster

There is a saying, "Put your money where your mouth is." This is the time to do just that in Family Cluster. This is the time to implement the plans you have made for Family Cluster, to practice what you have been preaching, to do what you have been planning.

Your session agenda plan is ready to go. That means you have determined the insight on which you wish to focus for a given Cluster session, the principle from which that insight is derived, the objectives related to the activities you wish to share with the Cluster members, and the activities related to gathering, the meal (if you have one), the Cluster meeting, the game, the theme experience, and closure.

Before Cluster Begins

Even if you have printed all the signs, have all the supplies ready to go, and have your session agenda plan well in mind, it is *important* that you be in the Cluster room with your coleader to make preparations *at least one hour* before Cluster begins. Have clearly in mind exactly where furniture will be located, where signs will be hung, and the schedule you wish to follow to make preparations. Have the "geography" of your session agenda clearly in mind. Anticipate what should come next. Be ready for families to arrive 15 minutes before Cluster begins. If they don't arrive early, this will give you 15 minutes to relax and perhaps rest before the first family arrives.

Be "all there" when the first family arrives. Allow your whole self to be available for this session. "Be available." Greet each Cluster member individually, with a smile, with enthusiasm, and with something unique about the individual, if possible. If the weather is cool outdoors, show people where to put their wraps. The gathering activities should be invitingly displayed somewhere in the room and the instructions should be accessible to people as they enter the Cluster room. They should be easy to read. If people are forced to stack up at the same table to do a gathering activity, they will get cramped in a hurry. Spread activities out so people have room to breathe and move, and get a sense of self and a sense of what is going on. If a meal will be eaten later, show people where to put their meal containers while they engage in gathering activities. Help each Cluster member to feel welcome. This is "home away from home."

Both leaders should be very much involved in gathering activities. Even though one has the responsibility for "conducting" this experience, it is important that both be available to support and greet each Cluster member.

Here are some suggestions for conducting various activities of Cluster.

Transitions

Cluster can get noisy and messy. When people get involved in activities, they like to talk while they are "doing." The informality of the activities often spurs pleasant conversation among family members and across families. If such things as clay or finger paints are being used, there needs to be a place to wash up in a hurry to get on with other things. Wastebaskets should also be available for disposal of waste paper, after-meal items, paper towels, and so forth.

People in Cluster become accustomed to routines. That is, they learn what to expect next. That's one of the reasons for having a set schedule such as gathering, meal, Cluster meeting, and so on. Routine helps people to establish boundaries, to recognize when a change may be coming. But you, the leader, are responsible for notifying the Cluster members when those changes, or transitions, are about to happen.

I don't like to be interrupted when I'm in the middle of something I'm enjoying. Most people, I would guess, are the same way. However, if I know in advance that within a given time period I need to be ready to move on to something else, it is easier for me to make the psychological adjustment. In other words, I like to have some warning that change is about to take place so I can prepare myself for it. Most people, I have found, like to have the same kind of warning within an established routine. Perhaps three or four minutes before the end of a gathering experience, you might tell the Cluster members that the gathering will be ending and the meal beginning (or the Cluster meeting, if there is no meal). People need time to finish what they are doing and to clean up. Be sensitive to the involvement of members of the Cluster and the time it might take to prepare adequately for the next item on the agenda.

Getting the attention of the group, especially when it is noisy and involved in an activity, may be a daunting task. So what do you do? Yell at the group? Yelling has never worked for me and, besides, I don't like people yelling at me. Children probably hear enough of that anyway. There is a difference between yelling and speaking in a loud voice. Sometimes a loud voice isn't necessary. Perhaps a soft voice will get all the attention you need.

There is a principle of physics called inertia. That is, when a body is in motion, it tends to stay in motion. When it is still, it tends to stay still. To get a moving body to stop or to get a motionless body going can be tasks requiring lots of energy. If people in the Cluster are given adequate warning and are acquainted with the routine, they usually make the transition from one activity to the next rather smoothly. Sometimes a pat on the back and calling someone by name will motivate them to make whatever change is necessary. Perhaps you need to comment on what you have seen and compliment people on what you have noticed. If people know they might be reinforced for something, you might get their attention in a hurry.

Observe those in the Cluster who seem to have the most difficulty making the transition from one activity to another. Perhaps they need more affirmation from you, some indication that you are noticing something special about them. Some people are perfectionists and won't leave a task until it is "perfect." No amount of prodding can move them. Maybe the task was too time-consuming. Learn from your observations what to do next time.

We had this very problem in a Cluster with one of our adolescent girls. She was a perfectionist. She was always the last one finished with anything. She seemed to do this to "control" her family. It often bugged other members of the Cluster. We leaders decided to give her as much verbal affirmation as possible. We also planned simpler tasks for the various activities. Before our Cluster ended, she had modified her perfectionist behavior considerably.

However, Cluster should be a place where a person can be individual, be a separate person from others. It is not necessary to be cut from the same cloth as everyone else in the family and the Cluster. Diversity can be valued by focusing on the unique strengths of each individual. When such individuals persist at tasks, for whatever reason, the best thing to do is to go on to the next item on the agenda and ignore the perfectionist who is not finished. This avoids power struggles and allows the free flow of Cluster activities.

However, it is important to allow Cluster members the time they need to make the transition from one activity to the next. Sudden change is not desirable, nor will it work.

Developing Cluster Contracts

It is easy to skip over one of the most important activities of Cluster—the Cluster contract. The Cluster contract is the set of ground rules by which the members of the Cluster live during their sessions together.

Just as families live by rules, so do Family Clusters. When rules are developed and signed by the members of the Cluster, Cluster members are more likely to live by those rules. It is *very important* that Cluster ground rules (a contract) be developed for *each* Cluster, probably during the second session of the Cluster (the first session should be devoted to getting-acquainted activities).

A big mistake Cluster leaders can make is not spending time during the first two or three Cluster sessions with Cluster members planning the ground rules of the Cluster. (Sawin, 1979, calls this "contracting," a very important process in the early part of Cluster that should not be overlooked.)

Every family operates by rules, whether implicit or explicit. Cluster should provide role models for families in setting explicit rules and agreeing to abide by those rules. The process of setting Cluster rules should be the major theme activity of the second, and possibly the third, Cluster session.

A Cluster contract is "an outward manifestation of an inner commitment" (Sawin, 1979, p. 44). A Cluster contract should include the rules by which the Cluster members wish to abide, which include

(1) the purpose of the Cluster;
(2) the dates of Cluster sessions and the time each begins;
(3) expectations regarding attendance;
(4) how adults, children, and teenagers are expected to interact with each other;
(5) the roles of the leaders;
(6) expectations of family members; and
(7) how to manage such Cluster activities as cleanup tasks, refreshment assignments (if they want them), how to manage anticipated problems with young children, when bathroom breaks will occur, and so on (Sawin, 1979).

Exhibit 12A is an example of a set of ground rules for one Cluster I led with a coleader. The members of the Cluster determined as families how they would sign this "contract." One family signed with their thumbprints in various colors of watercolor paints. One family drew their hands in a concentric circle and each person signed his or her hand.

It is easy to skip the Cluster contract. The price may be chaos or at least disgruntled Cluster members whose expectations were not met during Cluster. Probably the best source of Cluster contracting "how to's" is from the founder of Family Cluster herself, Margaret Sawin (1979).

Before the members of the Cluster sign the Cluster contract, there probably should be discussion of what it means to sign a contract. If members agree to attend each Cluster session, for example, and absenteeism occurs, then some important lessons about keeping commitments can be learned. By the way, it is important to notice when Cluster members are keeping their commitments. Indicate what specific Cluster rules they are keeping and let them know how you feel about it. The focus of Cluster is on the positive, on strengths, not on weaknesses. Cluster is to affirm, not to punish.

It is appropriate, however, to confront those who are absent by simply reminding them individually of the contract and that they have been missed. If they continue their absences, perhaps their absence is telling you something about not meeting expectations or not reinforcing the keeping of contracts.

Some people don't like the word *contract*. There are other terms that can be used, such as *ground rules, agreement,* or *pact* (Sawin, 1979). Whatever it is called in the Clusters you lead, there should be a time set aside (no later than the second session) to plan and agree on the rules to be followed in the Cluster. A sample session agenda plan relating to Cluster contracting is at the end of Chapter 8 (Exhibit 8B).

Conducting Singing in Family Cluster

Perhaps you are one of those people who feel they can't carry a tune in a bucket, perhaps you sing only in the shower, you wouldn't be seen dead singing in public. Never fear; you've got lots of company. One of the nice things about leading singing in Cluster is that you don't have to have a solo singing voice or be able to play an instrument. If you get a kick out of singing in informal groups, you can lead the singing in Cluster. The most important qualifications for leading the singing are (a) enthusiasm and (b) knowledge of the words and tune.

Singing can be a terrific way to settle people down for a new activity. In one Cluster I led, I printed the words to a funny song on newsprint and hung it up for everyone to see. Then I sat down on the rug and started to sing the song, strumming a few chords on my guitar. Pretty soon, the children were gathered in a big circle around me. Before I knew it, everyone in Cluster had sat down in a big circle and was singing along with me. What I had planned for that song and what it turned out to be were two very different things. That song became a favorite in the group because we could make up the wildest ways we could think of to get to Cluster, even on pink elephants or purple turtles! There developed a silent competition among the children to see who could come up with the most outlandish mode of transportation. We laughed a lot when we sang it. It has been several years since we all sang that song together, but I'll bet if we ever got together again all I would have to do is sit down and start playing and singing that song and, before long, everyone in the Cluster would be involved.

I suppose what I'm suggesting is that some of the warmest memories related to Cluster can be derived from the experiences Cluster members have singing together. Sing the songs you enjoy singing. Make up words to familiar tunes, if you like. Encourage Cluster members to do the same. A Cluster that sings together, stays together.

Telling and Reading Stories

Chapter 10 is almost exclusively devoted to picture books that are appropriate for use in Family Cluster. But how do you read a picture book to a Family Cluster? The same way you read it to children. Generally, it's a good idea for everyone to be seated on the floor and for you to be seated in a low chair, such as a child-size chair. Hold the book in one hand comfortably so everyone in the Cluster can see the pictures. If little children say, "I can't see!" encourage them to move up to the front of the group, right in front of you. Then read exactly what is on the page.

Sometimes the members of the Cluster enjoy saying some of the repeated words with you such as Wanda Gag's (1928/1977) "Hundreds of cats, thousands of cats, millions and billions and trillions of cats." It is important to read the words that are on the page because some children, particularly the younger ones, may become upset if you don't. Even though they can't read, they may be familiar with the story (including the words). To little children, the words of a story are sacred and should not be changed.

Read the story at a moderate pace and in a voice everyone can hear, turning the pages with the hand not holding the book. Sometimes changing the pitch of your voice or the intensity of your reading may add to the interest. Allow yourself to get lost in the story. Everyone else will, so you might as well too.

If you are telling a story with visual aids, such as a flannel-board story, be sure you have all the visual aids available nearby and in the order you need them. Otherwise, you will lose the interest of your group while you fumble around for the visual. Also be sure you know how to place the visual. If you are using a flannel board, be sure adequate material is on the back of each picture to attach the picture to the flannel. Pictures that keep falling off can disrupt your train of thought and the attention of the Cluster members.

If you are telling a story without visual aids, maintain eye contact with Cluster members as you are telling the story. Modulate your voice to fit the action of the story. Keep the story moving. Maintain the suspense until time to give the "punch line." Tell the story and then quit. Process the story when appropriate to do so (see Chapter 13 for processing suggestions).

Remember that a storybook or story is a tool, a means to an end. The end or desired outcome for each Cluster session is insight related to some family strength that you and Cluster families have determined earlier needs improving (see Chapter 7 on goals and objectives).

Conducting Games in Family Cluster

There are two major qualifications for successful leadership of games in Family Cluster: (a) thorough knowledge of the details of each game and (b) enthusiasm.

Games are effective tools for discovery learning, which is what the experiential education of Family Cluster is all about.

Knowledge

Conducting a game and playing it are two very different things. It is easy to get caught up in the competition and excitement of a game. With such involvement, keeping the rules seems to be second nature.

Conducting a game is a different matter. It helps to have played the game before. However, you have played enough games in your life that you don't really need to have played the game in order to conduct it effectively.

Know the rules of each game in detail. That is, don't leave anything to chance. Know exactly what people should be doing, and where and when. That is, know the "geography" of each game. Picture in your mind what the members of the Cluster will do, the order of events in the game. If any materials, supplies, or equipment will be used, know what is needed and when it should be handed out to Cluster members.

Rehearse in your own mind how you will direct the activities of the game. Anticipate any special challenges that Cluster members might face. Anticipate their needs and how you might help them meet the challenges.

Enthusiasm

Games generally require a high degree of energy output by the players. You can model this energy level by your own enthusiasm as you lead each game.

If you are enthusiastic about the game, show it in your voice as you give instructions. If you are enthusiastic about the game, show it with your body as you demonstrate what to do. Enthusiasm is contagious. You will find Cluster members imitating your enthusiasm as they engage in the game.

The four Cs of an effective game in Cluster are *conflict, control, closure,* and *contrivance* (Stolovitch & Thiagarajan, 1980).

Conflict. Conflict is the element of suspense, usually provided by the competition required in the typical game. However, because competition can defeat the purpose of games in Cluster, often other means of conflict can be introduced, such as setting a time limit to the game. A time limit should be set for every game in Family Cluster. Competition is appropriate but overemphasis on competition can destroy the purpose of the game.

Control. Control refers to the rules of the game. The rules of the game control the behavior of the players.

Closure. Closure refers to the means for terminating the game. These include arriving at the time limit for the game, achieving the criterion score originally set for the game, eliminating players, or acknowledging single or multiple winners.

Contrivance. Games vary on a continuum from completely unlike reality (such as Bingo) to very similar to reality (such as simulation games). This continuum between reality and nonreality is contrivance. Every game must have some degree of contrivance.

The effective leader of games in Family Cluster makes sure the four Cs of effective games—conflict, control, closure, and contrivance—are involved in each game played in Family Cluster.

As you conduct or lead any game in Family Cluster, keep the following guidelines (Stolovitch & Thiagarajan, 1980) in mind:

(1) Prepare carefully and "play it by ear." Avoid leaving plans to chance or assuming that just because you have read the instructions you know how to play and conduct the game. Allow the play of the game to go through your mind, play by play. Imagine who will be doing what and when. Go through the game with some friends or your family so you can become familiar with the sequence of the game and receive feedback about what will work and what will not work. Anticipate any emergencies. Relax when you lead a game in Cluster, allowing yourself to observe what is going on and to enjoy what is taking place. After your careful preparations, "play it by ear" once the game is under way. Do what your intuition, your feeling, tells you to do along the way, even if it means changing the game slightly in the middle of play. If any materials or supplies are needed for the game, have them ready and at your fingertips to be used when needed during the game.

(2) Introduce the game briefly and describe the rules clearly and concisely. Accept the possibility that some Cluster members will be confused at first. Reassure them that they will "see the light" before the end of the game. Show by your actions how to play the game so Cluster members can imitate your actions. If some rules don't work, modify them on the spot. Stay out of the game so you can be the leader and, especially, cheerleader. Give players lots of verbal encouragement (such as "Nice try!" or "Keep it up—you'll make it!").

(3) Keep the game moving at a moderate pace. Slow games are boring. Hectic games may miss the point, get out of control, and disturb young children. Stick to your timetable. However, if players are finished before the time is up, stop the game and move on to the next activity. If you sense that the players are rushing and missing the point of the game, slow it down or start the game over again.

(4) Head off overemphasis on competition as well as indifference among players. If the game seems to be too competitive for some or all members of Cluster, stop the game to talk about it or change the rules on the spot. If some players begin acting indifferent, perhaps you need to increase the ways that more people can win or change the criteria for success for different players (for example, younger players may need more lenient rules than older players). Find ways that *each* player can be motivated and highly involved in the

game. Your verbal encouragement may keep indifference to a minimum.

(5) Make certain that the game is an exciting one. If players become too excited, stop the game and discuss ways to moderate the excitement. Verbally encourage players as they play. If the game becomes boring, spice it up with bonus points, bluff-and-challenge rules, a faster pace, or increased chance elements.

(6) Individualize the game as much as possible. When pairing individuals, make sure they are as evenly matched as possible (for example, you wouldn't pair a child with an adult in a physical push-ups game). However, in team games, achieve as much imbalance as possible (such as by mixing adults and children); this makes it possible for team members to teach and learn mutually. Identify players who are shy or very young and provide special roles for them (such as judges, scorekeepers, or people to shout out numbers). If there are any show-offs in the group, help them channel their energies positively through special roles, such as scorekeeper, judge, or maker of new rules.

(7) Stay out of the way of the play of the game. Stay nearby to provide encouragement, change the pace when needed, or assist individual players when needed. Observe and note what players do to help you prepare for your role later when processing (see Chapter 13) the experience. If you need to make an announcement (such as a rule change) during play, make sure that all Cluster members are listening (sometimes turning off the lights briefly is a good way to get attention).

Here is a checklist you might use at the end of a Cluster session to determine how effective the game has been.

Game Effectiveness Checklist

(1) The game fit the theme of the Cluster session.

(2) Materials, supplies, and equipment needed for the game were prepared well in advance and were available when needed.

(3) Each member of Cluster participated in the game.

(4) Each member of Cluster seemed to enjoy the game.

(5) The pace of the game was moderate, neither too fast nor too slow.

(6) Shy members, young children, and show-offs were assigned special roles that were motivating and involving.

(7) The members of the Cluster followed the rules with ease.
(8) The game accomplished the purpose for which it was planned.
(9) The game was not overly competitive.
(10) No one became overexcited during the game.
(11) The game was individualized.
(12) I enjoyed conducting the game.

If you wish additional information about game possibilities for Family Cluster or helpful hints for conducting games, you might want to check some or all of the following sources at your local public library or college or university library:

Carney, T. F.(1976). *No limits to growth*. Winnipeg, Canada: Harbeck and Associates Ltd. ["Mind-expanding" techniques and games.]

De Vries, D. L. and associates. (1980). *Teams—games—tournament: The team learning process*. Englewood Cliffs, NJ: Educational Technology Publications.

Diagram Group. (1975). *The way to play*. New York: Paddington. [Describes hundreds of games from around the world.]

Fluegelman, A. (Ed.). (1976). *The new games book*. Garden City, NY: Dolphin/Doubleday.

Fluegelman, A. (Ed.). (1981). *More new games!* Garden City, NY: Dolphin/Doubleday. [Both books edited by Fluegelman come out of the New Games Foundation but can be ordered through the YMCA—see the end of Chapter 11 for address. There are numerous games for small, medium, and large groups for indoor as well as outdoor play. Both books are excellent resources for games appropriate for Family Cluster.]

Horn, R. (1976). *The guide to simulations/games for education and training*. Cranford, NJ: Didactic Systems. [Listings and descriptions of over 1400 games and simulations for all subjects and ages.]

Sackson, S. (1969). *A gamut of games*. New York: Castle Books. [Unusual games by a "diabolically clever" game designer.]

Thiagarajan, S., & Stolovitch, H. D.(1978). *Instructional simulation games*. Englewood Cliffs, NJ: Educational Technology Publications.

When It Isn't Your Turn to Conduct

Generally, it's a good idea for the two leaders of Family Cluster to take turns conducting the various activities on each session's agenda. It is *not* recommended that one leader lead an entire session and then trade off for the next session with the other leader. You should work together as a team during *each* Cluster session.

The person who is conducting an activity needs more eyes and ears than his or her own. It is so easy to get so deeply involved in an activity that you don't really observe what is going on around you. This is where the coleader, the one not conducting the activity, can really shine. Perhaps you have missed a child struggling with something who might need some form of affirmation. The coleader can inform you of this. Maybe the time is getting away from you (I can't emphasize enough how important it is to stick to a time schedule, or how easy it is for time to slip by when people are deeply involved in activities, as they usually are in Family Cluster). Sometimes just a signal, such as pulling at your ear, pointing at your watch, or making a "T" (for time) with a couple of fingers, is all that is needed to show that it is time to move on in the activity.

At the end of the Cluster session, both leaders should get together while the events of the Cluster are still fresh in their minds to discuss what happened and where some modifications need to be made or where more emphasis needs to be placed to meet the needs of members of the Cluster.

When you are not conducting a Cluster activity, you can be carefully observing the entire Cluster and zeroing in on people who might need a bit of cheerleading, a helping hand, or even a wink that encourages them on.

Energy Level

Cluster leaders note differences in energy levels of Cluster groups from one Cluster session to another. My own experience tells me that I need to come to Cluster ready to take my whole self into it. If I am dealing with other issues, such as grievances against others, feelings of guilt because I haven't done something I expected to have done by now, or a sense of pressure or confusion because

I am not prepared for the evening, the energy level in the Cluster will be exactly my own level. Leaders play a major role in maintaining the energy level of a Cluster. Other issues should be resolved before Cluster begins. A leader needs to take his or her whole self into Cluster. If a low energy level seems to be a pattern in a given Cluster, I suggest the leaders first look to themselves. What possible unresolved issues may be contagious within the Cluster? Am I too tired to conduct a Cluster? Am I feeling too overwhelmed to conduct a Cluster? Am I doing this out of a sense of duty or because I want to? Do I enjoy leading Cluster sessions? A Family Cluster whose leaders enjoy leading Cluster is likely to be a Cluster where the members enjoy themselves.

Leading Family Cluster is not necessarily backbreaking work, but it can be exhausting work. Sometimes the most exhausting things I do are the most satisfying. Leading Family Cluster is one of those exhausting, satisfying things I do. It drains me of psychological and physical energy, but it feeds my spirit, the inner me. It can do that to Family Cluster members too.

If you are a teacher by profession, you may wonder if you have done any "teaching" in Family Cluster. Family Cluster is not formal education. You are a teacher, but only in a technical sense. You lead Cluster members to the threshold of their own experience and help them to discover what is already there.

References

Gag, W. (1977). *Millions of cats*. New York: Coward, McCann. (Original work published 1928)

Sawin, M. M. (1979). *Family enrichment with family clusters*. Valley Forge, PA: Judson.

Stolovitch, H. D., & Thiagarajan, S. (1980). *Frame games*. Englewood Cliffs, NJ: Educational Technology Publications.

Exhibit 12A *SAMPLE CLUSTER GROUND RULES (CONTRACT)*

1. The purpose of Cluster is to experience growth and love together, to support one another in growth, and to enrich some of our family strengths.
2. There will be 10 Cluster sessions, held on successive Monday evenings, beginning at 6:00 P.M. and ending at 8:00 P.M.
3. The Cluster will begin on Monday, *(date)* , and end on Monday, *(date)* . Cluster will not be held on Monday, *(date)* , because it is a holiday.
4. At each Cluster session, each member will participate in ALL Cluster activities.
5. Cluster members will greet each other at each Cluster session.
6. Each Cluster member will assist with "child tending" as needed. The primary responsibility for "child tending," however, is within each child's family.
7. Cluster sessions will begin on time (6:00 P.M.) and end on time (8:00 P.M.).
8. Cluster members will eat a "sandwich meal" together at each Cluster session following the gathering activity. Each family will be responsible for its own meal at each Cluster session.
9. If any children need a bathroom break, and need assistance, they can ask any adult in the Cluster.
10. Each Cluster member will attend EACH Cluster session unless *(Leader's name)* is notified BEFORE a necessary absence.
11. Each Cluster member is responsible for what he or she gets from/gives to Cluster each week.

13. Processing a Cluster Experience

Perhaps your most important task as a Cluster leader is to process the experiences of Cluster members. Every theme experience should be processed. In addition, there are times during a Cluster session when "incidental learning" might occur, when the "learning moment" has arrived and you need to stop the activity of the Cluster and focus attention on something that you perceive is going on—especially when you think it might lead to important insights by Cluster members.

The main purpose of each Cluster session is the development of insight by members of the Cluster. Insight is an individual thing. What may result in insight for one person during an experience may be entirely different from what someone else learns. That's the chance you take as a leader in a Family Cluster. You need to plan the Cluster activities carefully in such a way that insights can occur. However, you need to trust the members of the group to develop whatever insights they need from a given experience.

Insights are those components of subject matter (and we *do* have subject matter in Cluster sessions) that answer the question:

> *How does this have value for me in my life?* (e.g., "I can see, now, that no one can fill my needs but myself." "I can see I don't like to do x, so I will do y, which makes me happier and gives me a greater sense of accomplishment." "I can see that when I accuse x of causing my feelings, she becomes defensive, so I will own my own feelings." "I can see that I haven't been successful because I haven't been clear in the past about what I want to do, so I will clarify my intentions.")

An insight is a selected piece of knowledge which a person applies to his or her own personal life after having had a deeply personal experience with that knowledge at an intuitive level. This piece of knowledge looks like it could have special value in the person's life. The person sees that if this knowledge is put to work it could prevent something from occurring that the person does not want to happen, or it could enhance the person's life in some worthwhile way. The continued application of the insight would give the person a clearer understanding of self (Mace, 1981). An insight is represented by the following model:

"If I do x, then y (*something desirable*) will happen."

OR

"If I do x, then y (*something undesirable*) will NOT happen."

Making such a change in a person's actions, however, always involves a risk. It is always a step into the unknown. (Mace, 1981)

The theme experience in each Cluster session should be an "insight" experience (that is, an opportunity for Cluster members to risk emotionally relative to a given content such as self-esteem or communication). This "insight" experience should be planned in such a way that issues related to inclusion, control, and affection can be dealt with effectively, in such a way that members of the Cluster can play a variety of task and maintenance roles, and in such a way that it will not be necessary to withdraw or become dependent, to fight or attempt control, or to "pair up." Emotional risk should be possible in the theme experience. That is, it should be "safe" to take emotional risks; members of the group should trust each other enough to take whatever risks are necessary. You, the leader, can set the pattern by role-modeling and providing a "safe" atmosphere in which Cluster members can participate.

Once the members of the Cluster have had a theme experience (including any other experience related to the theme that is designed to provide insight, such as a game, story, or song), they are ready for "processing." Processing allows the members of the Cluster to develop the insights that can be derived from the theme experience.

"Processing" is a dynamic process that, in itself, is risky because it deals with feelings and possible conflicts that may have come to the surface as a result of the theme experience provided for the Cluster members. Again, remember that the Cluster is not an attempt to focus on group therapy (i.e., to deal with things that don't work). It focuses on things that *do* work, even in embryonic form. You as the leader can do a great deal through the "processing" of a theme experience to focus on things that "work."

Processing consists of four steps, the EIAG (or Experience-Identify-Analyze-Generalize) steps.

Experience: This is the structured opportunity for the Cluster members to share with one another a task related to the theme.

Identify: This is looking back to identify what happened during the experience. Members of the Cluster should be invited, following an experience, to share with one another what happened to them as they "experienced" the structured opportunity during the theme activity. The focus should be on what happened to the person during the activity. Essentially, this is asking, "What happened to __________ when __________ did such and such?"

Analyze: Analyzing is commenting about *how* and *why* something happened (for example, "How did you decide to make your family sculpture?" "Why do you think you decided this way?" and so on).

Generalize: This is drawing conclusions about what happened during the theme experience and how it could be generalized to other situations. This is the "ah hah" experience, or the *insight* that was gained from the experience. It is a form of hypothesizing about what *has* happened and *can* happen in the future. This is the point not only where insight can take place but where behavior change is possible relative to the insight. Questions to assist in this generalizing or hypothesizing process might include

(1) What conclusions can we draw?
(2) What is a principle that might be of help in similar situations?
(3) Who could summarize what we have learned from this experience?

Generalizing is moving from the learning derived from a specific situation to something that can be done in a larger category of similar situations. In other words, it is going from the specific to the general.

Example of Processing in a Family Cluster

Matthew and Alice had conducted five sessions of their first Family Cluster. The 8 adults and 16 children were beginning to "jell" as a group. That is, they were beginning to initiate conversations with others outside their immediate families, including leaders; to appear at ease with routines of Cluster; and to laugh more freely than they had during the first session.

Tonight's Cluster session focused on the Family Strengths Inventory cohesion item: "We feel closer to one another in our family than we do to people outside our family." The theme was "To Be a Part or Apart?"

For the theme activity, each family was given a large clump of red clay (about five pounds for each family), was given 10 minutes to decide as a family what they were going to make with the clay that represented the family, and then spent 20 minutes making the clay structure, with instructions not to speak to one another during the activity. All the families sat together on the floor in one large group. Each family had been asked to put its "sculpture" in front of them and to sit together as a family. Each "sculpture" was on a thick piece of cardboard about two feet long and one foot wide.

Alice processed this activity and sat on the carpet surrounded by the four families. She began the processing by focusing on one family at a time so they could talk about their experience "sculpting" while it was still fresh and so they could share more freely with the other members of Cluster.

The Kenyon family, with Chad (40), a distribution manager at a soft-drink company, Mary (37), a homemaker, and their four children Ted (16), Linda (13), Monica (10), and Tami (7) (the focus family in Chapter 2), had made a sculpture of their home, which was placed in front of them during processing so everyone could see it. Tami kept touching up spots here and there while Linda kept telling her to "Leave it alone!"

The Crowley family sat next to the Kenyons in the circle of families. Mark (39) is a professor and his wife Ellen (36) is a full-time homemaker. Their five children sat or laid on their backs or tummies or laid back on their elbows to participate in the processing. They include Marni (15), Bill (13), Jimmy (9), Nathan (6), and Sandy (3)—the family "buzz saw." Their family sculpture was a large van (the family has one), a tent, and a campfire, with the sculptures arranged into a "camp" setting.

The Dart family was next, with Bill (43), an insurance salesman, and his wife Susan (40), a social worker, surrounded by their four boys, Bill, Jr. (17), Jared (14), Cam (11), and Andrew (7). Their sculpture was a representation of the family seated around the dinner table.

The fourth family, the Bradshaws, with Ken (39), a carpenter, his wife Ruth (36), a nurse, and their three children Robin (12), Danny (10), and Matt (8), focusing proudly on their sculpture, a large and handsome canoe, with each member of the family seated in the canoe. There was also a sculpted tent that looked rather hastily assembled. Alice focused on the Bradshaw family first.

Identify Phase

Leader: Let's start with the Bradshaw family. Someone tell us about your sculpture.

Robin: [age 12] (After considerable poking of one another to go first, Robin starts talking.) We made a canoe 'cause we like to go canoeing when we go camping. Right in the front here (pointing to sculpture) is Daddy. Mommy is back of Daddy. I'm here (pointing to middle) and Danny is here (pointing to spot just in back of the middle slot) and this is Matt (taking up the last slot in the canoe). Here is a tent (pointing) 'cause we sleep in a tent when we go camping, except we have two tents in our family. Mommy and Daddy sleep in one tent and Danny and Matt and I sleep in another tent.

(Cluster members are "oohing" and "aahing" the sculpture, which is extremely well made. Some are looking a bit sheepish, saying things like, "We aren't that talented," and "We sure could have used their help in making our sculpture.")

Leader: Tell us how you decided to make your sculpture.

Robin: (She continues speaking for the family.) Well, Daddy had the idea. We didn't think we would be very good, but we did it anyway.

Leader: Who decided your sculpture should be a tent and a canoe to represent the family?

Both parents: (Speaking at once and pointing to each other) She did. He did.

Leader: Matt, who do you think made the decision?

Matt: Dad did. He always decides what we're gonna do.

Analysis Phase

Leader: [Staying with the feeling expressed by Matt—this is getting into *analysis*—the LIT doesn't agree or disagree, simply helps Matt to identify and express his feeling.] Matt, you said your dad always makes decisions about what you are going to do in the family. Could you talk about that for a minute?

Matt: Dad *always* tells us what we're going to do and when we're going to do it (disgustedly). (Robin and Danny nod their heads in agreement. Mom and Dad look surprised.)

Leader: I get the feeling you wish your dad wouldn't make all the decisions for you.

Matt: Yeah! (heatedly) *I'd* like to make some decisions once in a while!

Leader: Robin, I see you nodding your head agreeing with Matt. Talk about your feeling for a minute.

Robin: Daddy won't let me grow up. He's always telling me what to do.

Danny: I wish we could just talk about it instead of having to do what Dad says all the time.

Leader: Thank you, Robin, Matt, and Danny, for sharing your feelings. [This is not therapy; however, some feelings have been expressed and the leader wanted the children to learn that expressing feelings is OK and safe to do in a Cluster. She'll come back to the parents and their feelings later. A Cluster ideally should be a model of a healthy home/family, where feelings—*any* feelings, whether pleasant or unpleasant—are openly discussed and accepted by family members, where feelings are *heard* and not "plopped" or ignored.] Let's talk about your experience making your sculpture. Ruth (the mother), why don't you tell us what you did as a family when you couldn't speak while you were making your sculpture. [Here the leader goes back to the *identify* phase of processing.]

Ruth: I surely wanted to talk and kept having to bite my tongue so I wouldn't tell the kids what to do. I wanted to show them how to do it and then have them do what I did—but I'm not very good at sculpturing (nods of sympathy from most other members of the Cluster).

[At this point, Sandy Crowley, age 3, begins to have a tantrum. His mother quickly picks him up, takes him out in the hallway, and closes the door. Sandy's screams, however, can clearly be heard by all members of the Cluster. This is one of those unexpected, possible "learning moments." The leader, Alice, calmly pauses in the discussion to deal with Sandy's situation inasmuch as it is clearly disturbing the other Cluster members and this might be a "learning moment" for the Cluster.]

Leader: (Sandy's screams can be heard like a wailing siren in the background. Cluster members seem to be uneasy at this point.) Sandy had a bad dream last night and he didn't get very much sleep. Sometimes when I haven't had very much sleep and I'm around people I don't know very well, I want to cry. Do any of you ever feel that way?

Andrew: [Andrew, in the Dart family, is 7 years old.] Yeah, but I don't cry, because I'm big and I don't have to cry.

Leader: Sandy is 3 years old. It's awfully hard not to cry when you are 3 and you are scared.

(The children in the group nod their heads in vigorous agreement.)

Leader: (She continues) . . . I wonder if we can let Sandy have the cry he needs right now and go on with what we were talking about. Is that OK with everybody?

[Here the leader has dealt with a situation that was very disturbing to the group. She handled it calmly and accepted the fact that Sandy needed to cry and was having some scared feelings. Her example was an effective model for the rest of the group. Possibly, the Cluster members learned during this "incidental learning" experience that it is OK to talk about feelings in Cluster.]

Leader: We were talking about the experience of the Bradshaw family when they couldn't say anything to each other while they were making their sculpture.

Ken: (The father) I kept taking Matt or Danny's hand to show them how to do it. They kept pulling away.

Analysis Phase

Leader: Ken and Ruth, now that the job is all done, how do you feel about the sculpture you made as a family?

Ruth: I think we did a pretty good job. All of us in a canoe surely represents us when we go on an outing. The tent even looks like our tent.

Ken: I probably didn't need to show Matt and Danny how to do the job, but I was afraid it would look terrible and we would have the worst sculpture in the Cluster. I wasn't worried about Robin and what she would do at all.

Matt: Robin never does anything wrong around our house!

Danny: Yeah, but I sure get in a mess of trouble! Matt does, too!

Generalize Phase

Leader: I'm getting the feeling the boys feel they never do anything right, but that Robin gets to do what she wants to do.

Matt and Danny: (Speaking together) Yeah! You're not kidding!

Robin: (Getting on the defensive now) Daddy tells me what to do, too! Sometimes, I don't like it, but I do it anyway. Sometimes he doesn't like what I do, but I just try to do better.

Leader: Ken and Ruth, what has this experience been telling you?

Ruth: I didn't know the kids felt so strongly about Ken making the decisions in our family. I guess we need to help all participate in the decisions that are made in our family, even when the children seem too young to make them.

Ken: I'm feeling a little embarrassed because I didn't know the kids felt so strongly about my making decisions. I guess I'd better let them participate in the decision-making process. I made the decision that we were going to come to this Cluster. Ruth and I talked about it and decided it would be a good experience for all of us. Maybe we should have all talked about it.

Leader: Thank you for sharing your feelings, Ken and Ruth [reinforcing the parents for expressing their feelings]. I wonder if you could tell us what you have learned about the way you communicate as a family without talking to each other.

Robin: (She cuts in before her parents have a chance to say anything.) I can tell how Daddy feels and what he wants us to do by just looking at his face. I can tell when he is mad at somebody, too.

Ruth: I think Robin is right. We tell people in our family what we are thinking or feeling just by the looks on our faces. I think I can tell what the kids think and feel just by looking at their faces.

Ken: But I don't want people just assuming they know what I'm thinking or feeling just by "reading" my face and actions. I want them to tell me about it.

Leader: Ken, that's called "mind-reading." I hear you saying that you get really uncomfortable when people try to read your mind. What would you like them to do about it?

Ken: If what they are "reading" is going to be a problem, I want them to tell me.

Leader: (She hurries to speak, because other family members are getting ready to speak.) Ken, I wonder if one of the reasons the members of your family don't say anything to you is because they are afraid of what you will say or do when they tell you what they think might be a problem. (Family members are nodding their heads in the affirmative.)

Robin: I'm scared to say anything to Daddy because he might not like what I'm gonna say. (The boys, Matt and Danny, agree, "Yeah! Yeah!")

Leader: It's a little scary, I suppose, because Daddy might reject you. (Robin nods her head in vigorous agreement.) Let's have one of the other families talk about their experience with the sculpturing. How about the Dart family?

At this point the leader could have continued a discussion of feelings. However, Cluster is *not* therapy. Therapy tends to be quite confrontational and to deal with the problems that come up in an individual family group. Cluster revolves around common strengths and problems. The leader at this point is wise to move on in the processing. Other Cluster members will talk about this experience for some time to come if it had any meaning for them. If not, that is the chance taken with a theme experience. Sometimes people gain valuable insights into their own experience in the family. Sometimes no insight is gained at all. Alice continued processing by focusing on the other families, first the Dart family, then the Crowley family, and finally the Kenyon family. Then she turned to the entire Cluster for the second phase of processing (see "Case Study, Part C," at the end of this chapter).

Processing is done instead of typical "teaching" kinds of things. That is, instead of telling everyone what they are going to learn, it is the responsibility of Cluster leaders to provide experiences from which Cluster members can gain individual insights. The temptation is to step in and say something like, "Did you notice ______? That's an example of what I was talking about in our lesson today." This is not to suggest that such comments are not appropriate. However, Cluster focuses on *insight*. Insight is derived from experiences—from active involvement with a principle in such a way that Cluster members find themselves learning without consciously realizing it. It is "discovery" learning at its best.

Processing is an easy Cluster experience to skip because leaders often feel uncomfortable with it, and some leaders have had so little experience processing that they would rather skip it. They may decide to go on to other Cluster experiences rather than processing an experience just experienced by the Cluster members. However, this would be a big mistake because the opportunity for insight might be lost.

How do you develop processing skills? One way is to do lots of role-playing. Set up imaginary experiences and practice with other LITs how you would process such experiences.

Remember, Cluster is *not* therapy. It is an education experience, an enrichment experience for entire family groups. Processing might be the most important contribution you as a leader make to each Cluster session.

Case Study, Part C

After processing each individual family, Alice turned to the Cluster as a whole and asked them some questions to help them explore their experience "sculpting" something that represented each family.

Identify Phase

Leader: Your instructions at the beginning suggested that you take some time to discuss and plan in your family how and what you would make before you made it because you wouldn't be able to talk while making your sculpture. I noticed some of you went right to work discussing what you were going to do. Others waited a while before they got going. What was happening after I gave you the instructions?

Mark Crowley [39]: There were so many things that could have represented us as a family. We just brainstormed for a while. It wasn't hard to get into the swing of things at all.

Ellen Crowley [36]: I was concerned about Sandy. He didn't want to come to Cluster. He was afraid he'd have another bad dream tonight.

Nathan Crowley [6]: Sandy's a big cry baby! He's always messing things up for us.

Marni Crowley [15]: (Disgustedly) And I usually end up picking up behind him!

Leader: [She avoids focusing on Sandy, who has the reputation as the Crowley family "buzz saw." She doesn't want to punish anyone for their feelings. She still addresses the Crowley family.] What made you decide to make a van and tent and campfire?

Bill Crowley [13]: That's easy. We always use our van when we go anywhere. Our favorite thing to do when the weather is nice is camping.

Jimmy Crowley [9]: Yeah, and we all know where our place is in the van. (The other four children nod their heads in agreement and begin to poke and shove each other teasingly.)

Leader: How about some of the other families—what did you do after you heard the instructions?

Bill Dart, Jr. [17]: We just kinda looked at each other for a while. Finally, Mom [Susan] said, "Well, what do we do together more than anything else?" It didn't take us long to figure that one out. We're always eating (everyone laughs). So we decided to make our family sitting at the table.

Ted Kenyon [16]: We didn't really want to do anything with clay—at least I didn't (several in Cluster shake their heads in agreement). Mom [Mary] and the girls [his three younger sisters] are the artists in our family. I was kinda hoping they'd come up with an idea.

Chad Kenyon [40]: Ted and I joked about playing basketball so much in our backyard basketball court. Then one of the girls suggested we make our house. That sounded easy, so we all decided to do that.

Analysis Phase

Leader: You have told us what you did to plan your sculptures and even why you did it. Now, let's explore a little bit how you did what you did. I noticed some grumbling at first, but you all settled right to work when it was time to build the sculptures and be silent. How did you go about building something you had agreed on when you didn't feel very skillful with clay?

Monica Kenyon [10]: I don't really know how to make anything with clay but the clay felt so good when I got my hands in it, I didn't want to stop. (Several others nod vigorous agreement.)

Tami Kenyon [7]: Yeah, I liked the gooey feeling of the clay (several nod their heads in agreement, both adults and children).

Bill Dart [43]: It was a real challenge to build that table without saying anything. We had all agreed we'd make our own selves sitting in a chair, and we didn't seem to have any problem with that. But once cooperative effort was required, we used gesture like crazy to communicate with each other.

Jared Dart [14]: (Proudly) And it worked—we did it!

Jimmy Crowley [9]: I was in charge of building the so-called forest around our camp. It was tough at first, but kinda fun. I needed more clay, but didn't know how to get it without talking.

Ellen Crowley [36]: That was my biggest challenge—keeping my mouth shut. Maybe we planned something too complicated with our one wad of clay (several nod in agreement).

Leader: (To the Bradshaw family) I haven't heard anything from the Bradshaws. How about it? How did you go about building your canoe?

Robin Bradshaw [12]: I think we've said enough (the other Bradshaws nod in vigorous agreement)!

Generalization Phase

Leader: [She doesn't press the issue with the Bradshaw family. This isn't therapy.] You've been doing some good thinking about what you've been doing with your sculptures tonight. Now let's just shift the focus a little bit. Did any of you notice the theme for tonight?

(Several raise their hands.)

Leader: Say it all together, those who raised your hands.

[About half of the Cluster members:]

"To Be a Part or Apart?"

Leader: What do you think that means?

Bill Crowley [13]: We're asking whether we're going to be a member of our family or not.

Linda Kenyon [13]: We're asking more than that. We're asking if we *like* being a member of our family (several nod in agreement).

Leader: What do you think the family sculpture experience was telling you about being a member of your family?

Danny Bradshaw [10]: That there are things we like doing with our family over and over.

Cam Dart [11]: Yeah, and we like doing it with the family better than with anyone else (several nod vigorously in agreement).

Jared Dart [14]: But sometimes I don't want to do things with my family. I don't think there is anything wrong with me when I don't want to do things with my family (several other children say, "Yeah!").

Ken Bradshaw [39]: Maybe we need to let everybody know when something is coming up in the family so they can plan for it and get ready for it. I like to be able to plan ahead for something. I'm more likely to include it in my plans.

Susan Dart [40]: Maybe when we let people know what's coming up so they can plan ahead, they'll enjoy things more with the family (several nod in vigorous agreement).

Leader: These are all excellent ideas. What did you learn from your family sculpturing experience this evening?

[The leader is now helping the Family Cluster members to firm up their conclusions about the theme experience and to pinpoint some of their insights.]

Marni Crowley [15]: I enjoyed making the sculpture. I found out we worked really well together as a family. I'm glad I did it with my family.

Ted Kenyon [16]: It took me a while to get into this messy business (snickers and nods of agreement from some of the other children). Gee, I found out I liked it once I got going. We didn't do a bad job at all.

Ellen Crowley [36]: I was amazed how well all seven of us worked together and had so much fun with such a seemingly difficult task.

Leader: Would someone like to summarize what you have learned from this experience?

Mark Crowley [39]: It doesn't really matter what we do as a family as long as we do it together.

Ruth Bradshaw [36]: We enjoy doing things together in the family, especially when we all feel we've had a say and been "heard" in the planning.

Bill Dart, Jr. [17]: Families doing things together can be just about the best thing ever.

Leader: You all have had a challenging experience together in your family. Thank you for sharing so much with all of us. Now it is time for a favorite closing song.

The leader brings processing to a close. A few Cluster members have expressed their feelings and insights. More learning will go on in private and perhaps in later conversations with one another. Processing has helped Cluster members to focus on their experiences and explore the meaning of these experiences. The leader makes a smooth transition to closure, a favorite Cluster song.

During their evaluation of tonight's Cluster session, Alice and Matthew expressed considerable concern about Sandy Crowley (3), who had a temper tantrum during Cluster. Before Cluster started they had prepared some simple wooden puzzles on a table in the "quiet corner" with some picture books and had put some soft blocks and stuffed animals on the floor in case Sandy needed to leave any of the Cluster activities for a short while. Sandy tends to use the blocks and puzzle pieces as missiles to throw at Cluster members. In general, Cluster members ignore him. However, he is living up to his reputation as a "buzz saw." Tami Kenyon (7) has taken Sandy under her wing. She seems to be a calming influence on him. She also considers it her job to "tend" Sandy. Alice and Matthew want Cluster to be a good experience for *both* Tami and Sandy. They have decided to continue as usual for the next session and observe Sandy before making any change in Cluster plans to fit Sandy's rather "hyperactive" nature.

In the meantime, Matthew reminded Alice what a good job she did with processing tonight. Alice could think of a dozen things she "should have said," but, thanks to Matthew's reminder and encouragement, she focused on her strength during tonight's session, not her weakness.

Reference

Mace, D. (1981). The long, long trail from information-giving to behavioral change. *Family Relations, 30*(4), 599–606.

14. Group Dynamics in Family Cluster

Perhaps your biggest challenge in leading a Family Cluster is to be aware of what is happening in the group as a whole, what patterns of communication are being used, who is being left out, who does the talking and to whom, the implicit messages that are sent from one member to another, how Cluster members respond to each other, where communication challenges exist, how Cluster members and families are "fitting in," and so on.

A successful Family Cluster has several things working against it from the beginning.

Group Barriers

Most important, each family who is part of the Cluster has its own long *history*. That is, there are routines and rituals that are simply accepted as part of the makeup of the family, which are probably not seriously questioned by any family member. When this history comes up against another history (that is, another family), barriers to communication may go up automatically. It is risky to share one's boundaries with someone else. In most cases, family members would be hard-pressed to put their hands on just what those boundaries are. Most families play "games," instead of taking the necessary risks to lower the boundaries. There is no point in lowering boundaries until you "test the water," until you find out if you can trust the other families, whether or not it is "safe" to lower the boundaries. It takes time and experience together before such trust can be developed.

A second barrier in building an effective Cluster is the fact that *each member of each family plays expected roles within that family*. If I, accustomed to playing my usual roles in my family, now play out my roles in view of an audience, I may close down my act because of self-consciousness. I find it difficult to be whatever I am when I know I have an audience. That's like analyzing what I do when I walk. After a while, the analysis becomes the focus and I stumble and fall. I don't want to do that for an audience.

A third barrier is closely related. When I become aware of even my most mundane and habitual behaviors, I begin to change. If I am a member of a family, my family members have become so *accustomed to my patterns of behavior* that I become a "predictable" person. That is, their behavior becomes dependent on mine and vice versa. If they see me changing my behavior, my expected roles, their roles become uncomfortable and noticeable. That is, my behavior has become an integral part of the functioning of the entire family system. The behavior of my family's members has become an integral part of my own functioning. If I make any changes in my behavior, especially major ones, like a house of cards the whole functioning system of the family is disrupted (comes tumbling down). Therefore, the other family members rush in, automatically, to "pull me back into line." My overtures or attempts to reach out to other families may upset my family functioning so much that the entire family, like a flock of birds that seems to turn together to an unheard signal, puts whatever pressure is needed to bring my behavior back to that which is expected and typical for me. It is the very unusual family that is aware of these subtle shifts in patterns of family functioning. Like the ill child who gets better, sometimes a family "needs" that child to be sick, so the family colludes in a strange drama to make the child sick again. My changed behavior when first entering a Cluster may "need" to be reversed by my family so that the family can continue to function as it always has.

A fourth barrier is typical of any group in a new situation. *People resist change*. People become defensive in the face of change. Maybe it is the old law of physics, inertia. That is, objects that are still tend to stay still. Objects that are moving tend to stay moving. If family members are accustomed to things going a certain way in their family group, they will automatically resist any pressure to change. This happens in any well-established group situation. About a year ago in another country, the mother in the family where I was living suggested that we invite Ruth X to lunch one Sunday. I had never met Ruth. I had cooked something special for the family and the thoughts of sharing that special dish with a stranger didn't excite me at all. As a matter of fact, I resisted the idea, doing everything I could think of to prevent the invitation—without coming right out and saying, "Ah, shucks, let's not invite her. I don't want her to come. I'd lots rather share my special dish just with the family." Ruth X came to lunch after all. She became one of my dearest friends, but not without a good deal of psychological resistance on my part to begin with.

These are four barriers against a Family Cluster before the Cluster even begins. Your job, as a leader of a Family Cluster, is, first, to recognize the symptoms of these barriers when the families first come together and, second, to find ways that will ease the lowering of these barriers by the family members involved in any given Cluster. It is important to remember that these are *natural* and *typical barriers* that probably exist outside the awareness of most, if not all, family members. Your recognition of the reality of these barriers to effective group functioning in a Cluster will help you plan activities that will assist family members to "ease into" new relationships with people who may be strangers at first. Before coming together, Cluster members have contracted that they will come together for a given number of Clusters, at a given time, on a given day of the week.

There may be resistance to the contract, especially if things do not go well for some individuals during the first couple of Cluster sessions. Such resistance is normal. Occasionally Cluster members need to be reminded of their contract to attend *every* Cluster session. However, when parents and their children are so very busy from day to day, we need to be cautious about building guilt by pressuring people to keep their contracts. We simply need to find a way to let them know they will be missed—or that they *were* missed. The important thing to do is to face this up front at the home visit when people in each family agree to come to each Cluster session—when the Family makes its contract to attend and participate in Cluster. It also needs to be included in the Cluster ground rules (contract).

Therapy Versus Enrichment

As discussed in Chapter 1, it is important to remember that a Family Cluster is *not* a form of group therapy, although there may be experiences that will be therapeutic for some or all of the members of the Cluster at times. (Remember, therapy focuses primarily on rehabilitation—what doesn't work—whereas a Family Cluster focuses on enhancement of family strengths—on *what works* and helping it to work better.) Family Cluster is a family educational experience, focusing on the development and enhancement of skills and knowledge already in embryonic form within the family. Therapy, on the other hand, focuses on "overcoming" or changing behavior patterns that have become "dysfunctional" within a family. As a general rule, there is far more individual confrontation of family members in therapy, usually by the therapist, than in a Family Cluster, where confrontation generally should be minimal and where the *emphasis* should be on *learning* (i.e., growing) and the *prevention of dysfunctional behavior*. There also should be lots of fun and laughter. A Family Cluster can become a strong support group for the families within its umbrella as they share educational experiences together and reinforce each other in the family growth process of relational living.

One thing different about a Family Cluster, compared to an adult support group, is the fact that the group consists of people from a wide range of ages—children, adolescents, adults.

Who Should Be in a Family Cluster?

In Chapters 1 and 6, I discussed who could and should be in Family Cluster. Here are a few additional thoughts about Cluster membership.

When planning a Cluster, I would suggest that, in addition to the adults (parents) in the Cluster, age groups of the children probably shouldn't span more than two or three developmental stages. For example, if school-(elementary) age and teenage children are involved in the Cluster, the needs of everyone are more likely to be met than in a Cluster composed of children ranging in age from infancy to late teens (such a group spans infancy, toddlerhood, preschool, school age, and adolescence—five developmental stages). It is my experience that, when children in more than two neighboring developmental stages are involved in a Family Cluster, children in one of the developmental stages will receive the major focus of the Cluster. For instance, in a Cluster I once led where the children spanned the five developmental stages, the "needs" of the adolescents (especially one very demanding—and needy?—adolescent) received major focus by the leaders. This is something that seems to happen unconsciously. When families volunteer for Clusters, be aware of these possible barriers to effective functioning and avoid problems before they begin.

What about Clusters including "never-married" persons or single parents and their children? If "never-marrieds" have roommates, I would suggest a Family Cluster composed of four or five sets of roommates. I would suggest the same thing for single parents and their families. Single-parent families probably face similar challenges and might like the support that comes not only from other single parents but also from children within single-parent families. At the same time, most single parents are mothers who often long for male role models for their children. Remember that a Family Cluster is an enrichment process, not a therapy process. Focusing exclusively on "problems" (which may happen almost unconsciously and exclusively in a group of single-parent families) may focus the Cluster on a therapeutic experience or, even more of a disadvantage, on the "person" in each family perceived as the "target" or "cause" of the "problems." I once wanted to run a Family Cluster for stroke patients and their families, until I recognized this pitfall of focusing on a "target" individual within the family.

I am suggesting that Clusters might be held for those who experience similar challenges, such as families with preschool-age children and younger children, single-parent families, stepfamilies, "empty-nest" families, single roommate "families," and so on. However, remember that the focus of Family Cluster is what works (strength), not problems (weakness, or what doesn't work). Family Cluster is *not* therapy.

Group Dynamics Within a Family Cluster

Every group develops its own patterns of relationships. That is, every group has its own patterns of interaction. Sometimes these patterns are "functional" (that is, they lead toward growth and learning by each member and by the group as a whole); group satisfaction with the process is its hallmark. Sometimes these patterns are "dysfunctional" (that is, they do not lead toward growth and learning but tend to pull the group into conflict and emotional dishonesty; there is not a sense of individual growth, a sense of trust or responsibility). Members of the group probably are not satisfied with the group experience. These typical patterns of relationship are referred to as the *dynamics* of the group because they are constant and flowing, and can be observed, and even changed, if necessary.

Here are some dynamics that typify Family Clusters:[1]

(1) Every group has a *climate*. Some group climates are cold, hostile, unfriendly, formal; others are warm, friendly, joyful, informative, and the like.

(2) There are *patterns of communication*—there are some who may be very vocal (that is, do lots of talking), some who do not talk in the group, perhaps even some silent ones who clobber the whole group or individuals outside Cluster sessions.

(3) There are patterns of *flight or engagement*. That is, some groups avoid discussing threatening or distasteful subjects or constantly change the subject being discussed (i.e., flight behavior). Some groups are quite open and deal openly with conflict or other threatening or distasteful subjects. They remain "on task" (i.e., they are "engaged" groups).

(4) Occasionally groups engage in *competition*. That is, there may be members who seem to be jockeying for leadership in the group, or vying for attention. Such behavior is dysfunctional to group maintenance.

(5) Some group members occasionally or frequently deal with their own *hidden agendas* during a Cluster session. Perhaps they wish for higher self-esteem, greater trust of self, greater trust of the group. At any rate, their behavior can be quite dysfunctional in a group because they don't realize what they are doing and the

group may unconsciously reinforce these hidden agendas. If I have needs to be "included" in a group, I need to learn how to tell the group, openly and honestly, that I need more nurturing and attention. People who bring their hidden agendas (and we all do, at times) to a group expect group members to "read their minds." They often are disappointed because most people are so busy with their own needs they don't heed—or "read"—what others want unless the wishes and wants are made known explicitly. Then the group can decide if they want to help the individuals accomplish their wants or not. In other words, the hidden agendas become open (i.e., explicit) agendas that are open for negotiation. There is no negotiation possible in a hidden agenda. Negotiation might mean I won't get what I want because the group would rather work on something else. It becomes my own problem whether I want to risk such openness and a threat to my own self-esteem. If I read such behavior by the group (not being willing to meet my wants) as a personal affront to my self-esteem, that is *my* problem, not the group's.

(6) Sometimes what a group member says is ignored by the rest of the group. This is called the *plop*. Ignoring what others say is not uncommon in most families—even so-called "healthy" (or "functional") families. In Clusters, even the most functional Clusters, important (i.e., to the person who says it) information gets ignored. If it is important, and if Cluster members have developed a sense of trust, they will call the attention of the group to their perception that something has been ignored. Cluster leaders can develop sensitivity to what is being ignored—and call it to the attention of the group, if necessary—and role-model how to deal with the problem of being ignored. No one wants to be a plop or be the recipient of a plop.

(7) Each Family Cluster has its own *trust level*—how members feel about taking risks with each other (i.e., sharing ideas, sharing feelings) and the possibility of having such risks ignored or even made fun of, the degree of faith and confidence in each other that exists in the group. Trust means I'm willing to take the necessary emotional risks to become a contributing member of the group—I'm willing to be ignored at times and to have my ideas and feelings rejected. If I trust my Cluster members, I don't take personally what they might do or say.

(8) Each Family Cluster has its own *responsibility* level. That is,

do *all* members of the Cluster participate in planned activities or do some of them hang back and wait to be invited? Do Cluster members "own" their own ideas and feelings by explicitly expressing them as "my" feelings? Do members "respond" to one another's ideas and feelings? Are ideas and feelings clarified and explored?

These are just some of the possible dynamics that might be observable in a Family Cluster. Remember, the group is always fluid—"in process," growing. What you observe during one session may not be observable in another session because something has happened to change the dynamics of the group. That's what "dynamics" are all about, fluidity and change.

Inclusion—Control—Affection

There are three issues (Schutz, 1967) that each member of the Cluster will deal with before he or she leaves the Cluster, regardless of the person's "personality" and regardless of the level of satisfaction that the person experiences in the group. These issues are *inclusion, control, and affection*; and, according to the theory, a person's feelings may focus on any of these issues at any given point in time during a Cluster experience.

Feelings are not the exclusive focus of Clusters. However, every Cluster leader needs to take into consideration the feelings related to inclusion, control, or affection when planning effective Cluster experiences.

When a Cluster is in its formative stage (that is, when the members first come together and get acquainted), the focus of member behavior will be *inclusion* concerns, such as

- Who else is here?
- How can I relate to them?
- What are the (emotional) costs of joining?
- What am I willing to pay?
- Can I trust myself to these Cluster members?
- Will they hold me up if I fall?

When the concerns for inclusion get some answers, the Cluster probably will move into a second phase, which is the phase dealing primarily with concerns about *control*, such as

- Who "calls the shots"?
- Who is in charge?
- Can I influence the group and how much?
- What requirements are placed on me?
- Can I say what I think?
- Can I take it if they say what they think?
- How does each leader function?
- How am I to function?

When the concerns for control have some answers, the Cluster probably will move into a third phase, which is the phase dealing primarily with concerns about *affection*, such as

- Am I willing to care?
- Can I show my caring?
- What if no one cares for me?
- What if someone cares for me?
- What if I don't ever care for anyone in the group?

These three phases of the group tend to overlap and even reverse themselves, especially when the end of the Cluster experience is approaching.

Task and Maintenance Functions in a Group

Possibly because of the struggle group members have with the three issues of inclusion, control, and affection, and because most people are socialized to believe that every group must have a "leader," the idea that an effective group is the result of members playing a variety of roles is almost blasphemous to many people. Most people think that a group without a designated leader will fail. However, the truly effective group, where individuals feel satisfied with their experience and where each person has grown, stretched emotional muscles, and achieved new insights (i.e., growth has occurred), is a group where the role of "leader" changes frequently.

Every group has two things going for it. First, every group has a *task*, a job to do, some goals to accomplish. A Cluster is planned by the leaders to provide opportunities for *each* member of the Cluster to be involved and to play a variety of roles in each experience. Even though the Cluster session has a theme (such as "self-esteem" or "nonverbal communication"), there are varieties of activities in which Cluster members can try out new roles. Even a game has a purpose, or task, to be accomplished. Here are some *task functions* that, ideally, should be shared by members of the Cluster.

- *Initiating*: proposing tasks or goals; defining a group problem; suggesting procedures or ideas to accomplish tasks or goals
- *Seeking information or opinions*: requesting facts; seeking relevant information about group concern; asking for expressions of feeling; requesting a statement or estimate; soliciting expressions of value; seeking suggestions and ideas
- *Giving information or opinions*: offering facts; giving relevant information about group concerns; expressing feelings; giving an estimate; stating a value or rule; giving suggestions or ideas
- *Clarifying and elaborating*: interpreting ideas or suggestions; clearing up confusions; defining terms; indicating alternatives and issues before the group
- *Summarizing*: pulling together related ideas; restating suggestions after the group has discussed them; offering a decision or conclusion for the group to accept or reject
- *Consensus testing*: asking if the group has "heard" a decision; sending up trial balloons to test a possible conclusion

Every group, in addition to focusing on a task, needs to focus on the relationships within the group. This is called group *maintenance*. It is easy to ignore what is happening to the individuals within a group, to allow conflicts and feelings to be "plopped." No group can function successfully unless group members share the following *maintenance functions* frequently:

- *Harmonizing*—attempting to reconcile disagreements; reducing tension; getting people to explore differences
- *Gatekeeping*—helping to keep communication channels open; facilitating the participation of others; suggesting procedures that permit sharing remarks

- *Encouraging*—being friendly, warm, and responsive to others; indicating by facial expression or remark the acceptance of others' contributions (note: acceptance does not mean agreement or disagreement; it simply suggests acknowledgment that something exists, such as a feeling or an idea)
- *Standard setting and testing*—testing whether the group is satisfied with its procedures; pointing out explicit or implicit norms that have been set to make them available for testing

Members in an effective Family Cluster will take turns with all of the task and maintenance functions. If the Cluster becomes dysfunctional, the following behaviors may become apparent in several or all group members:

(1) *Dependency/counterdependency*—"leaning" on someone in the group or expecting others to read minds (dependency); resisting what is happening in the group, especially the person(s) representing authority—that is, the leader(s) (counterdependency)
(2) *Fighting and controlling*—asserting personal dominance, attempting to get one's own way regardless of others
(3) *Withdrawing*—trying to remove the sources of uncomfortable feelings by psychologically leaving the group
(4) *Pairing up*—seeking out one or two supporters and forming a kind of emotional subgroup in which the members protect and support each other

Processing Experiences During a Family Cluster

Perhaps your most important task as a Cluster leader is to process the experiences with Cluster members (see Chapter 13). Every theme experience should be processed. In addition, there are times during a Cluster session when "incidental learning" might occur, when the "learning moment" has arrived and you need to stop the activity of the Cluster and focus attention on something that you perceive is going on—especially when you think it might lead to important insights by Cluster members.

The main purpose of each Cluster session is the development of insight by members of the Cluster. Insight is a very individual thing. What one person develops as a piece of insight about an experience may be entirely different from what someone else develops. That's the chance you take as a leader in a Family Cluster. Essentially, you need to plan the Cluster activities in such a way that insights can occur. However, you also need to trust the members of the group to develop whatever insights they need from a given experience.

The theme experience in each Cluster session should be an "insight" experience (that is, an opportunity for Cluster members to risk emotionally relative to a given content). This "insight" experience should be planned in such a way that issues related to inclusion, control, and affection can be dealt with effectively; in such a way that members of the Cluster can play a variety of task and maintenance roles; and in such a way that it will not be necessary to withdraw or become dependent (or counterdependent), to fight or attempt control, or to "pair up." However, emotional risk should be possible in the theme experience (that is, it should be "safe" to take emotional risks; members of the group should trust each other enough to take whatever risks are necessary; you, the leader, can set the pattern by role-modeling and providing a "safe" atmosphere in which Cluster members can participate).

Once the members of the Cluster have had a theme experience, they are ready for "processing." Processing allows the members of the Cluster to develop the insights that can be derived from the theme experience.

"Processing" is a dynamic process that, in itself, is risky because it deals with feelings and possible conflicts that may have come to the surface as a result of the theme experience provided for the Cluster members. Again, remember that the Cluster is *not* therapy (i.e., does not focus on things that need "fixing"). It focuses on things that *do* work, even in embryonic form. You as the leader can do a great deal through the "processing" of a theme experience to focus on things that "work."

Summary

Despite barriers to working together as a group, a Cluster session can be an important experience of growth for four or five families. However, leaders need to be aware that Clusters go through a process of growth as Cluster members participate together. It takes time for the group to become a cohesive group. Patience is an important characteristic for any Cluster leader to develop.

The theme experience is the activity planned during Cluster when family members can develop important insights about their family relationships and how they want to grow as a family. "Processing" is an important way to help Cluster members articulate the insights they gain during the theme experience. The "processing" activity consists of four closely interwoven phases: Experience (the theme activity), Identify, Analyze, and Generalize. The Cluster leader always conducts the processing of a theme experience. "Processing" can also be conducted for other Cluster experiences such as the "gathering," a "game," or even a "closure" experience.

A Family Cluster is a support group consisting of four or five families. Sometimes these families already know each other before they come together in a Cluster. It is not unusual for deeply bonding experiences to be shared by Cluster members and for friendships between families to develop that will last a lifetime. The dynamics of the group during Cluster make a big difference in the support/learning process.

Case Study, Part D

Matthew and Alice, after conducting seven sessions of Family Cluster, have noticed a big difference in the way Cluster members respond to one another and their Cluster experiences.

The four families (the six Kenyons, the seven Crowleys, the six Darts, and the five Bradshaws) now all know each other well enough to call each other by name. At the first Cluster session, Matthew and Alice noted how slowly and tentatively the members got going with activities and how closely they stuck to their family groups.

Now they are seeing freedom of movement between and among families. When she arrives, Tami Kenyon (7) always looks for Sandy Crowley (3). She seems to have taken responsibility for "tending" Sandy. She generally brings him a simple surprise each time, such as a balloon, a piece of licorice, even a card she had made for him in her second-grade class at school. Bill Dart, Jr. (17), and Ted Kenyon (16) have become good friends. Reportedly, they call each other on the telephone to talk during the week. Ken Bradshaw (39) and Chad Kenyon (40) have discovered a common interest in fishing and have made plans to go fishing together soon with their sons. Ellen Crowley (36) and Mary Kenyon (37) make it a point to have their families eat together at Cluster and they sit together and chat enthusiastically, most often about their common domestic challenges. Susan Dart (40), a social worker, and Ruth Bradshaw (36), a nurse, have found some common interests in their work even though their professions are very different. Often they find moments to chat together at Cluster. A "gang" of Cluster boys has formed, including Danny (10) and Matt (8) Bradshaw, Cam (11) and Andrew (7) Dart, and Jimmy (9) and Nathan (6) Crowley. At each Cluster they get together to discuss the latest toy on the market or neighborhood "adventure." Currently, they are excitedly planning a Halloween get-together. Jared Dart (14) and Bill Crowley (13) are just beginning to warm up to each other and discover some common interests. Marni Crowley (15), Robin Bradshaw (12), Linda Kenyon (13), and Monica Kenyon (10) form a loose "clique" that is just now beginning to jell with Marni as its leader, although there is some distancing between Marni and Monica, possibly because of the age and interest differences. Sandy Crowley (3) seems to "do his own thing" in his spaced-out sort of way. Fortunately, Tami Kenyon (7), his self-appointed babysitter, is usually nearby to listen with interest to his frequent, nonstop narratives. All of the parents and children in the Cluster seem to have established a growing support network.

The challenge of inclusion seems to be well met. Sandy seems to be testing out the limits, but the Cluster members seem to feel comfortable so far with the ground rules they established and signed during the second session of Cluster. Therefore, control seems to be no major issue.

It is taking longer now for families to leave Cluster at the end of each session. They almost have to be pushed out the door. There are frequent signs of growing affection among Cluster members.

Matthew and Alice are always exhausted at the end of each Cluster session. But enough is going right that they feel repaid for their considerable efforts to be effective leaders. They observe the group carefully each Cluster session. Currently they are watching the Bradshaw family closely, mainly because they appeared to be the "strongest" family of the four when Cluster began. When Alice conducted the processing of the theme activity during the fifth session (family sculpting with clay), she and Matthew became aware of some cracks in the family facade. They want to support the Bradshaws as they work to fill in the cracks.

They are concerned about 15-year-old Marni Crowley, who seems to be a cross between a loner and a leader. She seems either to lead the clique of girls or have nothing to do with them. She is "hot and cold."

Right now, Alice and Matthew are observing carefully, and planning Cluster activities to fit observed needs and talents of Cluster members.

Note

1. I acknowledge one of my own Family Cluster trainers, the Reverend Claude Pullis, for most of these ideas.

References

Mace, D. (1981). The long, long trail from information-giving to behavioral change. *Family Relations, 30* (4), 599–606.

Schutz, W. C. (1967). *Joy: Expanding human awareness*. New York: Grove.

15. Evaluating Family Cluster

At some point in Family Cluster, you need to pause long enough to answer some important questions. These are evaluation questions. When you plan Cluster sessions, when you use your observations to plan those sessions, when you ask yourself how you feel and how you did during Cluster, when you and your coleader decide what went well and what did not and how to improve things, you are evaluating Cluster. Evaluation is a process that helps you make decisions about the future of the Family Clusters you lead. Evaluation is an ongoing decision-making process. You receive your data from the members of Cluster to make these decisions.

Evaluation asks three major questions about Cluster:

(1) Do people like it? (appeal)
(2) How much time and money does it require? (efficiency)
(3) Does it work? (effectiveness)

This chapter will address how you answer each of these questions when determining the future of the Clusters you lead.

Appeal

Probably the most typical form of evaluation in Family Cluster is its appeal to those who attend. Appeal relates to those things that keep people coming back for more. It is those things that motivate Cluster members not only to attend Cluster, but to participate in

Cluster activities. Informal evaluations of appeal take place every time you observe someone in Cluster smiling or laughing, engaging enthusiastically in a Cluster activity, or telling you they like something about Cluster. Most likely, you unconsciously chalk up somewhere in the back of your mind a couple of categories related to Cluster: Things That People Like and Things That People *Don't* Like.

It might be a good idea at the end of the Cluster each week to have each person (or maybe half the members, rotated from week to week) complete a simple form designed to measure appeal. You could include some or all of the following items:

- My feeling about this Cluster session could best be described as

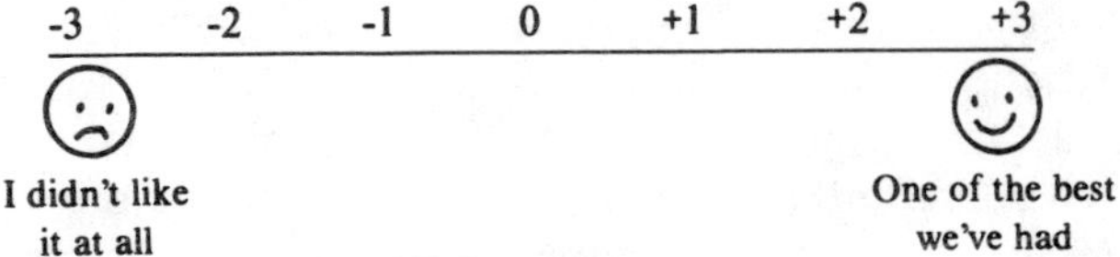

- The best part of this Cluster for me was
  ___________(name of the Gathering activity)
  ___________(the meal)
  ___________(name of something that happened in Cluster Meeting)
  ___________(name of the game)
  ___________(name of something that happened in closure)
- This Cluster could have been improved by
  [leave a space so the person can write his or her suggestions]

Perhaps you can think of others.

By the way, Cluster members should *never* be required to put their names on evaluation forms. What an individual says is not as important as the general sense of what people in the Cluster are feeling and thinking. These simple evaluation questions designed to determine appeal can help you get that sense.

Have evaluation forms and pencils readily available so Cluster members can easily complete them before they leave Cluster. The form should be *short* and easily completed. There should be a place where Cluster members can leave the forms when they are finished. It should not be easy for you to tell which Cluster member filled out which form. Confidentiality is important to lots of people, even children. If you want candid responses, evaluations should be confidential.

Preschoolers, toddlers, and infants, of course, cannot fill out evaluation forms. However, sometimes a parent or older sibling can help a preschooler to fill out an evaluation form. This helps the preschooler feel included by participating in an activity that generally would be exclusively performed by older people. Sometimes preschoolers, in their innocent candor, can provide ideas that might never be suggested by older Cluster members. Remember the old adage that begins, "Out of the mouths of babes . . ."

I remind my college students that I am capable of separating myself from what they feel or think. I do this to encourage them to be honest in their evaluations. Sometimes what they write stings, or is not stated very diplomatically. Sometimes they write suggestions that allude to the possibility I might have purposely done something in class to make life difficult for them. However, I recognize that this is the student's problem, not mine. In the meantime, I read for information that can help me make my classes more appealing to students. Anything else that students say I can let go of. I may not like it, but I can let go of it because I am not my classes. I am not my students. You are not your Cluster members. If you want honest evaluation, are you able to separate yourself from those in Cluster? Can you recognize information that you need without taking it personally?

Efficiency

Efficiency relates to *time*, the time it takes not only to plan Cluster but also the actual time spent *in* Cluster. If the Cluster session is designed for two hours each week, does it take longer, or does Cluster end on time? When people come to Cluster they expect to spend a given amount of time there. If Cluster goes beyond the contracted time period, Cluster members may arrive late at subsequent sessions or stop coming altogether, regardless of how appealing Cluster might be. It is important to contract with the Cluster how long each session will last, then make sure that the contract is kept. It is also important to contract for a given number of sessions and to stick to the contract. If the Cluster members wish to continue Cluster, then a new contract should be determined, including the number of sessions in the new Cluster term.

Efficiency also refers to the *money* it costs to operate a successful Cluster. Someone has to pay for leaders (personnel costs are always the largest expenditures in any organizational budget). Someone also has to pay for the space Cluster occupies. Lights, heat, air-conditioning, electrical equipment, water, and so on cost money. Most likely the sponsoring organization pays for these costs. Nevertheless, leaders must still determine if the organization is getting its money's worth. Are lights turned off when not needed? Do electrical appliances get used beyond what is reasonable usage? Are heat and air-conditioning used only to the temperature level deemed comfortable by Cluster members? Are custodial services overused for Cluster? Is there any waste of Cluster space, utilities, and so on?

Materials and supplies used in Cluster also cost money. These can be paid for by the families in Cluster. Is there enough paper? Glue? Masking tape? String or yarn? Are there enough colored markers (or crayons)? Scissors? Warm Fuzzies? Have you charged the families enough that you can purchase all the materials and supplies needed in Cluster?

Effectiveness

Effectiveness is the evaluation question: "Does Cluster work?" That is, does Cluster help families grow in strength according to the strengths needing improvement and agreed upon by the Cluster families? Are Cluster sessions designed to help Cluster members develop stronger families?

The questions about effectiveness are the most difficult to answer. It is too soon immediately following the close of any given Cluster session to measure any change in the family's strengths as a result of the sessions experienced by that Cluster. Each family needs time to reflect on the insights it has gained and to implement any desirable changes. Probably the best time to evaluate the effectiveness of Cluster is six weeks to two months following the last Cluster session. The Family Strengths Inventory (FSI) developed for the Cluster can be completed again by each of the members of each Cluster family. The leaders can arrange not only to deliver the FSIs to each family but to pick up the completed forms. After a new family profile on the FSI has been determined based on the results of this second completion of the FSI, the leaders can return to each home to show the new family strengths profile, to compare it with the first one, and to discuss how well the family improved on the SMITTIs (single most important things to improve) it had determined earlier (see Chapter 7). At this time, the family may wish to determine additional SMITTIs and how they wish to implement changes to bring about such improvements. Leaders can facilitate this process for each Cluster family. Perhaps the family will choose to work on their plan for six months or so and contract to retake the FSI a third time to check their progress toward their goals.

Evaluation Following Each Cluster Session

After each Cluster session, it is very important that the leaders get together alone to discuss the session. Generally I focus on the following three points:

(1) What went well? What did I like about this session? What did I observe that pleased me? How could I tell that the insight objective was being achieved? What did I like about what I did?
(2) What would I change about this session? Why would I change it? How would I change it?
(3) What did I learn during this session that I can apply to plans for the next session? Who or what family needs affirming? What issues are Cluster members struggling with? How can I help them?

Leaders can support each other and give ideas to one another as they evaluate following each Cluster session. It is important to do such evaluation *immediately following* the Cluster session while ideas are still fresh.

Evaluation is an important process. It should not be overlooked when planning and conducting Cluster. You are making your decisions on the basis of your evaluations all the time. Evaluation, however, should not be a "seat of the pants" or "off the top of the head" activity. You need data. The Cluster members are the source of that data.

There are three questions you need to answer when collecting data to help you make decisions about the future of Family Clusters you lead. First, you make *appeal* decisions (that is, "Do Cluster members enjoy Cluster?"). Second, you make *efficiency* decisions (that is, "Is Cluster time- and cost-effective?"). Finally, you make *effectiveness* decisions (that is, "Does Cluster work?"). All too often decisions about effectiveness are made on the basis of appeal—that is, the decision is made to make a change in the curriculum on the basis of what people *like*, not on the basis of what works.

Family Clusters you lead can be successful Clusters if you can adequately answer questions related to all three types of evaluation: appeal, efficiency, and effectiveness. Adequate answers to only one type of question are not sufficient.

The reason for Family Cluster is to support Cluster families in the growth of their family strengths. In order to be an effective leader, you need specific data from Cluster members to make decisions about appeal, efficiency, and effectiveness of Cluster.

Case Study, Part E (Last Part)

During the eleventh session, the members of the Family Cluster Matthew and Alice were leading decided by consensus that they wanted to continue Cluster. Alice and Matthew had informed the Cluster of other items ranked high by Cluster families when they took the Family Strengths Inventory (FSI) before Cluster began. The Cluster also decided to spend more time in the new Cluster on SMITTIs they had worked on during this first contract, specifically on the following:

Item 2 on *appreciation*: "In our family, we say things to each other that make us feel good about ourselves."

Item 10 on *appreciation*: "In our family, we do things for each other that make us feel good about ourselves."

Item 3 on *cohesion*: "We feel closer to one another in our family than we do to people outside our family."

Item 11 on *cohesion*: "Family togetherness is very important to us in our family."

Item 5 on *communication*: "Conversations in our family show lots of caring for one another."

Item 9 on *adaptation*: "In our family, parents and children discuss punishment together." [The children, especially, wanted this one.]

In addition, the following items from the FSI were selected as SMITTIs for the new Cluster sessions:

Item 20 on *communication*: "We are willing to deal with problems in the family when they come up."

Item 24 on *spiritual wellness*: "In our family, we practice what we preach."

The Cluster members wanted to spend two Cluster sessions on each of these eight SMITTIs so they contracted to meet for 16 more sessions.

Matthew and Alice had already agreed to begin a new Cluster made up of five additional families from the congregation. The new Cluster had been scheduled to begin just a week after the first Cluster ended and on the same evening of the week. (They had hoped they would have only four families, but a fifth family in the congregation was so insistent about joining that Matthew and Alice relented. Families in the first Cluster had spread the word about Cluster so enthusiastically throughout the congregation that Matthew and Alice could see themselves leading Clusters in the congregation for a long, long time.) The weekly meeting time was changed for the current Cluster to Tuesday evening. The only scheduling conflict was Ruth Bradshaw's, a nurse, who had to rearrange her shift at the hospital where she works so she could continue participation in Cluster.

The congregation board agreed not only to increase Matthew and Alice's compensation for leading the new Cluster as promised earlier but to compensate them adequately for continuing the first Cluster.

Matthew and Alice had discussed with their children, Matt, Jr. (10), and Cindy (6), the possibility of their spending two nights away from home instead of one with Cluster each week. Alice's mother, Grandma Stubbs, agreed to be with the children both Monday and Tuesday evening each week, so they wouldn't be without an adult at home. The children were enjoying their evening with "Grandma" once a week and readily agreed to having her with them twice a week now. The family had planned a trip to

Disney World during the Christmas vacation as a special bonus for adapting to Cluster two nights a week.

At the end of each session, Matthew and Alice had randomly selected Cluster members to complete an anonymous "evaluation" sheet of that session. They were only surprised about one thing. The Cluster members didn't like singing the "Whobody Song," which had been sung frequently in Cluster. Another short song the Cluster members liked was selected in its place. The presentation of Warm Fuzzies had become an established and much looked forward to ritual during the Cluster meeting each week. The Cluster especially enjoyed the "Warm Fuzzy Round" and had become quite adept at singing it. The children often requested it for a closure song. The Cluster members enjoyed singing camp and gospel songs together.

Matthew and Alice suggested during the eleventh session that, in addition to continuing the Cluster for another 16 weeks, the families in the Cluster could retake the FSI about 6 weeks following Cluster to find out how each family "improved" on Cluster SMIT-TIs. The Cluster families readily agreed to this suggestion. Alice and Matthew agreed to visit each family once the FSI results had been analyzed to show them their new family profiles on the FSI and to compare them with previous family profiles.

Alice and Matthew work hard preparing for Family Cluster each week. Now they will be leading two Family Clusters. This doesn't interfere with Matthew's work as a commercial artist. Alice, however, feels some stress because of her work as an elementary school teacher. She and Matthew have worked extra hard to make their time with their children during the week quality time. They are learning from their experiences in Cluster. They feel that their learning enriches their family life. Alice and Matthew are careful to maintain Friday evening as theirs exclusively, their "date night" each week.

In the meantime, they are satisfied with their performance as Cluster leaders. After each session, no matter how tired they feel, they take time to evaluate the session and to fit what they have learned into their plans for the next Cluster session. They have learned how true it is that being a leader of Family Cluster is "the toughest job you'll ever love."

16. "Mopping up"

When I was a child and young teenager, we had hardwood floors in our home. Hardwood floors gather dust in a hurry, especially when a large family lives in the home. One of my frequent tasks was "dust mopping" those hardwood floors. Using what we called a "dust mop," a broom made out of soft fabric or yarn, I would carefully dust the floors, including under and behind the furniture. Almost always when I "mopped" those hardwood floors I would find something valuable that someone had lost—money, jewelry, toys, even a diamond ring once! The owners were always glad to have the lost item returned. My reward, as I recall, basically was satisfaction in restoring what was lost to its owner. There was enough of the tease in me, however, that I occasionally brandished the "found" item and returned it only when ransom was paid!

This chapter discusses some important discoveries I have made about Family Cluster. Because they are in the closing chapter does not suggest they are unimportant items. None of these discoveries seemed deserving of an entire chapter. But each, in my view, is important information for the Cluster leader. At this point, I won't brandish my findings and then put them up for ransom. I'll let you decide for yourself how important these discoveries are.

When Cluster Is a "Bust"

Occasionally a Cluster session doesn't come up to the expectations of either leader. In other words, it is a bust. There is no point in hitting your head against a hard wall. What is past is past. You can't do anything about the past. But you can learn from the experience and implement what you have learned in the next Cluster session. Change is typical of every group. There is always the possibility of change. However, when we let a "busted" Cluster session defeat us, we are defeated as leaders. Learn from your mistakes and go on. Also remember that Cluster members are as responsible for what goes on as you are. Often when a Cluster session is a bust, and blame is important to establish (which it usually isn't), as a general rule it is the problem of the Cluster itself. Perhaps a "busted" Cluster session might be an effective discussion topic in the next session's Cluster meeting.

For example, I spent hours planning one closing Cluster session to prepare us to say good-bye to each other. That last Cluster was planned to revolve around a Hawaiian theme, primarily because one of our families in the Cluster was from Hawaii. I had Hawaiian music playing in the background and all kinds of exciting materials with which family members could make leis for each other when they arrived. Our family from Hawaii arrived late (the gathering experience focused on the Hawaiian theme) and only the father and his two teenage sons participated in the gathering experience—rushing because they were late. The mother and her two daughters didn't arrive at all. Later, during another Cluster activity, I went out in the hall to get some supplies. I discovered the mother and her daughters sitting on a nearby sofa talking. I was very angry. Why hadn't they at least put in an appearance? They hadn't kept their contract to attend the session. And I was terribly disappointed because they hadn't been able to participate in something that I had planned especially for them. I stuffed my anger for the entire session, taking personal responsibility for the conduct of the entire session, including the process that took place.

I kicked myself mentally afterward. Why didn't I say something during the session? Certainly the members of the Cluster sensed my anger. I could have stopped what was going on during the session and said something like, "I'm really missing X, Y, and Z. I wonder if anyone else is missing them too." If no one said anything, I could have let it go at that. But at least I would have shared with the group what I was feeling, instead of trying to stuff it inside myself (which never works, incidentally). I might have provided an opportunity for Cluster members to express how they were missing our members who had not arrived. Perhaps we could have talked about how we can deal with our feelings when we are disappointed or miss someone. I let a possibly important learning experience slip by.

Continuing the Family Cluster

Sooner or later the decision needs to be made whether or not to hold additional Cluster sessions beyond the number for which the Cluster members originally contracted. There are several things to consider when deciding whether or not to continue the Cluster and how to continue the Cluster.

Who makes the decision to continue? Before the last session of Cluster, Cluster members will give you verbal signals that they wish the Cluster to continue beyond the time for which you have contracted. When it is one or two Cluster sessions before the final Cluster, that might be a good time to address the possibility of holding Cluster for another contract period of time (at least eight weeks). The Cluster meeting would be the appropriate place to bring up the subject.

How is the decision to continue made? The decision to continue Cluster should be made by the members of Cluster. That's why discussing it during a Cluster meeting is probably a good idea. Simply indicate that you have heard several people talking about the possibility of extending (continuing) Cluster. Give the possibilities of continuing Cluster (that is, whether or not the space is available, whether or not the leaders are available, whether or not the sponsoring organization can continue to sponsor the Cluster, and so on). Allow the Cluster members to discuss the pros and cons of continuing the Cluster. You need to do some homework before discussing the subject with the Cluster members. For example, are you or other leaders available to continue the Cluster? Is the space you are meeting in now available for a continued Cluster? If not, what are the alternatives? Continuing Cluster will also require more materials and supplies. Are Cluster families prepared to pay the additional costs of Cluster? When will the Cluster be held? Does the Cluster wish to stick to the same schedule (that is, meet the same time on the same day each week)?

What are the advantages of continuing the Cluster? Cluster learning experiences generally are just getting to the place where people feel comfortable with them when the usual Cluster contract comes to an end (usually at the end of 10 or 12 weeks). Cluster members may wish to continue what they have begun. Cluster members are well acquainted with one another by now. The "wheel does not need to be reinvented." Cluster now has momentum. It is generally ready to move on with the good things it has already accomplished.

What are the disadvantages of continuing the Cluster? Sometimes the sponsoring organization cannot continue to sponsor the Cluster. Space might not be available. Perhaps some Cluster personalities clash and would prefer not to continue their relationships together. Perhaps the Cluster leaders feel burned out or might not be available to continue Cluster.

What should the focus of the continuing Cluster be? If the Cluster members decide to continue the Cluster, and the space and organizational sponsorship can continue at their current level, and the leaders are available to continue Cluster (with adequate compensation), the Cluster should continue to focus on family strengths, especially on those areas of improvement determined at the beginning of the Cluster when Cluster families determined their SMITTIs. The first session of the continuing Cluster should focus on the recontracting process. Later sessions should focus on areas of family strength determined by Cluster members to need improvement (derived from family profiles on the Family Strengths Inventory—see Figure 7.1 in Chapter 7).

How should the continuing Cluster be organized? It probably isn't necessary to reorganize the Cluster, unless one or more families wish to drop out and be replaced by other families on a waiting list. However, the families need to be reminded of their contracts, signed during home visits. If new families enter the Cluster, they change the entire system. Some way must be determined for welcoming them into the Cluster and getting acquainted with them. In that case, two or more families would have a history in Family Cluster whereas one or two families would not. You will need to be particularly aware of these differences. It may be better for the new families if they join a Cluster that you are beginning from scratch to avoid the problem of previous Cluster history. New people can get left out unconsciously. This can be a learning experience leading to growth for some, but not for all. You need to be sensitive to this possibility.

My own bias is to continue the Cluster as a unit or not at all. New families joining the Cluster while other families drop out change the personality of the Cluster. New families deserve the same start the old Cluster had. Putting new wine in old bottles is not a good idea, in my view, in Cluster.

If you are not available to lead the continuing Cluster, preparing new leaders to lead the Cluster is essentially starting the Cluster over from scratch. Adding new leaders is like adding new families.

By all means, continue the Cluster if the Cluster members wish it and if you are available to continue with the same Cluster and if *all* the Cluster families wish to continue. I personally have not led continuing Clusters, but I can see great advantage to them.

Ethical Guidelines for Family Cluster

Every profession providing human services has ethical standards to which those in the profession adhere as part of their willingness to be certified professionals. There are professional oversight committees whose function it is to determine where ethical problems might exist relative to the professional standards and how to weed them out.

Those who are trainers and/or leaders in Family Cluster are considered family life educators. The National Council on Family Relations (NCFR) at this writing has a task force in process preparing a code of ethics for those who are Certified Family Life Educators (CFLEs) through NCFR.

It is likely that many of the leaders in Family Cluster are nonprofessional people who have not pledged their support to any code of ethics. This by no means assumes that they have no personal codes of ethics. It simply means that they may not have pledged adherence to a systematized professional code.

In the absence of such a systematized code for family life educators (including leaders of Family Cluster), the following issues (Leigh, Loewen, & Lester, 1986) should be carefully considered by every Family Cluster leader.

(1) The leader's values. Although it is likely that most people share the same values related to honesty, hard work, responsibility, unconditional love, the importance of education, and so on, it cannot

be assumed that one's values are shared by all those whom one serves. These values become part and parcel of the way a leader plans Cluster, conducts Cluster, and interacts with Cluster members. For example, the Cluster leader might assume that effective communication in the home means that anybody can say anything about anything to anyone at any time in the family. Such an assumed value might fly in the face of what one or more of the families in the Cluster might hold near and dear. Perhaps there are secrets that should never be discussed, according to the implicit rules in some families. When planning Family Cluster and working with Cluster members, leaders need to be aware of their own values and how they might clash with those in the families with whom they work, and they need to determine how they might work out these value differences with the families.

(2) *Possible harmful negative effects*. There is an old saying, "If it ain't broke, don't fix it!" This is especially well known in the medical profession. Family Cluster does not exist to "fix" anything; it exists to make what works work better. Therefore, it is easy to assume that a Family Cluster experience could not possibly be harmful to those who attend. There is no evidence that Family Cluster harms people. Neither is there any published evidence that it helps (see Chapter 4). If there is no change for the "better" in a family's strengths as a result of attending Cluster, can it be assumed that Cluster does harm? It would be foolish to assume any such thing. However, Cluster leaders at least need to be aware how difficult it is to measure the kinds of interactive changes that go on in families, how small changes are likely to be on current measurements, and how easy it is to assume that because someone liked something it was not harmful. When family members begin talking about some of their interactive processes, this can be very threatening to other family members. Such openness can lead to conflict and perhaps to ultimate change for the better in the view of family members. But perhaps not. When Cluster leaders introduce ideas into Cluster that might create change, and thus conflict, they have entered a realm that can be very threatening to some. Perhaps there are people afraid to express their real feelings, even on confidential evaluation reports. Nevertheless, Cluster leaders need to examine the harmful possibilities of Cluster and determine whether they are confident that the camaraderie of Cluster and the structured learning experiences will outweigh the possible harm.

This is not to suggest that Cluster leaders operate out of fear of harming others. It simply suggests that leaders make an honest examination of what might happen and the desired end result of planned experiences. Perhaps this possible harm needs to be shared with the families who apply for Cluster experience.

(3) Responsibility to the client. Family Cluster leaders work with lots of clients at one time, the individual members of the families composing the Cluster. But for what is the Cluster leader responsible? Responsibility assumes that there will be some sort of exchange of service between the leader and client. Essentially, the leader is promising to provide an educational and enrichment service to the client, who in turn promises to attend Cluster and participate in the activities that provide that service. Does the responsibility of the leader go beyond this? The contract between the Cluster leader (including the sponsor) and the family should explicitly spell out these responsibilities.

(4) Informed consent. The Family Cluster families need to be informed of the following explicitly before they sign a contract to become a part of a given Cluster (Leigh et al., 1986): (a) how Cluster will operate (i.e., when it will be held, where and who conducts it, and what the routine will be), including any procedures used; (b) the role and qualifications of the leaders; (c) any reasonable risks resulting from participating in Cluster; (d) any possible benefits; (e) possible alternatives to Family Cluster that might provide similar benefits; (f) how questions that come up about Cluster will be handled; and (g) how withdrawal of consent is to be handled. Such information provides possible clients the information they need to become informed and to give informed consent (i.e., sign the contract).

(5) Confidentiality; privileged communication. The issue of confidentiality (privileged communication) might not be considered a problem in Cluster because it is an educational program and education is so public. Confidentiality might be considered the exclusive realm of therapy. However, Cluster leaders might learn of private information during home visits that should not be shared outside the context in which it was received. Cluster leaders have a major responsibility to build trust among Family Cluster members and between themselves and Cluster members. The effectiveness of Cluster is largely based on such trust. Cluster leaders need to determine how to handle privileged communication responsibly in

order to build and maintain trust. Cluster leaders might become aware of information that needs reporting, such as child abuse. When, how, and with whom to share privileged communication must be carefully considered by Cluster leaders. Cluster members often disclose information to one another and to the leaders that could be used to exploit Cluster members. The line between exploitation and confidentiality can sometimes be very thin.

Corey, Corey, and Callanan (1984) suggest four additional ethical issues that undoubtedly should be considered by Cluster leaders and trainers: (a) referral; (b) consultation with others; (c) extent of power and trust placed in the leaders; and (d) the development and assurance of competence.

(6) Referral. Even though Cluster is specifically designed for functional families, occasionally leaders might recognize dysfunctional behavior in members of the Cluster that might require professional assistance. Leaders need to be aware of referral resources available, when and how to refer people, how others can help Cluster members, and how to recognize when referral might be necessary. Leaders need to recognize their own limitations in dealing with dysfunctional behavior and need to know how to refer others for the assistance they might need.

(7) Consultation with professionals. Occasionally it might be wise for a Cluster leader to consult with a professional, such as a marriage or family therapist, a social worker, a medical doctor, an attorney. Some sensitive and difficult situations in Cluster might precipitate the need for such consultation. In some cases a referral might be the best way to handle a situation. Consulting with a professional involves the issue of confidentiality. (Codes of ethics do not consist of mutually exclusive categories.)

(8) Extent of power and trust placed in the leaders. Family members tend to place a great deal of power in the hands of the leaders because they are viewed somewhat as authority figures by members of Cluster. That authoritative power seems to come with the territory. The leader is not "one of the guys." The leader, even though working toward equality in the Cluster, is separate and apart from the others because of the role. Sometimes family members not only trust each leader a great deal but might become very dependent upon one or both. Dependency on the part of Cluster members means that the leader has the power to control the lives of others to some degree. To some, this is a powerful temptation.

However, no matter how benevolent the control, a major thrust of each leader's efforts should be independence—for the individual as well as for the family. Exercising dominion over others can be exploitative and tends to promote dependence, not independence.

(9) Leader competence. What makes an effective Family Cluster leader? The ethical issue of leader competence is a major one. It includes (a) how leaders are selected, (b) what they are taught, (c) how they are trained, and (d) the criteria for certification. Currently there are no professional certification requirements for Family Cluster leaders. The fact that a person is a CFLE (Certified Family Life Educator) is no guarantee that such a person is an effective Family Cluster leader. Successful completion of a leader training workshop or successful completion of a leader training course in college does not necessarily lead to effective Family Cluster leadership. What are the qualifications of a person who would most likely be an effective Cluster leader? (Chapter 5 describes some characteristics derived from my own personal experience.) What kind of training does a leader trainee require? How long should the training be? What kind of internship should be required? What are the criteria by which Family Cluster leaders should be certified? Who should certify Family Cluster leaders?

These nine ethics issues need to be addressed before an appropriate code of ethics can be developed for Family Cluster leaders. These issues, even before they are codified and standardized, need to be carefully considered by leaders of Family Cluster while they engage in "the toughest job [they'll] ever love."

Leading Family Cluster can be the greatest life adventure you've had yet. It is not without its challenges, its bumpy obstacles; but if we don't climb mountains, we'll never reach the peaks.

References

Corey, G., Corey, M. S., & Callanan, P. (1984). *Issues and ethics in the helping professions* (2nd ed.). Monterey, CA: Brooks/Cole.

Leigh, G. K., Loewen, I. R., & Lester, M. E. (1986). Caveat emptor: Values and ethics in family life education and enrichment. *Family Relations, 35*, 573–580.

Index

About the Author

BARBARA VANCE, a product of the mountains and deserts of the Mountain West and a whole flock of pioneer forebears, is a curious mixture of the adventurous, curious child and the quieter, more self-assured, more contemplative adult. Her doctorate at Stanford focused on psychotherapy. She prefers "preventive maintenance" (the focus of education and enrichment), however, to "rehabilitation" (the focus of therapy). That's why she is a Certified Family Life Educator (CFLE) through the National Council on Family Relations and has focused on international family life education. She has conducted leadership training throughout the United States, the South Pacific, and Southeast Asia for her church. For her profession, she has conducted family life education workshops in the Philippines, England, Scotland, Ireland, France, and Israel. She wears several professional hats: those of a developmental psychologist, instructional psychologist, and familogist (a new discipline). She is the author or coauthor of several books and the author of a wide variety of professional articles and research monographs. She is the oldest of five children and an aunt to 40 nieces, nephews, grandnieces, and grandnephews. Her hobbies range from reading mysteries to quilting, golfing, and traveling.

NOTES

NOTES